NEW CENTURY BIBLE COMMENTARY

General Editors

RONALD E. CLEMENTS   MATTHEW BLACK
(Old Testament)   (New Testament)

Romans

SECOND EDITION

THE NEW CENTURY BIBLE COMMENTARIES

Not yet available in paperback
Other titles are in preparation

NEW CENTURY BIBLE COMMENTARY

Based on the Revised Standard Version

Romans

SECOND EDITION

MATTHEW BLACK

WM. B. EERDMANS PUBL. CO., GRAND RAPIDS

MARSHALL, MORGAN & SCOTT PUBL. LTD., LONDON

Marshall, Morgan & Scott ISBN 0 551 01546 2

Library of Congress Cataloging-in-Publication Data

Black, Matthew.
Romans : based on the Revised Standard Version.

(New century Bible commentary)
Includes index.
1. Bible.   N.T.   Romans — Commentaries.   I. Title.
II. Series.
BS2665.3.B5   1989   227′.107   88-3978

Eerdmans ISBN 0-8028-0374-1

CONTENTS

PREFACE

The author of 2 Peter was not exaggerating when he said that 'there are some things in them (the letters of St Paul) hard to understand' (ch. 3:16). In some respects the Epistle to the Romans contains probably the hardest of all Paul's thoughts about his gospel. Certainly it is this Epistle which has presented generations of biblical scholars with some of their most challenging exegetical tasks. Moreover, the nature of some of the problems, where one may suspect, but can never be sure, that 'primitive error' or a textual corruption may be the source of the difficulties, does not make the exegetical task any easier.

The intention of the New Century Bible series is to provide, for the interested layman as well as for the clergy or theological student, an up-to-date account of the *status quaestionis* of the exegesis of the biblical writings, especially in those controversial areas of interpretation. In Romans this is a well-nigh impossible task; bibliographical items alone, over the past century, are more numerous than in any other New Testament book of comparable size. The attempt, nevertheless, has been made in the present commentary to give as wide and representative a selection of these as possible, from modern commentaries and articles which have appeared in the main European languages within the past seventy to one hundred years. The reader has thus additional reference material for his own reflection and exegetical decisions.

I am grateful to my secretary, Miss M. C. Blackwood, for her outstanding services in preparing the manuscript, through several drafts, for the Press.

To my colleague, Dr. A. J. M. Wedderburn, who has himself a special interest in Romans, I am indebted for a careful reading of the commentary in proof. My gratitude is also due to the readers of the Press for their care and attention to detail, in particular in checking references and ironing out inconsistencies. For the many imperfections that remain I am alone responsible.

MATTHEW BLACK

St. Mary's College, St. Andrews
29th March 1973

PREFACE TO THE SECOND EDITION

Since the publication in 1973 of the New Century Bible *Romans*, two major commentaries have appeared, the magisterial two-volume *International Critical Commentary* (the successor to Sanday and Headlam) of C. E. B. Cranfield of Durham, and the new *Handbuch zum Neuen Testament* of Ernst Käsemann of Tübingen. (For details of both works, see Select Bibliography below, pp. xv, xvi). Both these larger scholarly works contain a comprehensive survey of ancient and modern commentaries, monographs and studies of the Roman Epistle, including a substantial number of the latter which have appeared since 1973.

In view of the aim of the New Century Bible series to provide, for the interested layman as well as the clergy and theological student, an up-to-date account, in shortened form, of the exegesis of the biblical writings, a revised and expanded edition of *Romans* seemed both necessary and desirable, especially as this century approaches its final decade.

In my revision and expansion of the commentary (particularly in the later chapters of the Epistle), I am especially indebted to the work of C. E. B. Cranfield; if I have occasionally differed from him, and offered an alternative exegesis, it is usually the result of a close study of the evidence and arguments he has presented and deployed. The exhaustive recording of the views of ancient and modern exegetes in Ernst Käsemann's *magnum opus* I have also found extremely helpful. An indication of the extent of my own indebtedness to earlier, as well as to contemporary commentators and interpreters, will be evident to the reader from the many writers cited in the commentary. To survey and assess what has been written in the twentieth century alone on this classic document of the Christian faith would be beyond the powers of any individual.*

---

*In his *Index to Periodical Literature on the Apostle Paul* (Brill, 1960), B. M. Metzger lists some 3,000 items, mostly covering the first half of the twentieth century. In the decade 1532–1542, within the life-time of Luther, there were altogether thirty-five commentaries published. (See T. H. L. Parker, *Commentaries on Romans 1532–1542*, T. & T. Clark, Edinburgh, 1986.)

I am deeply grateful to Miss Evelyn Hood of St. Andrews for her invaluable help in the typing and preparing of this revised edition for the Press.

MATTHEW BLACK

40 Buchanan Gardens,
St. Andrews.
6th April, 1986.

ABBREVIATIONS

BIBLICAL

OLD TESTAMENT (*OT*)

Gen.	Jg.	1 Chr.	Ps.	Lam.	Ob.	Hag.
Exod.	Ru.	2 Chr.	Prov.	Ezek.	Jon.	Zech.
Lev.	1 Sam.	Ezr.	Ec.	Dan.	Mic.	Mal.
Num.	2 Sam.	Neh.	Ca.	Hos.	Nah.	
Dt.	1 Kg.	Est.	Isa.	Jl	Hab.	
Jos.	2 Kg.	Job	Jer.	Am.	Zeph.	

APOCRYPHA (*Apoc.*)

1 Esd.	Tob.	Ad.Est.	Sir.	S 3 Ch.	Bel	1 Mac.
2 Esd.	Jdt.	Wis.	Bar.	Sus.	Man.	2 Mac.
			Ep.Jer.			

NEW TESTAMENT (*NT*)

Mt.	Ac.	Gal.	1 Th.	Tit.	1 Pet.	3 Jn.
Mk	Rom.	Eph.	2 Th.	Phm.	2 Pet.	Jude
Lk.	1 C.	Phil.	1 Tim.	Heb.	1 Jn	Rev.
Jn	2 C.	Col.	2 Tim.	Jas	2 Jn	

DEAD SEA SCROLLS (*DSS*)

1QIs^a	First Isaiah Scroll
1QIs^b	Second Isaiah Scroll
1QLevi	Testament of Levi
1QpHab	Habakkuk Commentary
1QS	Rule of the Community (Manual of Discipline)
1QSa (= 1Q28a)	Rule of the Community (Appendix)
1QSb (= 1Q28b)	Collection of Benedictions
1QM	War of the Sons of Light against the Sons of Darkness

1QH	Hymns of Thanksgiving
4QFlor	Florilegium, Cave 4
4QpPs37	Commentary on Psalm 37
4Qtest	Messianic Testimonia
CD	Fragments of a Zadokite Work (Damascus Document)
DSH	(now designated 1QHab)

GENERAL

AV	*Authorised Version* (King James Version) (1611)
Bauer:	W. Bauer, *A Greek–English Lexicon of the New Testament and early Christian Literature* (Cambridge, 1957). Translated and adapted from *Griechisch-Deutsches Wörterbuch zu den Schriften des Neuen Testaments und der übrigen urchristlichen Literatur*, by W. F. Arndt and F. W. Gingrich.
B–D	F. Blass and A. Debrunner, *A Greek Grammar of the New Testament and other early Christian Literature* (Cambridge, 1961). Translated from *Grammatik des neutestamentlichen Griechisch*, by R. W. Funk.
Bib.	*Biblica*
BZ	*Biblische Zeitschrift*
BZNW	*Beihefte zur Zeitschrift für die neutestamentliche Wissenschaft*
CBQ	*Catholic Biblical Quarterly*
CIL	*Corpus Inscriptionum Latinarum*
EGT	*The Expositor's Greek Testament* (ed. W. Robertson Nicoll), 5 vols. London, 1897–1910
Ev. Theol.	*Evangelische Theologie*
ET	*Expository Times*
FRLANT	*Forschungen zur Religion und Literatur des Alten und Neuen Testaments*
G–K	Gesenius–Kautzsch, *Gesenius' Hebrew Grammar* (Oxford, 1910)
HThR	*Harvard Theological Review*
IEJ	*Israel Exploration Journal*
JBL	*Journal of Biblical Literature*
JJS	*Journal of Jewish Studies*

Liddell and Scott	*Greek–English Lexicon* (Oxford, 1968)
MM	J. H. Moulton and G. Milligan, *Vocabulary of the Greek Testament* (London, 1911)
Moffatt	J. Moffatt, *A New Translation of the Bible* (London, 1934)
MT	Massoretic text
NEB	*New English Bible* (1970; NT only 1961)
Nov. Test.	*Novum Testamentum*
NTS	*New Testament Studies*
RB	*Revue Biblique*
RSV	*Revised Standard Version* (NT, 1946; OT, 1952)
RV	*Revised Version* (NT, 1880; OT, 1884)
SB	H. L. Strack u. P. Billerbeck, *Kommentar zum Neuen Testament aus Talmud u. Midrasch* (Berlin, 1922–61)
SH	(see second item in Bibliography)
SJT	*Scottish Journal of Theology*
Stud. Ev.	*Studia Evangelica*
Stud. Theol.	*Studia Theologica*
TU	*Texte u. Untersuchungen zur Geschichte der altchristlichen Literatur*, 3. Folge (1883–)
TWNT	*Theologisches Wörterbuch zum Neuen Testament*, hrsg. v. G. Kittel u. G. Friedrich (Stuttgart, 1933–79) (Eng. translation by G. W. Bromiley, *Theological Dictionary of the New Testament* (Grand Rapids, 1964–76)
TZ	*Theologische Zeitschrift*
Theol. Ltzg.	*Theologische Literaturzeitung*
ZAW	*Zeitschrift für die alttestamentliche Wissenschaft*
ZNTW	*Zeitschrift fur die neutestamentliche Wissenschaft*

SELECT BIBLIOGRAPHY

OLDER COMMENTARIES

Bengel, J. A., *Gnomon of the New Testament*, Vol. III, pp. 1–198, Edinburgh, 1877.
Sanday, W. and Headlam, A. C., *A Critical and Exegetical Commentary on the Epistle to the Romans* (*International Critical Commentary*), Edinburgh, 1895; 5th edn., 1902, with many subsequent reprints. A full list of older commentaries is given ibid., pp. xcviii ff. Special mention may be made of two:
Vaughan, C. J. (Dean of Llandaff, 1879–97), 4th edn. (1874). Valuable for its philological learning, New Testament parallels, and Septuagint references.
Wordsworth, Christopher (Bishop of Lincoln, 1869–85) (1856–60). Especially valuable for its wide patristic learning.
To these should be added from the older commentaries:
Denney, James, *Commentary on Romans* (*Expositor's Greek Testament*, 2), London, 1900

MODERN COMMENTARIES

Althaus, P., *Der Brief an die Römer* (*Neues Testament Deutsch*, 6) Göttingen, 1966.
Barrett, C. K., *The Epistle to the Romans* (Black's New Testament Commentaries), London, 1957.
Barth, K., *The Epistle to the Romans* (trans. by E. C. Hoskyns, Oxford, 1933). Also: *A Shorter Commentary on Romans*, trans. by D. H. van Daalen, London, 1959.
Best, Ernest, *The Letter of Paul to the Romans* (*Cambridge Bible Commentary on the New English Bible*), Cambridge, 1967.
Bruce, F. F., *The Epistle to the Romans* (*Tyndale New Testament Commentary*), London, 1963.
Brunner, E., *The Letter to the Romans: a Commentary* (translated by H. A. Kennedy), London, 1959.
Cranfield, C. E. B., *The Epistle to the Romans* (*International Critical Commentary*), Edinburgh, Vol. I, 1975, Vol. II, 1979.
Dodd, C. H., *The Epistle of Paul to the Romans* (*Moffatt NT Commentary*), London, 1932; Fontana edn. 1959.
Gaugler, E., *Der Römerbrief* (*Prophezei*) I–II, Zürich, 1945, 1952.

Haering, T., *Der Römerbrief des Apostels Paulus*, Stuttgart, 1926.
Huby, J., S. *Paul. Épître aux Romains: traduction et commentaire*, Paris, 1940; new edn. with S. Lyonnet, Paris, 1957.
Käsemann, Ernst, *An die Römer (Handbuch zum Neuen Testament)*, Tübingen, 1973.
Kirk, K. E., *The Epistle to the Romans (The Clarendon Bible)*, Oxford, 1937.
Knox, John, 'Romans', in *Interpreter's Bible*, IX, Nashville, 1954.
Kuss, O., *Der Römerbrief übersetzt und erklärt, Röm. 1.1–6.11*, Regensburg, 1957, 1959.
Lagrange, M. J., *Saint Paul: Épître aux Romains*, Paris, 1916, repr. 1950.
Leenhardt, F. J., *L'Épître de Saint Paul aux Romains*, Neuchatel, 1957; English trans., *The Epistle to the Romans*, London, 1961.
Lietzmann, Hans, *An die Römer (Handbuch zum Neuen Testament)* 4th edn., Tübingen, 1933.
Manson, T. W., 'Romans', in *Peake's Commentary on the Bible*, London, 1962.
Michel, Otto, *Der Brief an die Römer (Kritisch-exegetischer Kommentar über das Neue Testament)*, 10th edn. Göttingen, 1955, 1966.
Murray, J., *The Epistle to the Romans (New International Commentary on the New Testament)*, Grand Rapids, 1959–65.
Nygren, A., *Commentary on Romans*, Eng. trans., London, 1952.
Pallis, A., *To the Romans: a Commentary*, Liverpool, 1920.
Rhys, H., *The Epistle to the Romans*, New York, 1961.
Ridderbos, H., *Aan de Romeinen*, Kampen, 1959.
Schlatter, A., *Gottes Gerechtigkeit*, Stuttgart, 1935; 3rd edn. 1959.
Schmidt, H. W., *Der Brief des Paulus an die Römer (Theol. Handkomm. zum Neuen Testament)*, Berlin, 1962.
Zahn, Th., *Der Brief des Paulus an die Römer (Kommentar zum Neuen Testament)*, Leipzig, 1910, 1925.

OTHER RECOMMENDED STUDIES

Allen, L. C., 'The Old Testament in Romans i–viii', *Vox Evangelica*, III, 1964, pp. 6–41.
Barrett, C. K., *Reading through Romans*, London, 1963.
Baur, F. C., *Ausgewählte Werke in Einzelaufgaben*, ed. K. Scholder, Stuttgart, 1963, I, pp. 147–266. Über Zweck und Veranlassung des Römerbriefes und der damit zusammenhängenden Verhältnisse der römischen Gemeinde, 1836.

Bultmann, R., *Theology of the New Testament*, London, 1955.
Cranfield, C. E. B., *A Commentary on Rom. 12–13 (SJT Occasional Papers 12)*, Edinburgh, 1965.
Davies, W. D., *Paul and Rabbinic Judaism*, London, 1948.
Delling, G., 'Zum neueren Paulusverständnis', *Nov. Test.*, IV, 1960, pp. 95–121.
Deluz, G., *La justice de Dieu: explication de l'Épître aux Romains*, Neuchatel, 1945.
Dinkler, E., *Predestination bei Paulus*, Neukirchen, 1957.
von Dobschütz, E., 'Zum Wortschatz und Stil des Römerbriefes', *ZNTW*, XXXIII, 1934, pp. 56–66.
Ellison, H. L., *The Mystery of Israel: an Exposition of Rom. 9–11*, Grand Rapids, 1966.
Friedrich, G., 'Römerbrief', in *Die Religion in Geschichte und Gegenwart*, V col. 1137–44.
Goppelt, L., *Jesus, Paul and Judaism*, translated by E. Schroeder, New York, 1964.
Hunter, A. M., *Romans: the Law of Love* (Torch Bible Paperbacks), London, 1955.
Jeremias, J., 'Chiasmus in den Paulusbriefen', *ZNTW*, XLIX, 1958, pp. 145–56 (esp. p. 154).
Jewett, R., *Paul's Anthropological Terms: a Study of their Use in Conflict Settings*, Leiden, 1971.
Käsemann, E., *Perspectives on Paul*, London, 1971.
Knox, W. L., *St. Paul and the Church of Jerusalem*, Cambridge, 1925.
Knox, W. L., *St. Paul and the Church of the Gentiles*, Cambridge, 1939.
Leon, H. J., *The Jews of Ancient Rome*, Philadelphia, 1960.
Lütgert, W., *Der Römerbrief als historisches Problem. Beiträge zur Forderung christlicher Theologie*, 17 (ii), Gütersloh, 1913.
Rigaux, B., *Saint Paul et ses Lettres (Studia Neotestamentica Subsidia 2)*, Paris-Bruges, 1962.
Schelkle, K. H., *Paulus: Lehrer der Väter: die altkirchliche Auslegung von Römer 1–11*, Düsseldorf, 1956.
Schmithals, W., 'Zur Abfassung und ältesten Sammlung der paulinischen Hauptbriefe', *ZNTW*, LI, 1960, pp. 225–45.
Scroggs, R., *The Last Adam: a Study in Pauline Anthropology*, Oxford, 1966.
Schürer, E., *A History of the Jewish People in the Time of Jesus Christ*, 6 vols., Edinburgh, 1898–1903; rev. edn., *The History of the Jewish people in the age of Jesus Christ*, ed. by Geza Vermes, Fergus Millar, Matthew Black, Martin Goodman, Vols. I–III (with Index), Edinburgh, 1983–87.

Schweitzer, A., *The Mysticism of the Apostle Paul*, Eng. trans., London, 1931.
Schweitzer, A., *Paul and his Interpreters*, Eng. trans., London, 1912.
Thackerary, H. St. John, *The Relationship of St. Paul to Contemporary Jewish Thought*, London, 1900.
Wiefel, W., 'Die jüdische Gemeinschaft im antiken Rom und die Anfänge des römischen Christentums: Bemerkung zu Anlass und Zweck des Römerbriefes', *Judaica*, XXVI, 1970, pp. 65–88.

THE STRUCTURE OF ROMANS

Bonnard, P., 'Où en est l'interprétation de l'Épître aux Romains?', *Rev. de Theol. et Phil.*, 3rd ser., I, 1951, pp. 225–43.
Dahl, N. A., 'Two notes on Romans 5', *Studia Theologica*, V, 1951–2, pp. 37–48.
Dupont, J., 'Le Problème de la structure littéraire de l'épître aux Romains', *RB*, LXII, 1955, pp. 365–97.
Feuillet, A., 'La Citation de Habacuc II.4 et les huits premiers chapitres de l'Épître aux Romains', *NTS*, VI, 1959–60, pp. 52–80.
Feuillet, A., 'Le plan salvifique de Dieu d'après L'Épître aux Romains. Essai sur la structure littéraire de l'Épître et sa significance théologique', *RB*, LVII, 1950, pp. 336–87, 489–529.
Grayston, K., '"Not ashamed of the Gospel": Rom. 1. 16a and the Structure of the Epistle', in *Stud. Evang.*, II (*TU* 87), 1964, pp. 569ff.
Jeremias, J., 'Zur Gedankenführung in den Paulinischen Briefen', in *Studia Paulina* (de Zwaan *Festschrift*), Haarlem, 1953, pp. 146ff.
Klein, G., 'Der Abfassungswerk des Römerbriefes', in *Rekonstruction und Interpretation*, Münich, 1969.
Luz, U., 'Zum Aufbau von Röm. 1–8', *TZ*, XXV, 1969, pp. 161ff.
Lyonnet, S., 'Note sur le plan de l'Épître aux Romains', *Melanges Jules Lebreton* (1951–2), pp. 301–16.
Manson, W., 'Notes on the Argument of Romans (Chapters i–viii)' in *New Testament Essays: Studies in Memory of T. W. Manson*, ed. A. J. B. Higgins, Manchester, 1959.
Ruijs, R. C. M., *De Structuur van de Brief aan de Romeinen: een stilistische, vormhistorische en thematische analyse van Rom. i:16–iii:23*, Utrecht-Nijmegen, 1964.

INTRODUCTION

to

Romans

INTRODUCTION

The Epistle to the Romans is one of the classic documents of the Christian faith, the theological Epistle *par excellence* in the New Testament; the only other comparable New Testament writing, both in epistolary form and theological content, is the anonymous Epistle to the Hebrews. But Hebrews is an epistolary homily: its theology is subordinate to its homiletic purpose. Romans is a theological affirmation of the Christian faith, composed in the form of the literary epistle (*epistolē*) of the period.[1]

This does not mean that Romans is an exposition of Christian theology in the same sense as Barth's *Dogmatics* or Bultmann's *Theology of the New Testament*. A more accurate characterisation is that given by Michel:[2] Romans is 'epistolary catechesis', or instruction in Christian doctrine, a *Lehrbrief*, i.e. an Epistle written to instruct its readers. This is a valid definition in so far as the Epistle does embody *didachē*, or catechesis, in what St Paul regards as the essentials of Christian belief and its implications for Christian life and doctrine. Its central theme is Christian 'righteousness' (*dikaiosynē*) or 'salvation' (*sōtēria*). But this instruction is communicated within the framework of a sustained argumentation directed against the antithesis of Pharisaic Judaism, that 'righteousness' or 'salvation' had as its foundation obedience to a revealed *tôrāh*, or divine revelation. 'Salvation' was adherence, not to a divine Law, but to a divine Lord, apprehended by faith.[3]

I. THE AUTHOR

The denial of Pauline authorship is now 'rightly relegated to a place among the curiosities of NT scholarship. Today no responsible criticism disputes its Pauline origin' (Cranfield, pp. 1f.). 'The authorship of the Epistle to the Romans is a closed question' (C. H. Dodd, p. 9).

Nevertheless, there is a problem raised by 16.22 (assuming

---

[1]This is not to deny that Romans is also a 'real letter' with some of the formal characteristics of the letters of the period (see below, p. 14f., p. 25, n. 1 & 2). But its *Gattung* is that of the Jewish-style literary epistle.
[2]*Kommentar*, p. 5.
[3]Cf. W. D. Davies, *Paul and Rabbinic Judaism* (London, 1948), p. 148.

chapter 16 to be part of Romans[1]): 'I Tertius, the writer of this letter, greet you in the Lord'[2]. Most commentators assume that Tertius was the amanuensis to whom the Apostle dictated the letter, and that it was later written out by him, in full, perhaps even from a shorthand copy of it. In an important study of the style and structure of the Pauline letters[3], however, O. Roller has argued for a more radical alternative, namely, that Paul entrusted the entire composition of the letter to his amanuensis on the basis of instruction from himself[4]. The formal characteristics of Romans, as contrasted with other Pauline letters, are alleged to support the theory: thus 1:8–15 begins with an epistolary prayer followed by a promise to visit Rome and at 15:28–33 the promise is repeated and elaborated and then followed by a concluding epistolary prayer, a chiastic arrangement which Roller thinks reflects the epistolary stylistic convention that the beginning and conclusion of a letter should correspond.

It is more than doubtful, however, if such a hypothesis adequately accounts for the manifestly Pauline style and contents, in particular the Pauline 'diatribes' the Epistle incorporates.[5] On the whole, it seems much more likely that Paul dictated the letter, either like Cicero, who once told his friend Atticus that he had dictated a letter to his fastidious friend Varro *syllabatim* to get his thoughts correctly expressed,[6] or else into short-hand which was then copied out in long-hand by Tertius.

But, at the same time, we must, in view of 16:22, and of the known habits of ancient amanuenses, allow for the possibility that Paul was assisted in composing Romans by a professional scribe, who could have contributed more to its composition than simply by copying out his short-hand or a dictated long-hand version.

2. DATE AND CIRCUMSTANCES OF WRITING

The date of the sending of Romans and the circumstances in which it came to be written can be determined with a fair degree of

---

[1]See below, p. 11f.
[2]See Cranfield, pp. 2f.
[3]*Das Formular der paulinischen Briefe: ein Beitrag zur Lehre vom antiken Briefe*, Stuttgart, 1933.
[4]op. cit., pp. 14ff., 295–300.
[5]See below, p. 29f.
[6]I am indebted to Cranfield (p. 3) for this parallel.

accuracy.[1] On the basis of a widely agreed interpretation of Rom. 16:23 and 1 C. 1:14, Paul is writing from *Corinth*, where he is the guest of his former convert Gaius, in whose house the Church in Corinth was accustomed to meet; moreover at 16:1 Phoebe, a deaconess of Cenchreae, the port of Corinth, is commended to the Roman Church. (She was probably the bearer of the letter.)

The actual circumstances of the writing of the Epistle are described at 15:22–32: Paul has now completed his work in Asia and Greece (v. 23), and is planning to mount a mission to Spain and, on the way, to visit Rome. But first he must 'back-track' to Jerusalem, with a relief fund subscribed by Macedonia and Achaia for the 'saints' there (the impoverished Jewish Christian community in the Holy City).

This statement of intentions and plans corresponds broadly with the account of St Paul's actual movements as reported by St Luke in Ac. 19:21–20:6. The Apostle's work in Asia, with his head-quarters in Ephesus is over or nearing its conclusion, and he is now planning to travel to Jerusalem via Macedonia and Greece; Luke even mentions Paul's intention to visit Rome after his journey to Jerusalem.

In this summarising report (Ac. 20:2–6) Luke informs us that Paul carried out his projected plan, and went first to Macedonia and Greece; in Greece he spent three months, before resuming his journey to Jerusalem. There is little doubt that it was during these three months in Greece, almost certainly in Corinth, that Romans was written, probably in the year A.D. 58.

The reason for his circuitous journey to Jerusalem (via Greece) had no doubt to do with the 'collection' for the Jerusalem Church (15:25f.; cf. Ac. 24:17). When he left Greece again, however, it was to make the same wide detour—through Macedonia and across Asia—this time almost certainly to avoid the hostile reception awaiting him in Syria, probably at Antioch (he could have sailed direct from Corinth to Antioch or Caesarea; Ac. 20:3). He may also have been deliberately avoiding a confrontation with Jewish pilgrims to the Passover Festival, who would be travelling by the direct routes.

Paul set out after his three months in Greece for Macedonia, as we now know, from Corinth; and, since he left in order to reach Jerusalem for the Passover Festival, we may presume that it was the winter months he spent in Corinth. There he occupied himself by writing the Roman Epistle.

---

[1]But cf. J. R. Richards, 'Romans and I Corinthians: their Chronological Relationship and Comparative Dates', *NTS*, XIII (1966), pp. 14–30.

The Letter was written, therefore, at the close of Paul's so-called 'Ephesian ministry' (c. A.D. 57).[1] We are in the year A.D. 58 when the Apostle sends his letter, perhaps in the early Spring.

The impression we receive from chapter 15 is that Romans was sent, among other reasons, to prepare the way for a future visit. Other, more powerful, motives, however, may have led to the conceiving and composing of this great Epistle. Paul was by no means certain he would ever see Rome: all reports underline the danger in which he stood, from the hatred of world Jewry and the tension and dissension in the Jerusalem Christian community (Rom. 15:31; Ac. 20:3). He could not be certain of the reception even a letter from him would get in Rome; and this may account for the absence of any greetings at Rom. 1:1, though mention is made of his amanuensis and other 'fellow-workers' at chapter 16 (Ac. 20:4, cf. Rom. 16:21–23). Paul bears sole responsibility for what he writes. He may also have thought that this, like his Master's last Passover, might well prove his own *via dolorosa et via crucis*. So, if he never preached in Rome, Rome (he determined) would, nevertheless, hear his 'Gospel' read to them, from his own living word. It really almost looks as if Paul set out, in these three months' breathing space in Corinth during A.D. 57–8, to write his last will and testament[2]—his final literary and theological testimony to the world, the supreme *apologia pro vita et doctrina sua*, the classic exposition of the 'Gentile Gospel', the 'Gospel according to St Paul', his liberal faith for the Gentile world.

3. THE READERS

St Paul is writing to a Church which had been in existence a number of years, perhaps a whole decade, before he sent his Epistle from Corinth in A.D. 57–8. He is evidently himself a stranger to the Church in Rome, and had never been there (1:10); he had certainly nothing to do with the founding of the Church in Rome. Traditionally the Church in Rome is connected with St Peter, not St Paul;

---

[1]The date, A.D. 57, for this stage in St Paul's career is fixed, first with reference to his encounter with Gallio at Corinth in A.D. 52—the one secure date supported by inscriptional evidence in the New Testament—and, thereafter, by a rough computation of the period occupied by the events described in Ac. 18:18–19:20 (five years may be too long).

[2]Cf. G. Bornkamm, *Paul* (London, 1971), pp. 88ff. and p. 96; also 'The Letter to the Romans as Paul's Last Will and Testament', *Austr. Bibl. Rev.*, XI (1963), pp. 2–14.

St Peter did probably at one time visit Rome, and may have been martyred there, but the actual founders of the Roman Church are unknown.[1] Their names may have been preserved in the list of persons greeted by the Apostle at chapter 16, if that chapter is a genuine part of the Epistle; Paul refers to, among others, a certain Andronicus and Junias who are 'of note among the apostles, and they were in Christ before me' (16:7). It may have been one or more of these notable pre-Pauline apostles who were the first to preach the Gospel in the imperial city.

The actual date for the foundation of the Roman Church is a matter for inference and conjecture. The main evidence is external, not internal: it consists chiefly of the report of the Roman historian Suetonius in his life of Claudius (25) of the famous edict of Claudius of A.D. 49 banishing the Jews from Rome on account of disturbances alleged to have been created by the instigations of a certain 'Chrestus'; Suetonius is evidently reporting a garbled version of riots, probably within the large Jewish community, produced no doubt by the preaching of the Gospel by early missionaries; we are probably to think of a situation similar to the riots which broke out about the same time in south Galatia (Derbe, Lystra, Lycaonia) as a result of Paul's preaching of the Gospel.[2]

On this view, the Gospel was planted in Rome by the preaching of the word. Dr. Cranfield argues for the alternative theory that the Gospel was more probably disseminated by Christians 'in the discharge of their ordinary, secular duties or business rather than through any specially undertaken evangelistic enterprise' (p. 17). The fact that no such enterprise is mentioned in Acts or Romans hardly means that it never took place. The decree of Claudius is more naturally understood if, in fact, it was the activity of Christian evangelists which caused the riots leading up to the famous edict.

Incidentally, we read of two Jewish exiles from the persecutions of Claudius at Ac. 18:1ff., the famous and well-to-do Jewish couple,

[1] Cf. H. W. Bartsch, 'Die historische Situation des Römerbriefs', *Communio Viatorum*, VIII (1965), pp. 199–208. See also *Stud. Ev.* iv.(1), *TU* cii, pp. 281–91.

[2] But cf. S. Benko, 'The Edict of Claudius of A.D. 49 and the Instigator Chrestos', *TZ* XXV (1969), pp. 406ff. Benko argues that the edict of Claudius was occasioned by the Jewish-Gentile *Kulturkampf* in Rome (Chrestos was a Jewish zealot agitator!). This was probably not the only occasion Claudius had difficulties with the Jewish colony in Rome. Cf. F. F. Bruce, *New Testament History* (London, 1969), pp. 279ff. on the report of Dio Cassius, *Hist.*, lx 6; see also W. Wiefel, 'Die jüdische Gemeinschaft im antiken Rom und die Anfänge des römischen Christentums: Bemerkungen zu Anlass und Zweck des Römerbriefes', *Judaica*, XXVI (1970), pp. 65ff.

Priscilla and Aquila, who must already have been Christians when they met Paul at Corinth.[1]

It is not surprising that there should have been a Christian Church in Rome at so early a period, for Roman Judaism presented a fertile soil for the Gospel. The Jewish community in Rome has been estimated in the first century B.C. at 40,000 to 60,000, with no fewer than thirteen synagogues.[2] The probability is that one of these was a Jewish–Christian synagogue; it is only in this way that we can satisfactorily account for the peculiarities of the early Roman Church.[3] A fourth-century Church Father, Ambrosiaster, has this to say about the ancient Roman Church:

> It is known that Jews lived at Rome in apostolic times, because they were subjects of the Roman Empire. Those of them who had become Christians passed on to the Romans the message that they should profess Christ and keep the Law . . . Without seeing displays of mighty works, or any of the apostles they accepted the faith of Christ, though with Jewish rites.[4]

We have no reason to disbelieve this picture of the early Roman Church.[5] When we add that, next to Jerusalem, it was probably the largest in the Empire (Tacitus, not many years later, speaks of Christians in Rome as an 'immense multitude'), we begin to under-

---

[1]Cf. A. Harnack, 'Probabilia über die Adresse und den Verfasser des Hebräerbriefs', *ZNTW* 1 (1900) pp. 33ff.

[2]Cf. H. J. Leon, *The Jews of Ancient Rome* (Philadelphia, 1960), pp. 135ff. J. Juster, *Les Juifs dans l'Empire Romain*, II (Paris, 1914), pp. 170.

[3]Michel (p. 2, n.3) thinks that there may have been several Christian centres, on the analogy of the numerous synagogues, and consequent on the Roman policy of 'decentralisation' of *'collegia'*, 'guilds', 'corporations'. See E. Schürer, *The Jewish People in the Time of Jesus Christ* (Edinburgh, 1901), II.ii, pp. 232ff.; edition Vermes, Millar and Goodman (Edinburgh, 1986), III.1, pp. 73ff.; J. B. Frey, 'Les Communautés juives à Rome aux premiers temps de l'Église', *Recherches de Science Religieuse*, 20, 1930, pp. 269–97; 21, 1931, pp. 129–68; see also G. La Piana, 'Foreign Groups in Rome during the First Centuries of the Empire', *HThR*, XX (1927), pp. 183–403, and 'The Roman Church at the End of the Second Century', ibid., XVIII, 1925, pp. 201–77. For the strong links between Roman Jewry and Jerusalem, see G. F. Moore, *Judaism in the First Centuries of the Christian Era*, I (1927), p. 106. One of the Roman synagogues was known as the *synagōgē elaias*, the 'Synagogue of the Olive Tree', cf. Schürer, II, ii, pp. 74, 248; edition Vermes, Millar, Black (Edinburgh, 1979), p. 445. Was the first Roman Christian congregation an off-shoot? See Ch. 11, below, p. 157.

[4]Cf. Dodd, pp. xxvii ff.

[5]But contrast Cranfield, p. 19 (foot) f. Was Ambrosiaster influenced by Marcion?

stand the challenge it presented to St Paul. Sir William Ramsay was no doubt right in arguing that St Paul was anxious to plant the Christian flag in the capital of the Empire, though he tended to overlook the fact that a Christian flag had already been planted there nearly a decade earlier—with a star of David, however, rather than a cross as its emblem. From St Paul's point of view the Roman Church was, like the Church in Jerusalem, a reactionary Church. He was ambitious to win Rome for his liberal Gospel, one prepared to admit Gentiles without first demanding that they become Jews. It is no coincidence that the main theme of Romans is 'Gospel and Law'.

Like all these early foundations, the Roman Church was of Jewish origin but of Gentile growth and, possibly, of predominantly Gentile racial composition.[1] It was, no doubt, a mixed community, socially as well as racially; some of the names at chapter 16 are those of emancipated slaves and freedmen, but others point to membership of the aristocracy ('the family of Aristobulus' at verse 10 is clearly a reference to members of the Herod family). The suggestion has been made, mainly on the basis of the evidence of 16:5, 14, 15, that there may have been several different groups or Christian cells in Rome, perhaps some form of 'house-church'.[2] It is certainly curious that the Apostle should mention groups, as at verses 14 and 15, as if they had a separate group identity. In view of the huge Jewish population in Rome with their thirteen synagogues, and the statement of Tacitus, that, at the outbreak of the Neronian persecutions, Roman Christians were an 'immense multitude' (above, p. 7) there may even have been a number of independent Christian–Jewish 'synagogues'. The language of the Roman Church appears to have been mainly Greek, and Greek seems to have maintained its position till well into the second century, certainly as a literary and probably also as a liturgical language.[3]

In the light of the character of the Roman Church, the reasons for St Paul's letter are quite simply two: (i) the Roman Church was an important Church; and (ii) it was still (from Paul's liberal standpoint) an imperfect and immature Church, still probably little more than a sect within Judaism. Its main doctrine, no doubt, consisted of a belief in the Jewish Messiah, Jesus, crucified and risen, side by side with obedience to the Law. Paul preached the

[1]But cf. Cranfield, pp. 20ff.
[2]Cranfield, p. 22.
[3]Cf. further, K. H. Schelkle, 'Römische Kirche im Römerbrief: zur Geschichte und Auslegungsgeschichte', *Ztschr. für katholische Theologie*, LXXXI (1959), pp. 393–404.

catholic Christ and emancipation from the Law: and he wrote to win over this influential centre to his Gospel.[1]

4. THE STRUCTURE OF THE EPISTLE[2]

While there is a general consensus among scholars, both ancient and modern, that Romans, in spite of its at times apparently digressive style, is not an entirely unplanned exercise—some more than others detect a carefully prepared 'outline' or 'plan'—agreement, even on the main structural lines of the Epistle, has never been complete; and differences of opinion are not likely ever to be fully or finally resolved.

Chapter 16, with its long list of greetings, presents its own special problems; and it may be that 15:14–16:27 should be treated together as marking the conclusion of the letter (see further below, p. 10).

Traditionally, especially in Protestant exegesis, chapters 1–8 have been regarded as the doctrinal heart of Romans, presenting the essential doctrine of the Epistle, 'justification by faith alone'. Within this section most exegetes have found a 'break', or 'caesura', in the developing argument at the end of chapter 5: chapters 1–5 deal with 'justification'; chapters 6–11, in the old Protestant terminology, with 'sanctification'—the Christian life ensuing on 'justification'.[3] Chapters 9–11 are regarded as a kind of appendix dealing with the problem of the final destiny of the ethnic Israel, so obdurately resistant to the appeal of the Gospel. Chapters 12–15 are Pauline *paraenesis*, i.e. attached Christian homiletic instruction.

Recent research has been challenging this traditional schema, especially in its analysis of the 'structure' of chapters 1–8, the 'great thesis' section; and, to judge from the amount of ink being spilled

---

[1]For modern discussion of the purpose of Romans (by Klein, Fuchs, Bornkamm, Marxsen, *et al.*) see K. P. Donfried, 'A Short Note on Rom. 16', *JBL*, LXXXIX (1970), pp. 441ff. No doubt Paul was anxious to have his authority as *the* Gentile Apostle recognised by this powerful Gentile community (Klein). Romans may also have been aimed, indirectly, at Jerusalem readers; cf. J. Jervell, 'Der Brief nach Jerusalem: über Veranlassung und Adresse des Römerbriefes', *Stud. Theol.*, XXV (1971), pp. 61–73. One might add that in view of the close links with Jerusalem (see above, p. 7, n. 3), Paul's *apologia pro doctrina sua* in Romans, especially *vis-à-vis* the Law, would stand him in good stead in Jerusalem.

[2]For bibliography, see p. xviii.

[3]Characterised as 'the classic plan' by Bonnard (p. 243); adopted by Godet, B. Weiss, SH, Goguel; and, among Catholic scholars, Lagrange, Huby. Cf. Dupont, p. 368. For Bonnard and Dupont, see bibliography.

on the question, the debate is likely to continue. As will be evident from the commentary, the present author favours the division at chapter 5:11–12, following the arguments of Dodd, Dahl, Feuillet and Dupont among others (see the bibliography). The theme of 'justification', while it reappears at different points in the later chapters (e.g. 8:1), has been central and basic in this first section: 1:17 (statement of theme)—5:11. The Adam-Christ typology (5:12–21) lays the foundation for the doctrine of the Christian life (life 'in Christ', i.e. within the Body of Christ, the new Adam; or life 'in the spirit', 'eternal life', the present possession of the 'justified sinner') (6:1–8:39). Chapter 7 is hardly a digression, since it deals with the 'old Adam'.[1]

Probably the most convincing, and certainly the most influential, of the many studies on the structure of Romans are those of Professor A. Feuillet of Brussels. Few will disagree with Feuillet's statement ('Le Plan salvifique', p. 337) that the theme of the Epistle is incontestably 'the salvation offered by God to all men through the faith of the Gospel'. This 'plan of salvation' the Apostle envisages first with regard to individuals (chapters 1–8), then for its bearings on the agonising problem of the unbelief of Israel (9–11). Feuillet further discerns a third section, viz. chapters 12–15, concerned with Christian life and community relationships. Chapter 15:14–16:27 is the conclusion of the Epistle.

In recognising these sections as each and all important parts of the 'grand design' of Romans, Professor Feuillet has made a significant contribution to the study of the Epistle.[2] The view that chapters 1–8 contain 'the great thesis', while the rest is appendix, is not likely to have been the perspective of St Paul; the destiny of his own people, who were rejecting his Gospel, was an agonising concern of the Apostle to the Gentiles. Similarly, chapters 13 and 14 dealing with attitudes within the typical hellenistic Christian community, including that at Rome, e.g. to the State and, especially to fellow Christians, in particular 'the weak' Jewish-Christian, still concerned about *kosher* foods, and the 'strong' Gentile—probably proselyte—

---

[1]For other views of chapters 6 and 7, see especially Dahl, Michel, Dupont: chapters 6 and 7 reply to questions about sin (6:1, 15) and the Law (7:7, 13), and together form a digression from the theme of chapter 5, which is resumed in chapter 8. (Cf. Nygren, *ad loc.*, for a further alternative.) On the 'question and answer' style, see below, p. 14f. These chapters can still contain replies to leading questions about sin and the law without being 'digressions'.

[2]Feuillet's arguments have clearly influenced the section divisions of the *Jerusalem Bible*; see Dupont, p. 365, n.4.

Christians, no doubt brought up under the restraints of the *tôrāh*, but now tending to throw off all restraint and taking up an antinomian or libertarian attitude.

Within chapters 1–8 M. Feuillet detects a structure, the key to which is supplied by Hab. 2:4, cited at Rom. 1:17 (the statement of the theme of the Epistle).[1] Feuillet agrees with the exegesis which understands the text as: 'The "just-by-faith" shall live', and sees in the rest of the section a literary structure built on the two concepts of the text, viz. *justificatio sola fide* and (eternal) life in Christ. The words 'just', 'justice' and 'faith', coming from the first part of the quotation as given by Paul, are of very frequent occurrence from 1:17 to 5:11, and almost entirely absent thereafter. On the other hand, the terms signifying 'life' (and 'death') occur regularly in chapters 5:12 to 7:1.

Only at one point does M. Feuillet's division and exegesis seem to require some modification. No less than at chapters 9–11, St Paul in chapters 1–8, and, in particular, from 5:12ff, is concerned, not simply with the salvation of individuals, but with the societary aspect of 'salvation'; the emphasis of the doctrine of 5:12–6:23 is on the redeemed *mankind*; the 'justified sinner' is thereby incorporated into the Body of Christ.

There is always, of course a danger in 'systematising' St Paul, and in this connection the observations of Professor J. Jeremias are of great importance.[2] The Pauline method of arguing a case with an imaginary opponent or objector has suggested that we have in Romans a piece of living missionary experience of the Apostle. Nevertheless, the arguments are conducted within the framework of the broad design of the Epistle, and do not materially affect its underlying structure, with its four central (and equally important) themes: salvation by faith; Christian life; the destiny of Israel; and the obligations of the Christian, especially to his fellow Christians of 'weaker' faith.

5. THE INTEGRITY OF ROMANS

Scholars have argued for more than a century that chapter 16 is no original part of what St Paul wrote to Rome, but is a fragment of another letter which St Paul wrote to the Church in Ephesus.

(i) It seems surprising that St Paul should have known and sent greetings to so many Roman Christians (some twenty-six persons

---

[1] *NTS*, VI (1959–60), pp. 52ff.
[2] See further below, p. 14f.

and groups of people are mentioned) considering that he had never himself been in Rome.

(ii) Several of the individuals named are associated with Asia and Ephesus, not Rome: at verse 5 a salutation is sent to Epaenetus described as 'the first convert in Asia for Christ', a description which seems more appropriate in a letter to Ephesus than to Rome.

(iii) Even more curious is the greeting at verses 3 to 5 to Prisca (Priscilla) and Aquila and the Church in their house. According to 1 Cor. 16:19, Aquila and Prisca were domiciled in Ephesus, and it was in Ephesus that the Church met in their house; greetings are sent here from Aquila and Prisca to Corinth from Ephesus, where that Epistle was written in A.D. 56.

To such internal considerations textual arguments have been added.

There is textual evidence that Romans circulated at one time without chapter 16. It consists of a reading of P^{46} (the Chester Beatty papyrus) which has the closing benediction of 16:25, not only at the end of this chapter, but also at the end of chapter 15. Since this benediction evidently formed the conclusion of the Epistle, it is argued that Romans did at one time end at chapter 15. Several Vulgate texts do not have chapter 16, but end with the doxology at 14:23.

The internal arguments for a connection of chapter 16 with Ephesus as a separate fragment can be answered, though the counter-arguments have been felt by some to be at times somewhat forced.

St Paul may have met the persons greeted in chapter 16 as 'displaced persons' from the Claudian persecutions of A.D. 49. Priscilla and Aquila had been driven from their home in Rome in A.D. 49 (Ac. 18:2), and had moved from Rome via Corinth to Ephesus where they were domiciled in exile (giving hospitality to the Church there, as no doubt they had done in Rome). With the proclamation of the general amnesty on Jews and Christians by Nero (the dawn of the *aureum quinquennium* in A.D. 54) Priscilla and Aquila had returned to Rome, so that nothing was more natural than that Paul should send greetings to them in his letter to Rome written from Corinth in A.D. 57-8.

If we can believe this possible—and it does not seem an unreasonable hypothesis—and do not find insuperable the difficulty of St Paul's acquaintance with so many Christians in Rome, then there is no compelling internal reason to reject chapter 16.

The textual evidence is more easily explained. According to this theory of chapter 16, it is interpreted to mean that Romans originally circulated without it; that chapter 16 was not in fact an integral part of the text of Romans, and therefore that it must be part of another letter.

The textual evidence, however, is capable of the alternative explanation that Romans did originally contain chapter 16, which was
later cut out simply because it consisted of a tedious list of names
no longer of interest when the Epistle was published and more
widely circulated. This is, in fact, how the evidence is best interpreted. It was noted that some mss. and versions (see Cranfield,
p. 6) without chapter 16 ended at 14:23, which is just before a long
Old Testament quotation. It is an unmistakable cut of the second
century Encratite (ascetic) heretic Marcion, who 'criticised the New
Testament with a sword' (*machaira*, Origen) (see SH, p. xc). It is
probable that the other textual evidence is to be explained similarly,
though the shortening of Romans in this way need not in every case
be attributed to Marcion.

The possibility that chapter 16 was not an integral part of the
original Roman Epistle, or had been dropped at an early date, has
given rise to various other theories about Romans. Lightfoot thought
that St Paul had shortened it himself, delocalising it for general use;
SH that Marcion shortened it for doctrinal reasons. These views are
summarised in A. H. McNeile, *St Paul: His Life, Letters and Christian Doctrine*, pp. 185–8.[1] A different solution was proposed by
Kirsopp Lake and accepted by F. C. Burkitt, that the short form
of the letter was original. 'Written by St Paul at the same time as
Galatians, in connection with the question of Jewish and Gentile
Christians, for the general instruction of mixed Churches that he
had visited.' 'Later on he sent a copy to Rome, with the addition of
the other chapters, to serve, as we should say, as a covering letter.'

There remains the view (Moffatt) that the Church shortened
Romans for general circulation; SH have shown conclusively that
Marcion did so, though no doubt mainly for dogmatic reasons.
Whether as the result of Marcion's influence or not, it is clear from
P^{46} that Romans did circulate without chapter 16 and, in G, one
manuscript at least lacks the personalia at 1:7, 15. Obviously the
general character of the Epistle, its suitability for all to read, and
the obvious place to make a cut of unnecessary material, led to the
removal of chapter 16 (and the doctoring of the text earlier) in
certain circles in the early Church. This is all the explanation we
require to account satisfactorily for the facts.[2]

[1] Cf. J. Knox, 'A Note on the Text of Romans', *NTS*, II (1955–6),
pp. 191–3.
[2] See T. W. Manson, *Studies in the Gospels and Epistles* (Manchester, 1962)
pp. 227ff., and K. P. Donfried, 'A Short Note on Romans 16' (above,
p. 9, n. 1) for discussion (and bibliography) on chapter 16. Cf. further,
N. A. Dahl, 'The Particularity of the Pauline Epistles', *Studia Neotestamentica et Patristica* (Cullmann *Festschrift*) (Leiden, 1962), p. 269.

6. THE STYLE OF THE EPISTLE

The Epistles attributed to St Paul present a considerable diversity
of style. In some respects the Epistle to the Romans is unique:

> This Epistle, like all the others of the group, is characterised
> by a remarkable energy and vivacity. It is calm in the sense
> that it is not aggressive and that the rush of words is always well
> under control. Still there is a rush of words, rising repeatedly to
> passages of splendid eloquence; but the eloquence is spon-
> taneous, the outcome of strongly moved feeling; there is
> nothing about it of laboured oratory. The language is rapid,
> terse, incisive; the argument is conducted by a quick cut and
> thrust of dialectic; it reminds us of a fencer with his eye always
> on his antagonist.[1]

A common explanation of this vivacious style of Romans is that it
has been influenced by the style of the spoken diatribe of the period
(see further below, p. 39). If it does show marks of the diatribe,
however, it is of a Jewish-style rhetorical discourse.

In his important contribution to the de Zwaan *Festschrift*,[2] J.
Jeremias drew attention to a formal characteristic of the style of
Romans which suggests that it owes much to the missionary experi-
ences of the Apostle, in which he was frequently interrupted in
mid-course by a Jewish hearer, who raised an objection to which
Paul was obliged to give an immediate answer.

While it seems very likely that Paul did carry this debating style
into his correspondence—Galatians is an obvious example—at the
same time his 'controversial' style probably also owes not a little to
the current rhetorical practices of the Stoic diatribe of the period,
especially as adapted by Jewish controversialists.[3]

The formal characteristics of this 'question–answer' style are:

(1) An objection is raised by the formula *ti (oun) eroumen* ('What
shall we say?') (3:5; 4:1; 6:1; 7:7; 8:31; 9:14, 30), or *ti oun* ('What,
then?') (3:1, 9; 6:15; 11:7). In the latter case, it would sometimes
seem that *ti oun* is simply a contraction of *ti oun eroumen* (e.g. 3:9
(?); 11:7); on other occasions it is incorporated into the syntax of
the sentence (e.g. 3:1).

(2) The objection is rejected with the formula *mē genoito*, which

---

[1]Cf. SH, p. lv.

[2]See above, p. xviii. Cf. also E. Trocmé, 'L'Épître aux Romains et la
méthode missionaire de l'apôtre Paul', NTS, VII (1960–1), pp. 148–53.

[3]Cf. R. Bultmann, *Der Stil der paulinischen Predigt und die kynisch-stoische
Diatribe* (Göttingen, 1910).

can be variously rendered: 'By no means', 'Heaven forbid!' (see note on 3:6) (3:4, 6, 31; 6:2, 15; 7:7, 13; 9:14; 11:1, 11).

At some places, Jeremias argues, Paul is replying to objections which are not expressly mentioned; e.g., chapter 4:1–2 is a reply to a 'hidden' objection that it was on the ground of his 'works' that Abraham was justified (the familiar rabbinical position—see note *ad loc.*).

The Jewish character of the Pauline diatribe or rhetoric is best seen in the extensive use the Apostle makes, not only of the Old Testament to provide scriptural authority for his position, but of familiar Jewish methods of employing or interpreting the Old Testament,[1] or simply of rabbinical methods of argumentation.[2] Among these are the use of the composite quotation (see note at 3:10), the scriptural argument by 'analogy' (Jeremias, op. cit., p. 149), or the adaptation of Scripture and its interpretation (*pesher*) in the somewhat free method familiar at Qumran.[3] In general, as Barth (following Luther) maintained, the proper understanding of the Old Testament was one of Paul's main reasons for writing Romans.[4]

The pervasive influence of the language of the Old Testament, its idioms and distinctive locutions, and, in particular, the profound influence both of the ideas and vocabulary of the Septuagint, including central theological concepts such as *dikaiosynē*, *sōtēria*, etc. has been frequently noted.[5] Nevertheless, Paul is a rhetorician, schooled at Tarsus as well as Jerusalem,[6] and there is really little foundation for John Chrysostom's complaint about the poverty of Paul's vocabulary or the 'artlessness' of his composition.[7] No distinctive Aramaic influence has been convincingly proved in Romans.[8]

---

[1] E. Earle Ellis, *Paul's Use of the Old Testament* (Edinburgh, 1957); J. Schmid, 'Die alttestamentlichen Zitate bei Paulus und die Theorie von sensus plenior', *BZ*, III (1959), pp. 161–73; G. Schrenk, 'Der Römerbrief als Missions-dokument', in *Studien zu Paulus, Abh. zur Theol, des alten und neuen Testaments*, XXVI (1954), pp. 81–106.

[2] See Bonsirven, *Exégèse rabbinique et exégèse paulinienne* (Paris, 1939).

[3] See Ellis, op. cit.; M. Black, 'The Christological Use of the Old Testament in the New Testament', *NTS*, XVIII (1970–1), especially pp. 8ff.

[4] *A Shorter Commentary on Romans*, pp. 11ff.

[5] Cranfield, p. 25.

[6] See especially W. C. van Unnik, *Tarsus or Jerusalem* (London, 1962).

[7] Cited in Cranfield, p. 26.

[8] But cf. the note on 13:8 (p. 184f.) and W. C. van Unnik, 'Aramaeismen bij Paulus', in *Vox Theologica* XV (1943), pp. 117–26.

COMMENTARY

on

Romans

EPISTOLARY PRESCRIPT AND STATEMENT OF THEME
1:1–18

(i) Apostolic Salutation and Epistolary Prescript 1–7
(ii) Thanksgiving and Personal Introduction 8–15
(iii) Adumbration of Theme 16–18

APOSTOLIC SALUTATION

1:1–7

The prescript of Romans is a somewhat elaborate form of the traditional Greek prescript, which we find at James 1:1, Acts 15:23, 23:26. For various reasons (see below), Paul expands this typical prescript, replacing the usual *chairein* ('greetings') with his own distinctive *charis kai eirēnē* ('grace and peace', 2 C. 1:2, Eph. 1:2, Phil. 1:2; Galatians has no prescript). The use of *eirēnē* = *shalom* alerts us to the influence of oriental as well as hellenistic epistolary prescripts, e.g., 2 Mac. 1:2. See further, below, on v.7. The prescript has a much more formal character here than in other Pauline Epistles (cf. the short, personal greeting at 1 Th. 1:1f., Phil. 1:1): the occasional absence of the definite article where it would normally be found is one such formal feature (e.g., at vv. 1, 4, 5; verse 5, *charin kai apostolēn eis hypakoēn pisteōs*), reminding us more of a Roman imperial mandate than a private letter. All this is quite deliberate: Paul (perhaps with the assistance of Tertius) is doing his formal best to impress the Roman congregation to which the letter would be read. There are several other reasons for this elaboration of the traditional form of prescript and salutation: (1) Paul was probably personally unknown to the majority of the Roman Church; and rumours had almost certainly reached Rome about this missionary iconoclast who was said to be challenging the Law of Moses, and making vast claims for himself as 'the Apostle to the Gentiles', putting himself on a level, as it were, with Peter and the Pillar Apostles. No such claim is here explicitly made: in describing himself as *klētos apostolos*, 'called as an apostle', Paul could be taken to mean simply 'missionary' rather than 'missionary extraordinary', like the Pillar Apostles, the Twelve. Nevertheless, he leaves his readers in no doubt as to his authority as an apostle set apart for the proclamation of the Gospel, as he says, 'among all peoples' (referring mainly to the Gentiles but including the Jewish people as

well). Certainly in Galatians Paul is making claims to be a
'missionary extraordinary' like the Pillar Apostles and St Peter
himself, but it would hardly have been tactful in this prescript to
the Roman Church to have made explicit claims to such a role: he
simply emphasises his divinely-appointed vocation as missionary
among the nations or peoples; and it is perhaps significant that he
puts function before status (*doulou Iēsou Christou*, 'servant of Jesus
Christ', before *klētos apostolos*, 'called as an apostle'). He also emphasises, as in the Galatian Epistle, that his apostolate is one of 'sheer
grace', *charin kai apostolēn* (hendiadys).

(2) Suspicion had been awakened in the Roman Church not only
about the person of this missionary Paul, but no less about his
message as in some way challenging the Law of Moses. Paul carefully formulates in the prescript in summary form his Gospel, in all
its essentials, in a statement which we have reason to believe may
have been deliberately adjusted to the capacity of his readers. (See
notes on verses 2 and 3.)

1. **servant** rather than 'slave' (*mg.*); the latter came to have
degrading associations absent from the term as used by the writer.
The expression 'servant of Christ' occurs not infrequently in salutations: this seems to be the first instance of it, but it is found also
in the salutations of Phil., Jas, Jude and 2 Pet. Did St Paul set the
fashion for other apostolic writers? The term does not here necessarily imply 'purchase by Christ', though St Paul does use this figure,
and that of 'manumission' elsewhere (1 C. 6:19, 20; 7:22, 23). Cf.
A. Deissmann, *Light from the Ancient East* (1910), pp. 327ff.

The expression 'servant of God/the Lord' is applied in the *OT*
variously to Moses (Jos. 1:2), David (Ps. 89:3, 20), and the prophets
from Amos onwards (Am. 3:7 to Jer. 7:25, Dan. 9:6 *et passim*). It
is probably reading too much into the expression to suggest that St
Paul is slipping the name 'Christ' without explanation into the place
of 'God' or 'the Lord', or is thus placing himself in the succession
of the prophets; that he regarded himself as 'bond-servant' of deity
in his service of Christ goes without saying. For the expression
applied to Christians by Paul, cf. Rom. 6:17, 22, 1 C. 7:22; Eph.
6:6; etc. The order 'Christ Jesus' is probably original, but it is
doubtful if any great significance is to be attached to it (cf. SH, *ad
loc.*); both forms have become titular.

called to be an apostle: In his apostolic vocation St Paul emphasises
that it is a divine calling (as is also—verse 7—the call to all 'saints',
i.e., Christians, cf. 1 C. 1:1; Gal. 1:1); in this he does stand in the
line of the servants of God of the *OT* (Abraham (Gen. 12:1–3);
Moses (Exod. 3:10ff.); Isaiah (Isa. 6:8, 9); Jeremiah (Jer. 1:4, etc.)).

At Gal. 1:15 Paul applies to himself what Yahweh said to Jeremiah (Jer. 1:5).

The term 'apostle' can be used in a lower and in a higher sense; in the former, it can apply to all the first 'missionaries' of the Gospel (e.g., Rom. 16:7). St Paul no doubt considered it applied to himself in the higher sense: he sets himself alongside the Twelve 'pillar' Apostles, an apostolate which had been conferred on him, not by election of men, but by the sheer grace of the special calling and revelation of God (cf. again Gal. 1:1), its sphere the Gentile world (verse 5); see A. Fridrichsen, *The Apostle and his Message* (Uppsala, 1947), p. 6: 'Obviously Paul pictures to himself the eschatological situation of the world in this way: In this world, soon disappearing, the centre is Jerusalem, with the primitive community and the Twelve, surrounded by the mission field divided between two apostles: one sent by the Lord to the circumcised, the other to the Gentiles. Peter and Paul himself are the chosen bearers of the Gospel, flanking the portal of the world to come.' Cf. Gal. 2:7, where Paul declares himself to have been divinely entrusted with the gospel to the 'uncircumcision' as Peter was to the circumcision. Similarly at 1 C. 15:8 he classes himself with James and 'all the Apostles', as the last Apostle to be a witness of the Risen Christ (although he tells us it was like an abnormal birth, so far as he was concerned); he is clearly referring to the appearance on the Damascus road. Now this was one of the primary qualifications— witnessing to the Risen Lord—according to Ac. 1:22 of the Twelve Pillar Apostles. Had a rumour reached Rome that Paul was classing himself with Peter and the Pillar Apostles? If so, it would certainly have given offence and been hotly disputed. Perhaps Paul is deliberately playing down his Apostolic Office in this verse, while, at the same time, if only by implication, maintaining his position as *the* Apostle to the Gentile world.

set apart for the gospel of God: lit. 'separated' (or 'singled out') 'for [the proclamation of] the Gospel'. Like the prophet Jeremiah, St Paul thinks of himself as 'set apart' in the purpose of God 'from his mother's womb' (cf. Gal. 1:15, 16; cf. Jer. 1:5); but he is also represented as 'set apart' at his conversion and by the appointment of the Church for its Gentile mission (cf. Ac. 13:2). There may be a cryptic allusion in this particular word to Paul's Pharisaic background (Phil. 3): the name 'Pharisee' was popularly explained as meaning 'one separated off (from the world)' and so 'set apart' (*parush*). If St Paul is here alluding to his former Pharisaic status, he is now declaring that his dedicated position is that of one separated from the world for the spread of the Gospel.

gospel of God: the expression is a very common one in Paul occurring some sixty times (with the variant 'gospel of Christ'). For an illuminating discussion of the term *euangelion* ('good news'), see Deissmann, *Light from the Ancient East*, pp. 370ff.

2. which he (God) promised beforehand through his prophets in the holy scriptures: the word *epangellesthai* ('to promise') and *epangelia* ('promise') are key terms in the *NT* for the 'promises' to Israel delivered by the Hebrew prophets, recorded in the sacred scriptures of the *OT*. These are now fulfilled in the Gospel, which is the 'promise fulfilled', the 'good news' of the advent of the Kingdom of God and his Messiah (cf. Mt. 4:23; Mk 1:14, 15; Ac. 13:32, 26:6; etc.). Note the characteristic paronomasia (*euangelion*, *proepēngeilato*). Cf. 2 Mac. 2:17; Ps. Solomon, 7:9(10) (the day of salvation *promised* to Israel), 12:7(6) ('the *promises* of the Lord' which the 'saints' will inherit).

3. concerning his Son: For the theory that Paul is drawing on an existing confessional formula in verses 3–4, see Cranfield, p. 57. 'Son', in 'Son of God', the highest christological designation, Jewish-messianic in origin (cf. Dalman, *Words of Jesus*, pp. 268ff., W. Kramer, *Christ, Lord, Son of God*. (SCM *Studies in Biblical Theology* 50) (London, 1966), pp. 183ff., F. Hahn, *Christologische Hoheitstitel: ihre Geschichte im frühen Christentum* (Göttingen, 1963), pp. 280ff. and E. Evans, *Tertulliani adversus Praxean liber* (London, 1948), p. 322. B. M. F. van Iersel, *'Der Sohn' in den synoptischen Jesus-worten, Nov. Test.*, Suppl. III (Leiden, 1961).

descended from David according to the flesh: St Paul is contrasting Christ's messianic status, on the human side ('according to the flesh'), with his 'spiritual' status ('designated Son of God', etc.). The Davidic descent of the Messiah was virtually axiomatic in popular Jewish messianism. It was part of Paul's gospel, according to 2 Tim. 2:8, and is appealed to as evidence for Jesus' messianic claims at Ac. 2:30. According to Mk 12:35f. and par., Jesus himself appears to have found difficulty with this popular belief, and to have taken exception to it;[1] he never used the term 'son of David' of himself. See also E. Schweizer, 'Röm. 1:3f. und der Gegensatz von Fleisch und Geist vor und bei Paulus', *Ev. Theol.*, XV (1955), pp. 563–71; and cf. E. Linnemann, 'Tradition und Interpretation in Rom. 1:3ff', *ibid.*, XXXI (1971), pp. 264–75.

It is doubtful if the Gospel would ever have commended itself

---

[1] Cf. however, D. Daube in *The New Testament and Rabbinic Judaism* (London, 1956), p. 163, where Mk 12:35f. is explained as a rabbinical type 'antinomy' to be resolved by referring each contradictory statement to its proper field of application, as here in Romans, 'son of David' according to the flesh; '"Son of God" according to the Spirit of holiness.'

to Jews, Palestinian or hellenistic, without this accepted article of messianic belief. If it was not original and primitive, it must have been incorporated at a very early stage into the Apostolic *kerygma*.

4. designated Son of God in power according to the Spirit of holiness by his resurrection from the dead: these words can only be understood when interpreted as a whole.

designated: the usual meaning of this verb is 'to define', 'to determine' and so 'decree', 'ordain' (cf. Ac. 10:42, 17:31; and *The Greek Anthology*, trans. W. R. Paton (1916–18), IV, p. 363 (xii, 158, 7): 'destiny decreed (ordained) thee (Eros) a god'). This fundamental meaning would seem to rule out the otherwise contextually suitable 'revealed', 'proved to be' (Chrysostom) for which there are other, regular Greek equivalents. The English versions 'declared (to be)', 'designated' would seem to derive from this basic meaning 'decreed'; 'installed' (Moffatt) is a somewhat free rendering. What is left vague by these renderings is in what way—when or by whom—we are to conceive that Jesus Christ was 'declared to be Son of God'. A recent suggestion of L. C. Allen ('The Old Testament Background of *(pro)horizein* in the New Testament', *NTS* XVII (1970–1), pp. 104ff.) is that the 'decree', proclaiming Christ's Sonship to which allusion is made here, is that of Yahweh at Ps. 2:6ff.: 'I will declare the decree; the Lord hath said unto me, Thou art my Son: this day have I begotten thee.' We would then render: 'whom God decreed Son of God' ('with power . . . through resurrection'). For this use of the passive, where the subject is God, see below, p. 27. Ac. 13:32 similarly connects Ps. 2:6ff., the divinely decreed Sonship, with the Resurrection (verse 32 also stressing the preaching of the gospel of the promise made to the Fathers). See further below for this 'primitive' Christology; and on this verb, cf. M. E. Boismard, 'Constitué Fils de Dieu (Rom. 1:4)', *RB*, LX (1953), pp. 5–17.

in power: the 'Son of God', begotten from David's line on the human side, is also declared by divine decree 'Son of God' in power, on the side of the Spirit, the Holy Spirit—i.e. on the divine, supernatural side. The phrase 'in power' can be taken closely with 'Son of God', or as qualifying the whole expression 'decreed', 'miraculously decreed Son of God through Resurrection'.

according to the Spirit of holiness: St Paul is contrasting the status of Christ's Sonship on the man-ward side (born of the seed of David, according to the flesh) with his status on the 'spiritual' (supernatural) side; Spirit (Holy Spirit) proceeds from God. The expression could be interpreted to mean also: 'through the operation of the Holy Spirit', and connected with 'through resurrection'. According to common Jewish belief, the resurrection of the dead was to be the work of the Holy Spirit (cf. I. Hermann, *Kyrios und Pneuma: Studien*

zur Christologie der paulinischen Hauptbriefe (1961), pp. 117ff.).
Christ was divinely decreed Son of God 'in power', i.e. miraculously,
by a mighty act of God, through the work of the Holy Spirit
effecting his Resurrection; cf. Lk. 1:35.

'Spirit of holiness' is not the normal phrase for Holy Spirit (*hagion
pneuma*), and has been taken subjectively to refer to a spirit of
transcendent holiness possessed by Christ. This seems unlikely.
'Spirit of holiness' looks like a primitive, 'hebraised' phrase (*pneuma
hagiosynēs = ruah haqqodesh*). For a similar expression, cf. *Test. of
the Twelve Patriarchs, Levi* XVIII. 7. Cf. further, B. Schneider, '*Kata
Pneuma Hagiosynēs, Bib.*, XLVIII (1967), esp. pp. 377ff.

by his resurrection from the dead: 'by' can mean 'by reason of',
'on the grounds of', 'through', or 'by' Resurrection; it may also
mean 'since'. The expression is a general one, 'Resurrection from
the dead', though the reference is to Christ's Resurrection. But cf.
S. H. Hooke, in *NTS*, IX (1962–3), pp. 370–1.

For the view that this verse implies a primitive Christology, see
Dodd, pp. 4ff. Dodd holds that the christological position here
defined is 'scarcely a statement of Paul's own theology. He held that
Christ was Son of God from all eternity, that He was "in the fullness
of time" incarnate as a man, and that by His resurrection He was
invested with the full power and glory of His divine status as Lord
of all. This is put most fully and clearly in Phil. ii:6–10; but there
is no reason to suppose that it belongs only to the later period of
Paul's theological thought. It is implied in this epistle, viii:3, as well
as in 2 C. viii:9 and Gal. iv:4. The present statement therefore, falls
short of what Paul would regard as an adequate doctrine of the
Person of Christ. It recalls the primitive preaching of the Church,
as it is put into the mouth of Peter in Ac. ii:22–34.' Cf. also
Ac. 13:33. Was it a deliberate accommodation to an early form of
Christology current in the Roman Church? If so, it was later
corrected and developed; the *Apostolic Tradition* of Hippolytus
('Canon of the Eucharist') reads: *quique in utero habitus incarnatus
est et filius tibi ostensus est* ex spiritu sancto *et virgine natus* (emphasis
mine); cf. R. H. Connolly in *JTS*, XXXIX (1938), pp. 357ff.

Jesus Christ our Lord: for the history, background and significance
of this full title, see Vincent Taylor, *Names of Jesus* (London 1953),
p. 22: 'in the majority of cases St Paul and St Peter use "Christ"
as a personal name'.

5. grace and apostleship: may be hendiadys, meaning 'grace
of apostleship', thus referring to the peculiar character of Paul's
apostleship as due to the totally unmerited act of grace in the divine
revelation to him through Christ (cf. above, p. 19). Cf. N. Turner,
Grammar of New Testament Greek, Vol. III, p. 335.

to bring about the obedience of faith: lit. 'an apostleship for faith and obedience among all Gentiles'. The words define the purpose and sphere of Paul's special apostleship: it was to bring the Gentile world to an obedience which springs from faith, in contradistinction to an obedience based on the external observance of Law. The genitive is an adjectival one. Cf. G. H. Parke-Taylor in *ET*, LV (1943-4), pp. 305-6.

As W. D. Davies has so well brought out (*Paul and Rabbinic Judaism*, p. 148), a great deal in Paul is only fully intelligible if we replace the Jewish ideal of the *tôrāh*, or Law, by the ideal (or Person) of Christ. The whole inspiration of Jewish life was the Law and obedience to it; the inspiration of Christian living is Christ, apprehended by faith, and obedience to the Risen Lord.

among all the nations: Is Paul here referring to the Gentiles, excluding Israel, or to the nations of the world generally, including Israel? The first is suggested by Paul's definition of his role as Apostle to the Gentiles. But he may be deliberately vague, even avoiding any specific claim to be *the* Apostle to the Gentiles by using the word here in the inclusive sense. Cf. Michel *ad loc.* who cf. 16:26f., parallel to Mt. 24:24; 28:19; etc.

including yourselves: along with 1:13ff. and 15:15ff. this verse provides the strongest support for the thoroughly, if not predominantly, Gentile character of the Roman church. (cf. Cranfield, p. 20).

for the sake of his name: Paul's apostolate to the Gentiles is not only for their sake—never for less. It is also 'for Christ's sake', unless, with Michel, we take 'name' as surrogate for God—it was 'for God's sake'.

6. called to belong to Jesus Christ: God calls; Christians belong to Christ—a possessive genitive (cf. Barrett). Cf. verse 7.

7. in Rome: G 1739^mg. pc. omit the words here and at verse 15; at verse 7 G it vg^mss change 'beloved of God' into 'in the love of God'. For the significance which has been attached to the omission, see note on the integrity of Romans, above, p. 13.

who are called to be saints: the divine calling is not only to the high office of the apostolate (cf. verse 1: 'called to be an apostle'): it embraces all believers, described at verse 7 as 'saints' (*hagioi*). The word 'holy' (*hagios*) originally denoted separation—in particular, separation for the service of God. (Lev. 19:2 'You shall be holy; for I the Lord your God am holy . . .'). Then *hagioi* comes to be employed in the *NT* virtually as a proper name for Christians (8:27, 12:13, 15:25; 1 C. 6:1; Eph. 1:15; Col. 1:4; Phm. 5); it undoubtedly derives from the designation the '*saints* of the most High' used to describe the Remnant or Son of Man at Dan. 7:13, 27, etc.

Grace to you and peace: this is a remarkable combination in what
is a distinctive Pauline salutation. 'Grace' (*charis*) rings the changes
on the common Greek salutation *chairein* ('greeting'), combining it
with the Hebrew salutation *shalom* ('peace'). 2 Mac. 1:2 is a
precedent. Cf. Mayor on Jas. 1:1 (pp. 30ff.). Yet both terms also
carry the full theological sense of the favour of God to man, and
the cessation of hostility between God and man which was the work
of Christ.

God our Father and the Lord Jesus Christ: Christ the Lord is
joined with God the Father as equal in status: here is the germ of
Trinitarian doctrine. It is also through Christ the Lord that God's
Fatherhood has been revealed to man and assured for him.

THANKSGIVING AND PERSONAL INTRODUCTION

1:8–15

Paul's letters generally open with an epistolary prayer for the well-
being of his readers, in which he singles out for thanksgiving some
special characteristic for which they are noted.[1]

The simple form of ordinary thanksgiving prayer in non-literary
correspondence has been elaborated by St Paul into a formal literary
pattern.[2]

The Apostle occasionally may introduce the main theme (or
themes) of his letter in this way (cf. 1 C. 1:7, 'spiritual gift'). At
times there seems a deliberate irony in the characteristics of the
addressees singled out for thanksgiving: in Romans it is their 'faith'
which is proclaimed 'in all the world'; in fact, they were probably
better known for their 'justification by works'. Thus, as early in his
Epistle as this point St Paul introduces its central theme.

In these verses Paul also intimates, prepares for, and justifies his
intended visit to Rome (cf. 15:23ff.). He desires both to confer and
receive some 'spiritual gift', though hitherto prevented from doing
so, for he is filled with zeal to proclaim the Gospel in Rome.

---

[1] For the Pauline epistolary thanksgiving prayer as a variation of a conventional epistolary form of prayer, see especially H. N. Bate, *A Guide to the
Epistles of St. Paul* (London, 1949), pp. 10ff.; W. Barclay, 'The New
Testament and the Papyri', in *The New Testament in Historical and Contemporary Perspective; Essays in Memory of G. H. C. Macgregor* (Oxford, 1965),
p. 70.

[2] See P. Schubert, *Form and Function of the Pauline Thanksgiving*, BZNW,
xx (Berlin, 1939); J. T. Sanders, 'The Transition from Opening Epistolary
Thanksgiving to Body in the Letters of the Pauline Corpus', *JBL*, LXXXI
(1962), pp. 348–62.

8. First, I thank my God through Jesus Christ for all of you.
First (of all): the adverb modifies the verb; Paul puts thanksgiving
to God first: yet the words also convey the thought that he also puts
his Roman readers first in his prayers. Or: 'my thanks to God for
you all must come first'.

through Jesus Christ: Origen comments on these words: 'To give
thanks to God: this is to offer a sacrifice of praise: and therefore
(Paul) adds: "through Jesus Christ", as it were through a great High
Priest.' (See SH, *in loc.*) This is probably to read a great deal more
into his words than Paul meant; the formula 'through Jesus Christ
(our Lord)' means simply that the thanksgiving which Paul offers
he makes, like his Roman readers, as a disciple of Christ.

your faith is proclaimed in all the world: the Roman Church was
possibly better known throughout the Roman Empire for its
legalism than for its faith. See above, and Introduction, p. 7f.

**9. For God is my witness, whom I serve with my spirit in the
gospel of his Son:** 'God is my witness' is an Old Testament form
of asseveration, 1 Sam. 12:5, Jer. 42:5, but also Homer, Od. 1.273;
Polyb. 11.6. Cf. Barrett, *Romans, ad loc.* For the same formula, 2
C. 1:23, Phil. 1:8; 1 Th. 2:5, 10. The verb 'to serve' here (*latreuō*)
is especially associated with the 'liturgical service' of God, in Temple
or synagogue, by priest and people. The organ of Paul's service is
his 'spirit': its sphere the Gospel. Cf. 15:16.

'with my spirit' has given difficulty to commentators. The interpretation adopted is that of SH, 'spirit' as indicating that by using which
he accomplishes his service. Cranfield tests some five other possible
meanings for this:

1. As referring to the Spirit of God dwelling in him. (W. G.
   Kümmel). The addition of 'my' makes this most unlikely.
2. As indicating a spiritual = Christian service in contrast to a
   pagan even Jewish service, i.e., whom I serve (*latreuō*) as a
   spiritual priest. This is a possible nuance in the phrase.
3. Pelagius *in toto corde et prompta devotione* = wholeheartedly. This
   seems unlikely.
4. 'Sincerely': Calvin, 'from the heart . . . with sincere devotion of
   heart, in contrast to mere outward appearance.' Again a possible
   interpretation.
5. As indicating the whole person so engaged: Michel, 'Dienst
   beansprucht den Geist, damit den ganzen Menschen, sein
   Denken, Wollen und Handeln.'

We have to ask what 'spirit', with 'my' attached, means in biblical
Greek. It corresponds to *Geist*, i.e., the distinctive organ of man,
his intellectual and spiritual (moral) being. Paul is referring to his
new 'cultic' service of God, its sphere the Gospel, and the organ of

service his whole mind and heart. For 'Spirit', see further below, p. 102ff.

without ceasing: 'continually, without intermission'. The adverb is stressed—so great is Paul's concern.

10. asking that somehow by God's will I may now at last succeed in coming to you: 'at last' seems to imply that Paul's Roman readers are aware of his plans to visit Rome; in fact they are not apprised of these till chapter 15. Cf. J. Knox, in *NTS*, 11 (1955–6), pp. 191ff. Paul had often planned to visit Rome but had been hindered hitherto (cf. verse 13). This is implied in this verse, verse 11 emphasising the intensity of Paul's desire to visit Rome. Though he no doubt intended to do so (cf. 15:32), the prospect is here left vague and uncertain: notice how indefinite his words are— 'if', 'perchance', 'at long last', 'sometime'. It was no doubt his fears and anxieties about the results of his forthcoming visit to Jerusalem which accounted for this feeling of uncertainty, as they would also for the words 'by God's will' (i.e. if God so wills it); God's will for Paul in Jerusalem was still unknown. Cf. 15:32. *RSV*'s 'by God's will', in both places means practically 'if God wills'. There is certainly nothing here to suggest that St Paul is coming to Rome; only that he has long wanted to do so. Cf. J. Knox, *loc. cit.*

11. For I long to see you, that I may impart to you some spiritual gift to strengthen you: the 'spiritual *charisma*' which Paul's purpose is to share (*metadō*, see Cranfield *ad loc* and note on 12:8) with the Roman Church is not necessarily to be defined as one or any of the 'spiritual gifts', e.g., those listed by him at 1 C. 12:1ff., though Paul could claim possession of miraculous gifts of the Spirit in a preeminent degree (1 C. 14:18). It is more probable that Paul is using the term in a more general sense of the 'benefaction' of his Gospel for the Gentiles.

12. to strengthen you, that is, that we may be mutually encouraged by each other's faith: *RSV* gives the correct meaning, not *RV* ('to the end that ye may be established'); *NEB*: 'to make you strong'. The word is used of the inner strengthening of mind and spirit imparted by God (cf. Rom. 16:35, 2 Th. 2:17, 3:3). The choice of the passive here may be deliberate: 'Not that I (Paul) should strengthen you, but that God should strengthen you.' For this use of the passive, cf. Jeremias, *Eucharistic Words of Jesus*, Eng. trans. (Oxford, 1955), pp. 122ff.

The previous verse might sound patronising, in spite of the use of the word 'share' where Paul might have said 'impart' (which is, no doubt, what he really meant); verse 12, with fine tact, qualifies verse 11: it was a common or mutual encouraging, or heartening or strengthening, he meant to be given and received 'among you', and it was by their commonly held faith—theirs and Paul's—that this strengthening and mutual encouragement was to be effected.

13. I want you to know: lit. 'I would not have you ignorant'. This is a favourite phrase (cf. 11:25, 1 C. 10:1, 12:1, 2 C. 1:8, 1 Th. 4:13) when St Paul wants to call attention to what follows; it is sometimes now referred to as a 'disclosure formula', or 'formula of transition'.[1]

have been prevented: at 1 Th. 2:18 Satan was the hindrance; here it seems to be implied that it is God—or Providence—preventing Paul's firm intention being carried out.

in order that I may reap some harvest: there is an ambiguity in the meaning, which again is an instance of Pauline tact. Paul planned to get results at Rome as elsewhere in the Gentile world; but his words could mean that he planned to come to receive some benefit from the Roman Church, as he had also elsewhere in the Gentile world.

as among the rest of the Gentiles: perhaps we should rather render 'as among the other peoples', thus not excluding the Jews, as a 'people', 'nation' or 'ethnic group'. Cf. the note above on verse 5.

14. under obligation: the noun is ambiguous: it can mean 'I owe a debt to', 'I am under obligation to'; and this fits well with the meaning of verse 13, that Paul planned his visit to Rome to receive some fruit from the Roman Church. The same noun, however, from meaning 'to owe something to' can come to mean 'to have a duty to' (cf. Gal. 5:3, Rom. 8:12), and this fits the other sense of verse 13. Paul planned his visit to Rome to impart the *charisma* of his Gentile Gospel; for he has a duty to Greeks and barbarians, wise and simple—to which latter category some Roman Christians may have belonged.

15. so I am eager to preach the gospel: the expression may be literally translated: 'as far as concerns me there is readiness', implying 'I am ready to do my part, whether or not you are'. Another version is: 'thus the readiness or inclination on my part (is) to preach the gospel', etc. This amounts, in effect, to the same as *RSV*, but the *impersonal* way of saying it may be deliberate: St Paul is keeping himself in the background.

It is not till chapter 15 that Paul discloses his plans, first to

[1]Cf. J. T. Sanders, op. cit. n.o), J. L. White, 'Introductory Formulae in the Body of the Pauline Letter', *JBL* XC (1971), pp. 91–7; also T. Y. Mullins, 'Disclosure: a Literary Form in the New Testament', *Nov. Test.*, VII (1964), pp. 44–50. White argues that the body of the Roman letter begins with verse 13, and that therefore the end of the Thanksgiving is at verse 12.

proceed to Jerusalem with his 'collection' for the saints (and all that this entails of trouble and delay), then to visit Spain via Rome. See J. Knox, *op. cit.* (above, p. 27).

to you also who are in Rome: G supported by the Old Latin (it^g) and Origen omit 'in Rome' as above at verse 7.

If we accept the argument of White that the body of Romans begins at verse 13 (see above, page 28, n. 1), then Romans is, in fact, Paul's Gospel which he had failed to preach in person: verse 15 introduces it, verses 16–18 adumbrate it, and the remainder of chapters 1 to 8 defines it and enlarges on it.

PRELIMINARY STATEMENT OF THEME

1:16–18

The 'great thesis' of Romans, 'justification by faith alone' is adumbrated in these verses.

16. ashamed: to the Greek the gospel was 'foolishness' (1 C. 1:23); it took courage not to be ashamed of it in Imperial Rome. Cf. further, K. Grayston, '"Not Ashamed of the Gospel"', *Stud. Ev.* II (1964), pp. 569–74; O. Glombitza, 'Von der Scham des Gläubigen', *Nov. Test.*, IV (1960), pp. 74–80.

power of God: the word 'power' (*dynamis*) is especially associated in the *NT* with supernatural manifestations (e.g., miraculous occurrences like the Resurrection, cf. verse 4): in the plural, 'powers', it is a synonym of 'signs' (*sēmeia*) and 'wonders' (*terata*) (cf. Ac. 2:22). Thus the Gospel as the 'power of God' is a unique manifestation of supernatural reality. Older commentators compare it with natural forces such as heat and electricity, but, if we use this analogy or translate by 'force', 'energy', etc., it must be remembered, (a) that such a force was conceived of in a category or concept of the supernatural—it emanated from beyond Nature as a divine force; and (b) that the divine 'force' or 'energy' of God which is the Gospel, by its very nature, is a *personal activity* of God on the human level—and this it is at the point of its manifestation, in Christ.

for salvation: the fundamental idea of 'salvation' (*sōtēria*) in Greek (profane or biblical) is—like the word's derivatives—that of any kind of deliverance from physical danger or death (e.g. 1 Sam. 11:13). In biblical Greek the word came especially to be appropriated to denote the great 'deliverances' of Israel by Yahweh, e.g. from the Egyptian bondage (Exod. 14:13, 15:2), the Babylonian Captivity and Exile (Isa. 45:17, 52:10). By a natural development, the word came to be used to describe the final deliverance of Israel when the Saviour or Deliverer came (e.g. Ps. Sol. 10:8, 12:6); and this deliverance came more and more to be interpreted in terms of an ultimate deliverance from the powers of Satan, sin, and death. This is the connotation of the word in the *NT*: it is God's deliverance of man from sin, death, and judgement. Cf. Rom. 5:9ff.; 1 C. 3:15; Phil. 1:28; 2:12; 1 Th. 5:8ff.; 2 Th. 2:13. While the negative character of salvation is mostly implied (cf. 5:9ff.), salvation can also take on a positive content. Phil. 3:20–21 refers, for instance, to the transformation by Christ, the Saviour (*sōtēr*) of our body, in its present humble state, to conform to his glorious body, i.e., the redemption or 'deliverance' of the body referred to at Rom. 8:23.

to every one who has faith, to the Jew first and also to the Greek: faith is the pre-condition of the effective working of the reality of God's saving power—and that reality goes out to every man, first to the Jew, since he was God's privileged man (cf. Ps. 80:17, where Israel is described as 'God's right-hand man', i.e. that branch of the human family specially chosen by God as the channel of his 'revelation'), then to Greeks; for this salvation by divine power given to faith is open to the believing Gentile no less than to the believing Jew. St Paul thus emphasises the universality of salvation by faith. When the response of faith is present, there is salvation—for every man, without exception. This universal availability of salvation to faith is emphasised again and again in Romans: 3:22; 5:18; 3:32; 10:4; 11:32. Paul would have no partial or conditional doctrines of salvation. See further below, p. 164.

Verses 16 and 17 contain an adumbration, if not a full statement, of the central theme of Romans 1–8. It has all to do with the 'salvation'—in both positive and negative senses—to which these verses introduce the reader. The ground and basis of 'salvation' is now indicated in the words 'to everyone who has faith (*panti tō pisteuonti*)': salvation comes of 'believing' (*pisteuein*) or of faith (*pistis*).

What may be described as the *locus classicus* for this 'great thesis' is Rom. 3:21–26, although the theme reappears, as a *Leitmotif*, throughout the Epistle. (See notes on 3:21–26, p. 58ff.). In none of these passages, however, do we find *pisteuein* or *pistis* explicitly explained or exactly defined. At 3:22 it is declared to be 'faith in Jesus Christ' (objective, not subjective genitive, see note *ad loc.*): Jesus Christ is, in some sense, the object of Christian faith. But in what sense?

A clue is supplied at Rom. 4:22–24 where 'to believe' (*pisteuein*) (here said to be the grounds for 'justification') is defined as belief in the God 'who raised Jesus our Lord from the dead.' A further analogous definition appears at Rom. 10:9ff.: grounds of salvation are again stated to be belief that God raised Jesus from the dead, accompanied by a confession of Jesus as Lord. Faith (*pistis*) seems, therefore, in Pauline usage, primarily and fundamentally—whatever else it comes to embrace in its semantic scope—a *credo*, i.e. belief in the 'mighty act' of God in the Resurrection of Christ. See the excellent definition in *TWNT Faith* (*Bible Key Words*, Bultmann and Weiser (London, 1961)), pp. 70ff. 'In Rom. 10:9 . . . Paul indicates the content of the Christian faith in one sentence in which he is consciously expressing, not a concept peculiar to himself, but that which is taken for granted by every Christian preacher: "if you confess (*homologein*) with your lips that Jesus is Lord and believe (*pisteuein*) in your heart that God raised him from the dead, you will be saved." . . . Christian faith consists in recognising Jesus as Lord, and at the same time accepting ('believing to be true') the miracle of the resurrection.' See also ibid., pp. 86f.

Thus 'faith in Jesus Christ' (cf. Rom. 4:24) implies the acceptance of the Resurrection Gospel, belief in the Risen One as Lord.

This comes to be extended, however, to include, as the very essence of Christian faith, a personal loyalty to and trust in the Risen Christ: but this is more clearly defined by expressions such as believing/trusting in, a trust in (*pisteuein* or *pistis eis/epi*) Jesus Christ. These are 'epitomising formulas' denoting 'a turning towards the person of the Lord, just as *pistis epi theon* . . . *pros ton theon* (1 Th. 1:8) denote turning to God from heathenism' (ibid., p. 74). In this respect there is no discontinuity with the Old Testament. 'Faith' in the Old Testament, where God is its object, is not just belief in God—such belief is almost universally taken for granted—but trust and loyalty to God (implying obedience as well as belief). Paul and the New Testament take over this fundamental meaning, but make Christ as well as God the supreme object of the believer's loyalty and trust.

These may all be regarded as variations and extensions of the same central idea of the Risen Christ as the object of the believer's faith; fundamental to all, however, and this cannot be sufficiently stressed—for Paul as for pre-Pauline tradition or common Christian usage—is the acceptance of the Resurrection Gospel, with its implications of a relationship to the Risen Lord.

Faith may, therefore, be succinctly defined as trust and loyalty to Christ whom we acknowledge as Lord and believe rose from the dead. Again, excellently defined by Bultmann and Weiser, *op. cit.*, pp. 68f.: the specifically Christian sense of *pistis* 'implies the sense of *giving credence*; and the elements of obedience, trust, hope and loyalty can also be included in the meaning . . .'

17. the righteousness of God: Righteousness (*dikaiosynē*, and its cognates) have a wider semantic range in the Bible than its familiar

English rendering. It does mean 'uprightness', 'virtue', 'moral integrity' like English 'righteousness'. But since Hebrew ethics is also a 'relational ethic' as much as an individualistic ethic, *dikaiosynē* (= Hebrew *ṣedhaqah*, *ṣedheq*) has also the sense of 'right relations' (within the community, family, tribe, etc.) and so 'justice'. (Hebrew relational ethics is not just what J. F. Fletcher advocates in his *Situation Ethics: The New Morality* (London, 1966), but at times it comes very close to it, e.g., Gen. 38:26.)[1] There is a third dimension to *ṣedhaqah*, viz., the relationship to God: biblical ethics has, in fact, always three aspects, for *ṣedhaqah* in its fully realised and experienced form is a relationship of loyal obedience to God, expressed in right relations to others in a life of uprightness and integrity; cf. Lk. 10:27; Dt. 6:5, Lev. 19:18: 'Thou shalt love the Lord thy God . . . and thy neighbour as thyself'; Mic. 6:8: '. . . what doth the Lord require of thee, but to do justly, and to love mercy, and to walk humbly with thy God'. In other words, no man is an island, and unless our communications with God and our neighbour are open and right we have little chance of achieving this positive quality of living which the Hebrews call *ṣedhaqah* or *ṣedheq*.

This brings me to a final important aspect of it: the concept of *ṣedhaqah* is soteriological, as well as ethical. It is bound to be so because of the vertical as well as its horizontal dimension. In theological language, within a theocratic society like Israel (or the Church) it implies a covenant relationship to God which guarantees his favour and blessing. For the Jew it is the covenanted *ṣedhaqah* under the *tôrāh*, which guarantees *berakha*, that mystic quality of life which is true well-being, always and essentially for the Hebrew mind morally conditioned. It is the well-being, *shalom*, of the God-fearing man who enjoys the divine favour and blessing; cf. Ps. 24:5;

---

[1] A classic example of Hebrew 'relational ethics'—and its 'righteousness'—is the story of Tamar at Gen. 38. Tamar's husband Er, Judah's eldest son, died and Judah promised Tamar his younger son, Shelah, in marriage when he should grow up. But the promise was never kept; and Tamar took her revenge on Judah by dressing as a 'woman of pleasure', and conceiving a son by her father-in-law. As proof that he had had illicit relations with her, she had obtained from Judah his seal and staff. When Tamar's 'sin' became known, Judah condemned her to death by burning—till she produced the evidence of her child's paternity. Gen. 38:25 (*NEB*) 'The father of my child is the man to whom these things belong'—and she produced the seal and staff. Confronted with the evidence, Judah declares 'She is more in the right (*AV*, 'more righteous') than I, because I did not give her to my son Shelah'. Tamar's adulterous act was *right* within the context of the continuing life of the tribe or community. She had done what Judah had failed to do, produced an heir in the family.

at Prov. 8:18 it means 'success'. Thus if *sōtēria* tends to emphasise
the negative aspect of 'salvation' *sedhaqah* = *dikaiosynē* underlines
its positive side: it is 'salvation for a quality of life', and eventually
'for eternal life'. But where it is present, in Jewish piety no less
than in Christian, it is always a positive quality of a life, focussed
on faith, guided by God in righteous living within a nexus of right
human relationships. It may be represented, in simple terms, as a
relationship, with a vertical dimension upwards (the relation to
God), a horizontal relation outwards (to one's neighbour) and an
inward relation to the conscience or self. The integrity of the individual, no less than the harmonious well-being of the social group,
depends always on the balance of these 'dimensions', as 'right
relations, up—out—in'. And for Christian 'righteousness' it is
upwards, under God, to the Lord Jesus Christ, outwards to the
Christian brother, and inwards to the Christian conscience.

But 'righteousness' is also an attribute of God; the 'righteous God'
performs acts of righteousness (Jg. 5:11). When attributed to God,
'righteousness' can mean 'right vindicated' (cf. *NEB*: 'God's way
of righting wrong')—hence 'triumph, victory, the victory of the
righteous cause'. The word thus comes to be nearly synonymous
with 'salvation', stressing the more positive aspects, not 'deliverance
from', but a vindication of, and so the *triumph* of, etc. (the righteous
cause). The expression 'the righteousness of God' comes especially
to be applied to the saving action or intervention of God in the
deliverance of Israel from Egypt (e.g. Ps. 103:6ff.), or the deliverance from the Babylonian captivity (Isa. 51:5; 'My righteousness
(triumph) is near; my salvation is gone forth . . .')

While this is the Semitic background of this rich word, we have
also to reckon with Pauline variations on it. The one which has
given a whole Reformed theology its key term is that which connects
the noun with the usage of the corresponding verb *dikaioun* (Heb.
hisdīq). Since Paul can use the verb *dikaioun*, meaning 'to pronounce
righteous' and so 'to acquit', at Gal. 3:11, in a context similar to
the present one (also using Hab. 2:4 as proof-text), it is not
surprising that the noun has come to be traditionally rendered by
'justification', in the forensic sense of *justificatio*, namely 'acquittal'.

Before any attempt can be made to try to define which of these
possible meanings were intended at verse 17, there are three other
expressions in this verse that require study.

is revealed: It is possible to understand 'is revealed' of *dikaiosynē*
in the sense of 'acquittal' or 'justification', or in the richer sense of
the word as full Christian 'integrity' under God as something now
becoming a present reality. At the same time, the term seems to
stress an outward 'demonstration' or 'manifestation', and, for this

reason, may be felt to describe more appropriately the '*dikaiosynē* of God' as the 'triumph of God', the revelation of God's Mighty Act in Christ. Similarly the parallel expression at verse 18, 'the wrath of God is revealed from heaven against all ungodliness', seems clearly to refer to the complementary Act of God in the impending Judgement, as something already in process of happening (see the note on verse 18). St Paul conceives of the eschatological drama as something which has already begun: the Judgement is so imminent that it can be spoken of in the present tense. On the other hand, the tense of the synonymous verb at 3:21 ('has been manifested') clearly indicates that Paul is thinking of the saving acts of God (the *Heilsgeschichte*) as a whole, as not only in process of realisation, but as, in fact, a present reality. (Cf. Rom. 8:14f., 23: 'adoption' as sons anticipate our final adoption. We are not yet fully 'sons of God', although we already are deemed to be 'sons of God'.)

through faith for faith: This phrase can be understood in one of five ways:

1. Barth translates 'For therein is revealed the righteousness of God from faithfulness unto faith: as it is written, But the righteous shall live from my faithfulness.' He comments: 'From faithfulness the righteousness of God reveals itself, that is to say, from His faithfulness to us. The very God has not forgotten men; the Creator has not abandoned His creation . . . the faithfulness of God to men still abides.'[1] This translation is open to the objection that Paul would then be using the same word *pistis* twice, in the same phrase, with a different meaning. Moreover, no *NT* manuscript reads 'from my faithfulness'. Nevertheless (as we shall see in the next verse), the LXX understood Hab. 2:4 in this way: 'The just shall live by *my* faithfulness', i.e. the loyalty of Yahweh to his people—and the quotation in Romans may be understood as 'the righteous shall live by faithfulness' i.e. the faithfulness of God.

2. Similar phrases at 2 C. 2:16 'from death to death' (i.e. 'from total death'), 'from life to life' (i.e. 'from life that is life indeed') (cf. also Ps. 84:7 (LXX 83:8)) suggest some such meaning as 'through pure faith' or 'through faith and nothing but faith' (so Nygren: *sola fide*).

3. Others interpret: 'from the faith (of a believer) to the faith of (others)—i.e. through the spread of faith', or

4. 'through the deepening of the faith of the individual' (see SH *ad loc.*).

5. This is one of a number of phrases in Romans where J. Hugh

Michael suspects a corruption by 'vertical dittography': *ek pisteōs* should be omitted as a dittograph from the following *ek pisteōs* in Hab. 2:4.[1] This would certainly cut the Gordian knot, both of the difficult phrase 'from faith to faith', but no less of the exegesis of I:17 as a whole. The verse would then be parallel to 16, and translated: 'a righteousness of God is being revealed to faith'. The construction would be analogous to 8:18: 'the glory that is to burst on us' (Goodspeed).

There are, therefore, five alternative understandings of the phrase: In it (the Gospel) the *dikaiosynē* of God is revealed:

1. from God's faithfulness to our faith;
2. through faith and faith alone;
3. through the spread of faith;
4. through the deepening of the faith of the individual;
5. (simply) to faith.

He who through faith is righteous shall live: Hab. 2:4. The original meaning of the Hebrew text of Hab. 2:4 is that 'the just or righteous man shall live (or survive) by *his* loyalty (to Yahweh)', i.e., the loyal Israelite shall escape or survive the impending political catastrophe—in this case the Babylonian invasion or captivity (586 B.C.). The text is quoted several times in the *NT*: by Paul again at Gal. 3:11, where the context requires us to understand 'the righteous man' as the one who will be acquitted and 'live (eternally)' at and after the Judgement on the sole grounds of his faith;[2] Heb. 10:38 cites the passage as: 'my just one shall live by faith (loyalty)'. The thought is similar to Hab. 2:4: loyalty to God will save the Christian ('my just one'), in this case, during the persecutions of the Church in the Roman Empire. (Whether the loyalty is to God or to Christ is not specified further.) 'Life' here has obviously come to mean more than the survival of physical life from disaster; it means: 'shall obtain or retain eternal life'.

How did St Paul understand Hab. 2:4 at Rom. I:17? Notice that he omits, in both places where the passage is cited, the *OT* pronoun: '*his* faith', or '*my* faith'. Feuillet[3] considers this to be deliberate: it has been done to enable Paul to take the words 'by faith' (*ek pisteōs*) closely with the preceding 'the righteous man' (*ho dikaios*), and to read, not 'the just shall live by faith', but 'the just-by-faith shall

---

[1] *JTS*, xxxix. (1938), pp. 150–4. See below, pp. 76, 200; also Michael's notes on 3:30, 4:12, 5:6, 6:16, 19, 10:9, 13:1, 4, 9, 14:12, 15:4, 5.

[2] Is there a possible suggestion here that 'the righteous man' is a term for the Christian? cf. David Hill, in *NTS* XI (1964–5), pp. 296ff.

[3] 'La Citation d'Habacuc II. 4 et les huit premiers chapitres de l'Épître aux Romains', *NTS*, VI (1959–60), pp. 52ff.

live' (or as *RSV*). What St Paul is primarily interested in is the kind
of 'righteousness' by which a man is to live, whether it is to be a
'righteousness' based on the Law, or a new kind of righteousness
in which the inner obedience of faith replaces obedience to the
external letter of the Law. The opposite and contradictory proposition to 'the just-by-faith' (*ho dikaios ek pisteōs*) would be contained
in such words as 'the just-by-law' (*ho dikaios ek nomou*). From the
subsequent argument of Romans it is clear that St Paul's main
purpose is to substitute for the obedience to the Law as the main-
spring of life (cf. Dt. 30:15ff.) a living obedience by faith in the
Risen Christian Lord (cf. 3:22, Phil. 3:9); for Paul no less than for
Hebrews, the 'life' to be so gained is eternal life.

We must understand and render therefore: 'the just-by-faith (in
Christ) shall live (now and for ever)'—and the words, of course,
mean 'enjoy fullness of life, now and for ever.'[1]

Feuillet has raised an important issue: Paul's omission of the
pronominal adjective '*my* (faith)' or '*his* (faith)' can only be a quite
deliberate piece of Pauline *pesher* or interpretation. But was it just
to enable the reader to make the combination 'the just-by-faith,' or
was it to allow him to interpret the phrases *either* of the faithfulness
of God (as the LXX) *or* of the faith of the individual? The Pauline
omission of the pronoun leaves open the possibility of understanding
the words as 'the just-by God's-faithfulness will live', or 'the just will
live by (God's) faithfulness'. Such a type of *pesher* is not unfamiliar in
the use of the Old Testament by Paul's contemporaries.

We return now to the exegesis of the verse as a whole. The
'righteousness of God' has been traditionally interpreted in this
context in two ways:[2]

1. In view of the following 'proof-text' from Habakkuk which
stresses the righteousness of the individual, the 'righteousness of
God' is understood to be an individual righteousness, 'imputed' or
'imparted' by God (*justitia imputata* or *infusa*), whereby, on the sole
condition of faith alone in Jesus Christ, the guilty party is 'justified'.

---

[1]Exegetes in favour of this view: H. Lietzmann, M. J. Lagrange, M.
Goguel, E. Kuhl, L. Cerfaux: for the older, traditional view, Th. Zahn,
SH, C. H. Dodd, O. Michel.

[2]For a comprehensive discussion, see J. A. Ziesler, *The Meaning of
Righteousness in Paul* (*SNTS* Monograph Series, Cambridge, 1972); Ziesler
stresses the relational aspect of Christian 'righteousness' within the New
Covenant societary unit, the Body of Christ. Cf. also S. Lyonnet, 'De
notione justitiae dei apud S. Paulum (Rom. 1:17 et 3:21–26; Rom. 3:5)',
Verb. Dei, XLII (1964), pp. 121–52.

This is then said to be revealed 'by faith and faith alone'. Thus the theme of Romans is stated as: *justificatio sola fide.*

In support of this interpretation, Rom. 3:22 is cited: 'the righteousness of God through faith in Jesus Christ', where a 'righteousness proceeding from God' and 'imputed' or 'imparted' on the grounds of faith in Jesus Christ seems the sense intended. Moreover, since 3:24 employs the verb in the sense 'being acquitted (freely by his grace)', the 'righteousness of God' in verse 21 must at least bear the meaning of 'divine acquittal'. A similar sense is claimed for Phil. 3:9, where Paul is again contrasting (as at Gal. 3:11) an 'acquittal' based on 'law' (i.e. legal works) with 'acquittal' which proceeds from God on the grounds of Christian faith.

2. 'It is well to remember that St Paul has all these meanings (of 'righteous' and its cognates) before him; and he glances from one to another as the hand of a violin-player runs over the strings of his violin.'[1] The problem is to determine the meaning appropriate to each context. In spite of the arguments for a forensic connotation at 1:17, the context, (especially the parallel at verse 18 which stresses the revelation of the judgement (wrath of God), tends, on the whole (without altogether excluding other meanings) to place the emphasis on 'the triumph of God (over Satan, sin and death)'.

The key to an understanding of Paul's essential thesis is his conviction of the total bankruptcy of contemporary Pharisaic 'scholasticism', which seemed to base the whole range of active right relationships within the Covenant ('righteousness') on the meticulous observation of the injunctions of the *tōrāh* as expounded and expanded in the 'tradition of the elders'. This was 'legalistic righteousness', a form of ethics based on a code, external and 'written', losing sight entirely of the gracious personal will of a holy and good God, of which it was originally intended to be the divine vehicle of expression. Paul would have had no quarrel with the pious Jew who sought to do the will of God as revealed in the *tōrāh*, without being hidebound at every turn by the 'prescriptions' of Pharisaic tradition. But he took a revolutionary step forward by proclaiming a new personal intervention of God in the history of salvation, Christ Risen and Returning, and faith in this act of God as the sole grounds for salvation in the eschatological present as well as in the impending, imminent Parousia.

On the whole, it seems to me that the Barthian insight in this case may well furnish the main clue to St Paul's chief thought, without excluding other nuances in a verse so pregnant with meaning.

[1]SH, p. 34.

The triumph of God, of right over every form of wrong, in the life of the individual as in the life of mankind, is disclosed for all in the Gospel, through God's eternal faithfulness to his creature, in raising Christ from the dead to be the life-giving object of man's faith.

We may then render verses 16 and 17 as follows:

16. For I am not ashamed of the Gospel. For it is the power of God for salvation to everyone who has faith, the Jew first, then the Greek.

17. For the triumph of God is revealed from (divine) faithfulness for (human) faith, as it is written, 'The just-by-faith(fulness) shall live'.

18. the wrath of God: verse 18 goes clearly with verse 17 and, at the same time serves as a transition to verses 19ff. The same verb is used of the 'revelation' of God's anger as in connection with the 'revelation' of his 'righteousness'. God's wrath is the manifestation of his righteousness. The God of the *OT* is on occasion an angry deity, but his anger is never capricious or arbitrary like the deities in Greek mythology: it is inflicted, for instance, on rebellion against the Covenant (Lev. 10:1–2), or on Israel for her transgression, on the Day of the Lord (Isa. 2:10ff.). In the *NT* the use of the term is 'eschatologised' (e.g. Mt. 3:7; 1 Th. 1:10; Rom. 2:5; Rev. 6:16, 17). But this does not mean that the wrath of God is manifested only on the great Day of Judgement; God's way of 'setting things right', which is also his judgement and the manifestation of his wrath, is also a present eschatological reality in the visible consequences of here-and-now evil-doing ('. . . salvation and wrath also were being anticipated in history (though each was still to be consummated in the future)' (Barrett)). This is the element of truth in Dodd's explanation of the wrath of God 'to describe an inevitable process of cause and effect in a moral universe' (*ad loc.*). Cf. also G. Bornkamm, 'The Revelation of God's Wrath: Romans i–iii', in *Early Christian Experience* (London, 1969), pp. 46ff.

For the wrath of God is revealed: The parallel with verse 17 is clear if only from the opening *gar*, 'for', which goes back either to 'I am not ashamed' or (more probably) to 'it is the power of God for salvation . . . for . . .'. For a full discussion see Cranfield, pp. 106f. The verb here, *apokalyptetai*, as in verse 17, is best taken as a continuous present: 'is being revealed'. Paul is thinking of the great eschatological drama as having begun already with the Resurrection: the *final* manifestation of God's wrath, viz. the Last Judgement, will ensue when Christ returns at his Parousia.

from heaven: it is to be a Judgement 'out of this world'. This is not God acting in history (as in the deliverances from Egypt and

Babylonia) but from 'beyond history'. The eschatology is a 'trans-
cendentalising' eschatology.

ungodliness and wickedness of men: 'ungodliness' is the human
condition which brings down the divine wrath, since it is a breach
of the first commandment, which is clearly Paul's main thought in
these verses: from 'godlessness' or 'idolatry' all human wrong-doing
springs.[1]

THE FAILURE OF LAW 1:19–3:20

THE CASE AGAINST THE GENTILES

1:19–32

The long section 1:19–3:20 is an indictment of the human race for
its tragic failure and folly. The first section (1:19–32) deals with
Gentile guilt. Though not possessing any revelation of God, the
Gentile world had a natural theology and a natural law: yet it failed
just as Israel failed.[2]

The literary structure of these verses is noteworthy. It is a Jewish
type of polemic by which St Paul carries forward his argument,
possibly influenced, in content and style, by Wis. 12:27, 13:1ff. (Cf.
E. Norden, *Agnostos Theos* (Darmstadt, 1956), pp. 128ff.) Verses
28–32 read like part of a spoken diatribe, and might well have
come from a Pauline missionary 'sermon': they resemble, in some
respects, the section in Attic comedy known to the ancient rhetor-
icians as the *pnigos*, a long passage to be spoken in a single breath.
There is a word-play in the Greek at verses 28 and 31 ('see fit'
(*edokimasan*); 'gave them up to' (*paredōken*); 'improper (*adokimon*)
conduct'; 'foolish' (*asynetous*), 'faithless' (*asynthetous*). Note, too, the
emphatic repetition of the word 'gave them up' (*paredōken*) (verses
24, 26, 28) and 'exchanged' (*ēllaxan*, *metēllaxan*) (verses 23, 25, 26).
The central idea is that of God's despair (*paredōken*, 'gave them up')
at human perversion (*metēllaxan*). Verses 18ff. develop the Stoic

---

[1] On the verse, see also C. E. B. Cranfield, in *SJT*, XXI (1968), pp. 330–5.
[2] Cf. S. Schulz, 'Die Anklage in Rom. 1:18–22', *TZ*, XIV (1958), pp. 161–73.
Cf. further, H. Ott, 'Rom. 1:19ff als dogmatisches Problem', ibid. XV
(1959) pp. 40–50; F. Flückiger, 'Zur Unterscheidung von Heiden und
Juden in Rom. i:18–ii:3', ibid., X (1954), pp. 154–8; A. Fridrichsen, 'Zur
Auslegung von Röm. i:19ff', in *ZNTW*, XVII (1916), pp. 159–68; M.
Barth, 'Speaking of Sin: Some Interpretative Notes on Rom. i:18–iii:20',
SJT, VIII (1955), pp. 288–96.

doctrine of knowledge of God through his works. Paul seems also to be familiar with pagan catalogues of the vices: they are grouped into (a) sensual vices (24–28), and (b) anti-social vices (29–31).

19. What can be known: (See H. Rosin on Rom. 1:19, in *TZ*, XVII (1961), pp. 161–5. Cf. also B. Gärtner, *The Areopagus Speech and Natural Revelation* (Uppsala, 1955); H. Bietenhard, 'Natürliche Gotteserkenntnis der Heiden', *TZ*, XII (1956), pp. 275–88; B. Reicke, 'Natürliche Theologie nach Paulus', *Svensk Exegetisk Årsbok*, XXII–XXIII (1957–8), p. 159; H. P. Owen, 'The Scope of Natural Revelation in Rom. 1 and Acts 17', *NTS*, V (1958–9), pp. 133–43; J. L. McKenzie, 'Natural Law in the New Testament', *Bulletin of the Research Council of Israel*, IX (1964), pp. 3ff.; D. M. Coffey, 'Natural Knowledge of God: Reflections on Rom. 1:18–32', *Theological Studies*, 31 (1970), pp. 674–91. For Stoic antecedents, see especially M. Pohlenz, 'Paulus und die Stoa', *ZNTW*, XLII (1949), pp. 69ff.)

plain to them: lit., 'manifest in (or among) them'. What was knowable about God was known to them. The sense 'plain in their minds and consciences' may be preferred, since the argument goes on to state that their minds 'had become darkened'.

20. Ever since the creation of the world: or: 'from the created Universe', i.e. from things created. The first sense is preferable, and the phrase is parallel to the expression 'from the foundation of the world' (Mt. 25:34) and 'from the beginning of creation' (Mk 10:6). Cf. Wis. 13:8.

his invisible nature, namely, his eternal power and deity, has been clearly perceived in the things that have been made: note the oxymoron: 'invisible', 'clearly perceived' (lit., 'seen'); and cf. (Ps.)Aristotle, *de Mundo*, 6: 'The invisible God is made visible by his works themselves' (*atheōrētos ap' autōn tōn ergōn theōreitai [ho Theos])*', with Philo, *de Praem. et Poen.*, VII, for the same paradox, no doubt a commonplace of Stoic natural theology; for the whole verse, cf. also Wis. 13:1ff., and for the connection with Wisdom, see Bornkamm, *Early Christian Experience*, p. 55. Bornkamm also rightly sees that 'natural revelation' for Paul is not the 'knowledge of God' by the use of rational faculties, but a God-given revelation to the mind of man (op. cit., pp. 50ff.)

eternal (*aidios*), here and at Jude 6 only. Cf. Wis. 2:23 for the noun *aidiotēs*, 'everlastingness, eternity of being'. *Deity, theiotēs*, here only in the New Testament (again, in biblical Greek at Wis. 18:9) denotes the divine nature and properties in contrast to *theotēs*, the divine personality (Col. 2:9). Cranfield, p. 115.

21. became futile in their thinking . . . were darkened: better 'became darkened' (note that both verbs are ingressive aorists).

The *dialogismos* ('thinking') may refer to the 'arguments', 'debates', 'disputations' of the Stoic philosophers. We may paraphrase: 'they lose themselves (ingressive aorist) in their futile disputations, and are plunged (ingressive aorist) in mindless darkness.'

22. On verses 22–32, see J. Jeremias, *Abba* (Göttingen, 1966), pp. 290–2. Cf. also E. Klostermann, 'Die adäquate Vergeltung in Röm. 1:22–31', *ZNTW*, XXXII (1933), pp. 1–6. The usual paragraph division at verse 24 is to be rejected: the literary structure is: verses 22–24 (the sin of idolatry); 25–27 (divine punishment]; 28ff. See also S. Lyonnet, 'Notes sur l'exégèse de l'épître aux Romains', in *Bib.*, 38 (1957), pp. 35ff.

became fools: again, ingressive aorist.

23. exchanged the glory . . .: men substituted idolatry for the worship of the true glory of God. In the background of the thought of this verse is Ps. 106:20, and also possibly Gen. 1:20; cf. Jer. 2:11; Dt. 4:15–18. Cf. N. Hyldahl, 'A Reminiscence of the Old Testament at Romans i:23', *NTS*, II (1955–6), pp. 285–8. Paul's thought is influenced here by Wis. 14:12, idolatry leads to moral depravity.

images resembling mortal men: cf. J. M. Bover, ' "Imaginis" notio apud B. Paulum', *Bib.*, IV (1923), pp. 174ff. See further, M. Hooker, 'Adam in Rom. 1', *NTS* VI (1959–60), pp. 297–306; XIII (1966–67), pp. 181–3. Cf. Wis. 14:12, 15:14f. Like the author of Wisdom, St Paul regards idolatry, the breach of the first commandment, as the *fons et origo* of all human evils. We must also remember that Paul's world, the hellenistic world of pagan cults, was dominated by idol-worship, in every shape and form, including animal worship. (Cults which were also closely associated with sexual licence).

24. lusts: in this context referring to sexual (or homosexual) passions.

among themselves: or 'between themselves'. This seems to mean 'with one another', and this yields a superior sense to the alternative interpretation which renders 'so that their bodies were dishonoured among them' (so *SH*).

25. the truth about God for a lie: in the *OT*, 'lie', 'lies', can be used with the sense of 'false gods', 'idols' (e.g. Jer. 13:25) and this may be the sense here—'for idols' (collective singular). In that case, 'the truth of God' is not the 'truth about God' as virtually 'the true God' (abstract for concrete: cf. 1 Th. 1:9). This does not, of course, exclude other and wider meanings, such as 'the true revelation of God (which God gave)' and 'falsehood' (i.e. the false world of idolatry). cf .3:7.

Bornkamm notes (*Early Christian Experience*, p. 53) that Paul agrees with contemporary opinions that 'idolatry and immoral life are the results of irrational and deficient knowledge of God'.

who is blessed for ever: a brief Jewish form of doxology. Cf. 9:5 and SB II, p. 310 and III, p. 64.

Verses 26–32 specify in detail the perversions which are consequent on idolatry. In 26–27 Paul describes the horrible homosexual practices of pagan society so obnoxious to Jews, though in specifying them first he may be giving them an even larger prominence than some of his compatriots did (cf. Letter of Aristeas, 152, in H. G. Meecham, *The Oldest Version of the Bible* (London, 1932), pp. 48, 297ff.).

26. dishonourable passions: corresponds to 'impurity' and the 'dishonouring of their bodies' in verse 24.

27. in their own persons: lit. 'in (within) themselves'.

error: the Greek word is stronger: it means their foolish apostasy.

28. base mind: the word-play in this verse (see above, p. 39) is reproduced by Barrett (*in loc.*): 'And as they did not see fit to take cognizance of God, God handed them over to an unfit mind.' The original word means 'tried and rejected', a meaning which is reproduced exactly by the translation 'reprobate'. Kirk (Clarendon Bible) renders much more freely: 'as they recked nothing of God, he gave them over to recklessness'.

and to improper conduct: lit. 'to do the things that are not fitting' (*kathēkonta*). The expression is a regular Stoic term, e.g. Epictetus, II, XVII, 31; Polyb. VI:6, 7. Cf. M. Pohlenz, *Die Stoa* (Göttingen, 1948–9), I, p. 487; and SH, *in loc*. Cf. also 2 Mac. 6:4 and 3 Mac. 4:16.

28–32. The list of vices may owe something to similar Hellenistic (or Jewish-Hellenistic) lists. There are similar 'catalogues' at Rom. 13:13; I C. 5:10ff., 6:9ff.; 2 C. 12:20ff.; Gal. 5:19ff.; Eph. 4:31; 5:3ff.; Col. 3:5, 8; 1 Tim. 1:9ff.; 2 Tim. 3:2–5. Cf. also 1 Clem. XXXV:5.

29. wickedness: (*adikia*); 'wrong-doing' or 'injustice' (*NEB*) is closer to the original. The word refers to all anti-social action or conduct, whereas evil (*ponēria*) is perhaps better rendered by 'wickedness': evil in general is meant. (*NEB* 'mischief' is too narrow a connotation for *ponēria*).

covetousness: *NEB* 'rapacity' is possibly too strong, though the Greek word can have this sense; in Plato it is the characteristic vice of the tyrant. The word means literally 'having more (than one's share)'—'selfishness', 'self-seeking', 'self-aggrandisement', 'greed', etc., according to context. A fairly common Pauline word; cf. Col. 3:5 where 'selfishness' is declared to be idolatry. This particular vice usually stands at the head of the hellenistic catalogue of vices, so that presumably it was one of the most common and most frowned-on of vices.

malignity: *NEB* 'malevolence'.

30. haters of God: the word could be understood in a passive sense meaning 'hated of God', as the Vulgate renders: *Deo odibiles*. Moreover, the word appears only to be attested in this passive sense (see Bauer, *in loc.*). On the other hand, the word is a comparatively rare one, and, as Barrett points out, the passage as a whole deals with human activities; the word, therefore, is better understood in an active sense: 'God-loathers'. (Cf. also I Clem. XXXV:5, where the noun has an active connotation.) It has been further suggested that we should take the word as an adjective with the previous noun: 'God-hating (hated) slanderers', a suggestion of Pallis, (*To the Romans* (1933); see Barrett, *in loc.*). The objection to this is that in the rest of the verse we have to do with single words (or compound expressions), all nouns (or nouns with a genitive), and this suggests that the word is to be understood as a noun by itself.

inventors of evil: an odd kind of expression. It is paralleled by Virgil's description of Ulysses as *scelerum inventor* ('crime-deviser'). Similar expressions at 2 Mac. 7:31 and in Philo *in Flacc.* X, 73.

31. foolish, faithless, heartless, ruthless: there is no logical link between the first two words: they are brought together for the sake of the word-play: *asynetous, asynthetous*.

32. There seems to be an anti-climax in Paul's 'not only . . . but': 'not only approve of those who do such things but do them themselves' would give the more appropriate sense: but the more difficult text is Paul's. The explanation is perhaps that we have to do with a sentence which 'has been taken over bodily by St Paul' from *Test. Asher* vi.2; see R. H. Charles, *The Greek Versions of the Testaments of the Twelve Patriarchs* (Oxford, 1908) *ad loc.* Cf., however, M. de Jonge, *The Testaments of the Twelve Patriarchs* (Assen, 1953), p. 19, who regards the sentence in Asher as an interpolation from Romans.

THE JEWS ALSO ARE ATTACKED[1]

2:1–29

Verses 1–7 establish that only a good life counts in God's sight, and this applies equally to Jew and Greek (verses 9–11). Obedience or

---

[1]That Paul has exclusively Jews in mind in this section has been challenged in recent discussion. Cf. H. W. Bartsch, 'Die historische Situation des Römerbriefes, *Stud. Ev.*, IV (*TU* 102, 1968) p. 286. See also Barrett, *ad loc.* (Jews and Stoic philosophers?)

disobedience to Law decide a man's destiny, and again nationality is of no account in God's sight, for the pagan world, though not possessing *the* Law, was not without some idea of law (their 'natural law', like their natural religion), obedience or disobedience to which would be rewarded or punished with the same impartiality as where there was a revealed Law (verses 11–16). The discussion about the equal responsibility of Gentile and Jew before God is continued in 2:17–3:20, with special reference to the alleged superiority of the Jew (3:1–9); 3:9–20 states the main conclusion, that both Jew and Gentile stand condemned in God's sight, and this is done with the help of a catena of *OT* quotations which clinch the argument with an effective rhetorical climax.

1. **another:** lit., 'the other man'. Barrett (p. 43) considers the thought here to be quite general: Paul is thinking of those who set themselves up as judges of their fellows (cf. *NEB* 'in judging your fellow-man', and verses 9f. and 12–16, which apply to both Jews and Gentiles). While there may well be a reference to 'others' in general, the immediate context seems to suggest that the writer has the Jews particularly in mind (see Cranfield *ad loc.*). Paul seems to use the term 'the other man' (*heteros*) virtually in the sense of 'neighbour' (Rom. 13:8; cf. 1 C. 6:1; 10:24), a meaning which is not directly attested outside biblical Greek (cf. Liddell and Scott s.v.); even in biblical Greek this meaning is rare but found (Prov. 27:17; Ec. 4:4). Occasionally, as here, the word may have the distinctive Hebrew meaning of '*aḥēr*, which it regularly renders in the LXX, i.e., the other who is different, the stranger, the foreigner— in this verse 'the Gentile'; cf. 1 C. 14:21 ('the lips of foreigners' *NEB*.)

2. **We know:** or, '**For we know . . .**' This is a familiar Pauline phrase (cf. 3:19; 7:14; 8:22, 28). Cf. the phrase *kathōs oidate* ('as you know'), especially in 1 Th. 1:5, 2:2, 5. Paul can assume a body of Christian instruction. See N. A. Dahl, 'Anamnesis: Mémoire et Commémoration dans le christianisme primitif', *Stud. Theol.*, 1, (1–2) (1947), pp. 69–95.

3. **Do you suppose:** lit. 'are you reckoning on this'.
you will escape: there seemed to be a widely held popular view among Jews that Jewish nationality by itself would confer exemption from judgement.

4. **presume upon:** lit. 'despise'. Cf. 1 Tim. 6:2 for a similar use.
riches of his kindness . . .: this expressive figure of speech occurs a number of times in different connections in the Epistles: e.g. 9:23, 11:33; Phil. 4:19; Col. 1:27, 2:2; it is especially characteristic of Ephesians (1:7, 18, 2:7, 3:8, 16). The figure is not found elsewhere in the *NT*. 'The full force of this accusation will be felt if we set

beside it words from Wisdom (which Paul evidently knew).'
(Barrett) Cf. Wis. 14:52–15:1–6.

is meant to lead you: this is an attempt to render what is called a
conative present: 'is seeking (striving, etc.) to lead'.

5. hard and impenitent heart: a hendiadys—'in your obstinate
unrepentant state of mind'.

you are storing up wrath: lit. 'you are "treasuring" up wrath'. The
kind of 'treasure' here being amassed is contrasted with the 'riches'
of verse 4. A 'treasury of wrath' was not what the Jew here addressed
believed he was accumulating. (Cf. H. St. J. Thackeray, *The
Relation of St. Paul to Contemporary Jewish Thought* (London, 1900),
pp. 81ff.) 'Your obedience to the Law and disbelief in the Gospel
is not leading to a treasury of merits with God but a treasury of
wrath'. For this metaphorical use of the verb, cf. Prov. 1:18 (LXX).

**on the day of wrath when God's righteous judgement will be
revealed:** lit., 'on the day of wrath and of the revelation of the just
judgement of God.' The word rendered 'just judgement' is a rare
one (*dikaiokrisia*), and it was this which probably led Moffatt to
render 'just doom'. It is a solemn and dignified expression: the
same meaning could have been conveyed by the two words 'just
judgement' (as at 2 Th. 1:5), but the style would have been the
poorer.

6. St Paul, here and at verse 13, assumes the current Jewish
doctrine of 'justification by works' (cf. 2 C. 5:10; Gal. 6:7; Eph.
6:8). For its relation to the doctrine of justification by faith in this
chapter, see the note on verse 7.

7. to those who by patience in well-doing: the sense here could
be simply that of persistence or determination to do what is right.
The word rendered 'patience' has an active as well as a passive sense
in Greek; here it is not only the active pursuit of the good life which
is meant (*NEB*: 'steady persistence in well-doing'), but possibly
also the patient endurance under difficulties which nevertheless
continues to do right, like the 'goodness' which St Peter commends
to the Christian slaves at 1 Pet. 2:20ff. (cf. Heb. 12:1).

seek for glory and honour and immortality: the last term is literally
'incorruption'. The motivation of goodness is the same as its reward;
to those who seek a glorious incorruption by patient suffering and
persistence in well-doing, will be granted eternal life.

In the parallel clause at verse 10, it is 'glory and honour and
peace' which are to be the reward of 'every one who does good'. Is
it possible that the original order of words at verse 7 was 'to those
who by patience in well-doing seek eternal life, (he will give) glory
and honour and immortality' (i.e. *zētousin zōēn aiōnion* after *kath*

hypomonēn ergou agathou)? Did a scribe perhaps object to the idea that eternal life could be sought by 'good works'?

In verses 7 and 10 Paul seems clearly to be stating just this general principle of 'justification by legal works'. Verses 12–16 develop this theme. Paul is, to all intents and purposes, affirming—and identifying himself with—a doctrine of justification by works. This plain meaning of the text, applying to both Jews and Gentiles, has caused difficulty for exegesis (as it may have for a scribe at verse 7), since it seems to be in flagrant contradiction to the Pauline *sola fide* doctrine. A closely related problem is Paul's claim, as it seems, that Gentiles are capable of fulfilling the requirements of the law 'by nature' (*physei*), i.e. that they possess a 'natural law' (see on verse 14). The answers currently being given to the problem raised by modern exegetes for verses 7–10 is that Paul is really thinking, in the first place, of Christians, and the 'good works' are not just 'legal deserts', but 'the expression of faith and repentance' (he may also have intended to include 'Old Testament believers' or 'heathens' in whom God 'might see evidence of a secret faith.') (See Cranfield, p. 152). Similarly at verses 14–16 it is argued that the Gentiles with a law in themselves are really also Gentile Christians.

Such an exegesis, in both passages, 7–10 and 14–16, emasculates the Pauline argument for justification *sola fide*. 'Justification' for Paul is by 'deeds' for Jews and Greeks alike—and Paul is thinking, in both cases, of non-Christians. The heathen nations do possess a law of nature, just as they have a natural theology. Paul accepts this current position of rabbinical theology, though he probably goes further than any of his Jewish contemporaries in his claim that Gentiles have a 'natural law'. His argument in this chapter is not that such a system of legal righteousness and such a 'natural law' were ideals incapable of realisation for most men: it was a divinely ordained order for all men, and one that was 'not too hard for you', not 'in heaven' but 'very near . . . so that you can do it.' (Dt. 30:11f.; cf. Rom.10:8.)

The whole thrust of Paul's argument in the following verses is that *all men had tragically failed to fulfil the just requirements of law, whether revealed or natural.* Paul, that is, does affirm in these verses a universally applicable doctrine of 'righteousness by works', but argues that this whole divine order has foundered on the rocks of human weakness and wilfulness, and that nothing less than a miracle of God's doing has been required to right this tragic human situation, *namely, the miracle of the Risen Christ,* faith in whom produces the enabling power of the Spirit by which the Christian believers could be justified, *sola fide,* indeed, but also, because of his faith, by his ensuing 'works'.

There is, therefore, no necessary contradiction with his own distinctive teaching about justification *sola fide*. The Pauline doctrine deals with the conditions of entering on the Christian life—that life rooted and grounded on faith alone. But in the life that follows, 'works', as the spontaneous expression of the life of faith (the 'fruit of the spirit'), are no less an integral part of the life which will one day be judged by God—only they are no longer simply the result of conformity to an external legal code.

8. for those who are factious: the *NEB* rendering, 'for those who are governed by selfish ambition', is closer to the original meaning of the Greek. The same expression occurs at Phil. 1:17. The noun here used *eritheia* is rare and probably means 'selfishness', 'selfish ambition', rather than 'strife': but commentators are divided. **the truth:** i.e. the way of truth.
wrath and fury: i.e. in the eschatological sense of these terms. Such evil-doers will be made to feel the full force of the terrible wrath of God in the coming Judgement.

9. tribulation and distress: these are both strong terms. The second means 'torturing confinement': *RV* 'anguish' is possibly better, because stronger, than 'distress': *NEB* (1961) takes the two words together as a hendiadys, and renders: 'grinding misery'.
for every human being who does evil: or who persists in evil-doing; the present tense may be pressed.

10. glory and honour and peace: a change in the earlier formula of verse 7. 'Peace' includes, if it is not confined to, the Pauline connotation of 'reconciliation with God' (cf. 5:1).

11. For God shows no partiality: lit. 'for there is no favouritism' (respect of persons, an *OT* expression) 'with God'—a principle enunciated also in *OT* Scripture, e.g., 2 Chr. 19:7; cf. also Sir. 35:13.

12. without the Law: i.e. outside the sphere of, or beyond the reach of, Law, but with the nuance 'lawlessly' and, in the second instance, 'as law-breakers (criminals) [perish]'. There is a deliberate parallelism in the clauses of this verse: the words might be a quotation from some well-known source. Moffatt brings this out well by rendering: 'All who sin outside the Law will perish outside the Law, and all who sin under the Law will be condemned by the Law.'

13. will be justified: i.e. will be acquitted at God's final assize.
14. Gentiles: i.e. *some* Gentile nations.[1] The absence of the article

---

[1]On this section, see J. Riedl, *Das Heil der Heiden nach Röm. 2:14–16, 26, 27* (Vienna, 1965); cf. *Scholastik*, XL (1965), pp. 189ff; F. Kuhr, 'Römer ii:14f. und die Verheissung bei Jer. 31:31f.', in *ZNTW*, LV (1964), pp. 243–61; cf. also Cranfield, pp. 155f.

is significant: '*The* Gentiles' would mean all or most Gentile nations. But Paul would hardly concede that *the* Gentiles do naturally what the law enjoins—some Gentile nations certainly, and even this is subsequently qualified.

do by nature what the law requires: 'the law' here is clearly the Mosaic Law. As a rule in these verses when Paul speaks of 'law' (without the definite article), it is law in general he means, though it may also refer to the Mosaic Law as one form of 'law'.

It seems probable that the Apostle is thinking of the Stoic 'natural law', i.e. reason, the immanent principle informing the *kosmos* (and converting it from *chaos* into *kosmos*), manifesting itself in the human mind as the power of discursive thought, able, among other things, to distinguish right from wrong. This is the meaning of 'conscience' in verse 15: it is the power of reason to make moral distinctions, and so decisions. See, further, note on verse 15.

The idea of 'natural law' goes back beyond Plato: in general it comes very close to the Hebrew ideal of the 'law written in the heart'. Cf. Plato, *Republic*, IV. 425a, 427a, Isocrates, *Areopag.*, 41 ('justice in the soul' contrasted with 'written statutes'—'let them fill their souls with justice and not the statute-books with new laws'); cf. also Plutarch (cited Wettstein); 'who shall govern the governor? . . . Law the king of all mortals and immortals, as Pindar called it; which is not written on papyrus rolls or wooden tablets, but is his own reason within the soul, which perpetually dwells with him and guards him, and never leaves the soul bereft of leadership'. (Trans. Dodd, p. 36)

they are a law to themselves: lit. 'these men (or individuals)'. The masculine demonstrative pronoun shows that Paul is not really prepared to concede even that *some* Gentile nations could rise to these heights, but only that a few individuals might do so.

The words 'they are a law to themselves' mean the very opposite of the popular expression about 'being a law to oneself', namely, *have law within themselves*. Cf. Aristotle, *Nicom. Ethics*, IV. 1128a.31: 'the cultivated and free-minded man will so behave as being a law to himself', i.e. he does not require rules to be imposed from outside, but has his own self-imposed discipline. Cf. further, M. Pohlenz, 'Paulus und die Stoa', *ZNTW*, XLII (1949), pp. 69ff. See also W. Kranz, 'Das Gesetz des Herzens', *Rhein. Mus. für Philologie*, XCIV (1951), pp. 222-41.

15. They show: lit. 'inasmuch as they . . .'—giving the grounds for the statement of verse 14. There are several possible ways of construing these words: (a) inasmuch as they *manifest* (i.e. show as qualities of character) the conduct required by the law as (something) written in their hearts; (b) the word translated 'show' is used specially in a legal connection (the noun *endeixis* means 'proof', and gives us the English word 'indictment'): the verb here employed means 'prove', 'produce as proof'. We may then render: 'inasmuch as they produce as proof . . .'; in favour of this alternative are the legal metaphors in the rest of the verse ('bear witness', 'accuse', etc.).

what the law requires: lit. 'the works (coll. sing.) of the Law', i.e. the conduct required by the Law.

conscience: Cf. for the same phrase, 9:1. See further, B. Reicke, '*Syneidēsis* in Rom. 2:15', *TZ* XII (1956), pp. 157–61; C. A. Pierce, *Conscience in the New Testament* (London, 1955); Cranfield, pp. 159f. W. D. Stacey, *The Pauline View of Man* (London, 1956), pp. 206f. In Pauline usage 'conscience' as 'knowing in oneself' (lit., 'to know with oneself') the difference between right and wrong and was no doubt guided and informed by the Law of Moses; cf. M. E. Thrall, 'The Pauline Use of Syneidēsis' in *NTS* 14 (1967–8), pp. 118f.

and their conflicting thoughts: lit. 'and with one another, their reasonings'; or 'their mutual debates', i.e., 'their argumentations with one another', an alternative which may be preferable, especially in view of the prominence of the words 'with one another'. (Is the reference perhaps to the Stoic (or current philosophical) discourses in the form of the Platonic dialogues, a view not necessarily excluding inner 'struggles of conscience'?)

16. on that day when: there is no justification for detaching the clause from its present place. (Moffatt places verse 16 after verse 13.) The verb in verse 15, 'they show that what the law requires', is a statement referring to the case of certain Gentiles *now, in the present*: they *do now* have this law written in the heart. But the following clauses refer forward to the future day of judgement: their conscience and their arguments with one another will be the joint witnesses for the prosecution or even for the defence on the day when God judges the secrets of men. (For the time-sequence of participles, see C. F. D. Moule, *An Idiom Book of New Testament Greek* (Cambridge, 1953), pp. 100f. (Semitic participles are timeless.) This is well brought out for this verse in the *NEB* which begins a new sentence with the participial clauses, beginning with 'Their conscience': '(. . . they display the effect of the law inscribed on their hearts.) Their conscience is called as witness, and their own thoughts argue the case on either side, against them or even for them, on the day when God judges the secrets of human hearts through Jesus Christ.' (Is Paul thinking of the need for two witnesses for a valid testimony (Dt. 17:6, Mt. 18:16)?)

God judges: or: 'God will judge'. The reference is to the future

Last Judgement in this verse, as earlier in the chapter at verses 3, 5–6. See H. Saake, 'Echtheitskritische Überlegungen zur Interpolations-hypothese von Römer 2:16', *NTS*, XIX, (1972–3), p. 486.

according to my gospel: this is sometimes connected with the following words 'by Jesus Christ', and to refer to the doctrine of the Parousia judgement as 'Paul's Gospel'. There is nothing, however, peculiarly Pauline about this idea. According to the immediately preceding verses, the Gentiles stand equally responsible before God for their guilt, and will be judged or exonerated (on the grounds of their conscience) at the Parousia—according to *Paul's* Gospel. The words refer to verse 11 (there is no favouritism with God), expanded at verses 12–15: *all* men will be judged by God through Jesus Christ—Jews by Jewish standards, Gentiles by Gentile standards—according to Paul's Gospel.

By Jesus Christ: the judgement at the Parousia is meant.

   17. The indictment is now brought *expressis verbis* to bear directly on the Jew. On 2:17–24 see especially O. Olivieri, in *Bib.*, XI (1930), pp. 188ff.

call yourself . . .: 'bear the name of Jew' (*NEB*).

rely upon the law: lit. 'have the Law at your back', 'lean upon the Law' (cf. Mic. 3:11)

boast of your relation to God: *NEB*: 'are proud of your God'. Sanday suggests a connection with Jer. 9:24: 'Let him that glorieth glory in this, that he understandeth and knoweth me, that I am the Lord' (SH, *in loc.*). The verb used here *kauchasthai* is a favourite with St Paul, occurring some thirty times. The cognate nouns *kauchēma* and *kauchēsis* also occur a number of times, all, with the exception of the latter at Jas 4:16, in St Paul. The only other occurrence of the verb in the New Testament is at Jas 1:9, 4:16. The verb in profane Greek means 'to boast', 'to be loud-tongued', 'to vaunt oneself', but in biblical Greek it is also used to translate the Hebrew verb *'alaz* (*'alas*) which means not 'to boast' but 'to exult in': 'glory in' of *AV* does convey something of this meaning, e.g., Ps. 149:5—'Let his faithful servants exult in triumph; let them shout for joy as they kneel before him' (*NEB*). Cf. also Ps. 5:11. At Rom. 5:3, 11 it seems to be this nuance which is intended, '. . . let us even exult in our present sufferings' (*NEB*). The two meanings tend to overlap (like *AV*'s ambiguous 'glory in'), but it is important to recognise this dimension of Pauline 'exultation' in his gospel of righteousness by faith. Cf. especially, 2 C. 10:17, Phil. 3:3; and in the present passage the idea of 'exulting' in God cannot be excluded (Hebrew *'alas*). The noun may similarly mean 'exulting', 'exultation'.

   18. approve what is excellent: *NEB* (1961): 'are aware of moral distinctions'; Moffatt: 'with a sense of what is vital in religion'; lit., 'prove the things that differ'. But proving leads to approving, and the latter to the making of distinctions. One might render: 'have acquired powers of moral discrimination'. Tyndale rendered: 'hast experience of good and bad'. Cf. *NEB* (1970).

because you are instructed in the law: *NEB* (1961) takes with 'approve what is excellent', but the clause goes more naturally with both the preceding statements: 'It is through the instructions which he has received from the law that the Jew knows the will of God and discerns the things which are essential.' (Cranfield, p. 166). The verb *katechein* 'to inform' (Ac. 21:21, 24) means also 'to instruct' used especially of the instruction (*katechēsis*) of Christian catechumens (Ac. 18:25; 1 C. 14:19; Gal. 6:6).

19. guide to the blind: cf. Mt. 7:3–5, 15:14, 23:16, 24. Some think St Paul is alluding to these sayings, but they may have been proverbial. Cf. Isa. 42:7, 19ff., 1 Enoch 105:1.

20. the embodiment of knowledge and truth: *NEB*: 'the very shape of knowledge and truth'. It is rather the essence or substance of true knowledge, which the Jew found in the Law. There may be a hendiadys in the words 'knowledge and truth', and they should be rendered as a single expression, 'true knowledge'; at 2 Tim. 3:5, the noun *morphōsis*, here rendered by 'embodiment', means 'outward appearance', 'outward show'; but it seems unlikely that this is the meaning here.

22. rob temples: the Jews abhorred idolatry, but were not above removing from pagan shrines their gold or silver idols for their own private use and profit; cf. Josephus, *Ant.*, IV.viii.10 (207), and Ac. 19:37, where the Town Clerk declares that Paul and his companion were not 'temple robbers'. In an anti-Jewish writing attributed to Lysimachus of Alexandria (*c.* 1st century A.D.?), in a passage purporting to describe the entry into Palestine of the 'Jewish people', pillaging and burning temples on their way, it is said that Jerusalem, which they founded, was originally named Hierosyla ('sacrilege'), but was later changed to Hierosolyma, to avoid the opprobrium attached to the original name. (Th. Reinach, *Textes d'auteurs grecs et romains relatif au Judaisme*, Paris, 1895, pp. 119ff.)

24. For, as it is written: the words which follow are a free adaptation of Isa. LXX, 52:5 'On your account continually is my name blasphemed among the Gentiles.' Cf. J. A. Fitzmyer, 'The Use of Explicit Old Testament Quotations in Qumran Literature and the New Testament', *NTS*, VII (1960–1), p. 324, 'a free adaptation of the text of Isaiah, which goes beyond the original sense of it.' Yet it is an 'explicit quotation', and carries the full authority of Scripture. See M. Black, 'The Theological Appropriation of the Old

Testament by the New Testament' in *SJT*, XXXIX (1986) p. 4; B. Lindars, *New Testament Apologetic* (London, 1961), p. 22.

25. your circumcision becomes uncircumcision: the meaning is not in doubt. It is worth noting, however, that the verb *gegonen* ('becomes') here may reflect a rabbinical nuance = 'is reckoned as', 'is in effect' (*logisthēsetai*, verse 26). Cf. SB, III, p. 119.

26. a man who is uncircumcised keeps: lit. 'if the uncircumcision keep': abstract for concrete.

27. those who are physically uncircumcised: lit. 'the uncircumcision by nature'; again, abstract for concrete.

you who have the written code and circumcision: lit. 'you with all your written code and circumcision'. The *dia* (here translated 'with') is the *dia* of attendant circumstances.

28–29. These verses show the familiar characteristics of Hebrew poetic style, and this seems intentional.

It is not the outward Jew that is a Jew;
Nor is external, physical circumcision true circumcision:
He who is one inwardly is the (real) Jew:
And circumcision is of the mind, spiritual not literal.

'Circumcision of the heart (mind)' is an *OT* expression; cf. Jer. 4:4; Dt. 10:16, 30:6. It means man's inward response to God, e.g., in repentance, or 'man's humble response to God's gracious love and election' (Dt. 10:16) (Barrett). It has been argued that 'external' as applied to 'physical circumcision' is redundant and has arisen by a dittograph of the same expression (*en tō phanerō*) in the previous clause ('the outward Jew'). Certainly this expression has crept into the text more than once elsewhere, e.g. Mt. 6:6, 18. See H. Sahlin, 'Einige Textemendationen zum Römerbrief', *TZ*, IX (1953), pp. 92ff.

29. His praise is not from men but from God: Barrett draws attention to a probably underlying word-play here: 'Jew' is *yehudi*, 'praise' is *hodayah*. He tries to reproduce it by rendering: 'He is a Jew, whose due comes not from men but from God.'

THE ALLEGED ADVANTAGE OF BEING A JEW

3:1–9

'If what St Paul is contending is true', an imaginary objector states, 'then there does not seem to be any advantage at all in belonging to the Jewish race.' St Paul replies to these objections, taking the opportunity at the same time to reply to the standard charges of antinomianism which were being brought against him.

The argument is conducted by a process of question and answer, the question being asked by an imaginary opponent or objector, and the answer coming from the Apostle.

As C. H. Dodd points out, the style is that of the contemporary popular preacher, the style of the *diatribē*, or philosophical conversation. This seems largely to have been a technique evolved by the Cynic and Stoic schools for popularising philosophical and ethical ideas. 'The best familiar example of its use is the *Diatribai*, or *Dissertations*, of Epictetus, which were actually taken down from oral delivery by his pupil Arrian. (His better-known *Enchiridion*, or *Hand-book*, is a compilation of selected sayings.) They are distinguished by a familiar and lively interchange of questions and answer, ironical apostrophe and personal appeal.' (Dodd, pp. 148ff.; see R. Bultmann, *Der Stil der paulinischen Predigt und die kynischstoische Diatribe* (Göttingen, 1910) on Rom. 9–11.) On the 'Question and Answer' style of Romans, see especially J. Jeremias, 'Zur Gedankenführung in den paulinischen Briefen' (above, p. 14). This feature of Pauline style has been taken as a guide to the literary structure of Romans, e.g., chapters 6 to 9 are the answer to three questions set out in 6:1, 7:7, 9:14; cf. J. Dupont, 'Le Problème de la structure littéraire de l'Epître aux Romains' (above, p. 14). Jeremias argues that the thought sequence of Rom. 1 to 11 is determined by these objections (p. 147).

Verses 9–20 set out the general conclusion to this long indictment, viz. that the whole human race, Gentile and Jew, stands condemned before God. This conclusion is most effectively stated in a long *catena* of interwoven *OT* passages—a well-known rabinical literary device (see below, note on verses 10ff.).

2. Much in every way. To begin with . . .: St Paul does not get beyond his first point; his mind is typically diverted by the thought of the 'untrustworthiness' of the Jews, as suggested by their first great advantage or superiority—viz. that they had been entrusted with the Scriptures. A full list of the advantages of the Jew is to be found at 9:4ff.

are entrusted with the oracles of God: the word here rendered 'oracles' (*logia*) means (a) primarily, the promises, especially the *OT* promises, about the coming of Christ; but it can also mean (b) the Scriptures, or (c) oracles (divine), which include both ideas. (For a detailed study of the word, see T. W. Manson, *Studies in the Gospels and Epistles* (Manchester, 1962), pp. 87ff.); J. W. Doeve, in *Studia Paulina* (de Zwaan *Festschrift*, Haarlem, 1953), pp. 111–23.

3. were unfaithful: the divine trust in Israel, in committing the Scriptures to her guardianship, recalls, by an association of opposites, Israel's faithlessness: the tense of the verb is the so-called 'ingressive aorist'—we may render, 'failed in their trust', 'proved untrustworthy'.

Does their faithlessness nullify the faithfulness of God: Paul makes effective use of the cognate terms 'were unfaithful' (*ēpistēsan*), 'faithlessness' (*apistia*), 'faithfulness' (*pistin*). Included in the 'faithlessness' of the Jews is their 'unbelief' (*apistia*) so far as the Gospel is concerned; and 'unbelief' rather than 'faithlessness' is the prevailing sense of this abstract noun in Romans (4:20; 11:20, 23). SH, followed by Cranfield, maintain that both expressions here 'were unfaithful' (*ēpistēsan*), and 'faithlessness' (*apistia*) refer to 'unbelief', although SH add: 'At the same time the one sense rather suggests than excludes the other' (p. 71). Rather, what we have here is a skilful—and by no means untypical—Pauline play on words in which the dominant thought is of the infidelity of the Jews to their divinely given vocation (having been 'entrusted' with the oracles of God), an infidelity which will not, however, mean the cancellation of the fidelity of God to Israel. But they 'failed in their trust'/'proved unbelieving', both meanings, conveyed by *ēpistēsan*, and continued in 'faithlessness/unbelief' (*apistia*).

The verb *katargein*, 'nullify, abolish, do away with, destroy', is a favourite Pauline verb (25 times in Paul; elsewhere only in Lk. 13:7, Heb. 2:14). The Pauline usage could reflect the common Aramaic verb *baṭṭel* (Heb. p r r, Hiph., *hephir*) (cf. Michel, *ad loc.*).

4. By no means: A familiar formula in the contemporary *diatribe*. It conveys a strong repudiation or denial of what has just been stated or agreed: 'Heaven forbid!' 'Never!' See Bauer, s.v. *ginomai*, 3a, Michel, *ad loc.*, and B-D, 128 (5).

Let God be true: the connection is clearer if we render: 'God must be true' (i.e. faithful to his promise) 'though every man be false' (i.e. untrue, faithless, unreliable—see note on 'falsehood' at verse 7). The verse echoes the thought of Zeph. 3 (especially verse 5). The last words are taken from Ps. 116:11 (LXX 115:2).

The quotation from Ps. 51:4ff. sits somewhat loosely to its context. '(Against thee, thee only have I sinned, and done that which is evil in thy sight), that thou mightest be vindicated in thy words (promises), and prevail when brought to judgement.' The purpose clause in Romans is attached loosely to the previous clause, simply confirming scripturally, in a general kind of way, the truth that God will always be found in the right over against men; cf. Barrett, p. 63: 'Paul, following the Psalmist, pictures a scene in court, where God and men plead against each other; when this happens, God is sure to leave the court in the right.'

5–8. The argument is a little tortuous, and very much in the disputatious style of rabbinical logomachy. But it enables Paul to

reply to the charges of antinomianism to which he had been exposed.
'If', the argument runs, 'our unrighteousness proves God righteous,
and, therefore, fulfils a divine purpose, how can God be a just God
in punishing wrong-doing?' 'But how', Paul counters, 'can God act
as the Judge of the world if he is unrighteous? For this function he
must be righteous. If God's faithfulness, nevertheless, redounds to
his glory by my faithlessness, why am I still judged as a sinner?
Can we not (as we are calumniously reported and some say we
declare) do evil that good may come? Of such persons the judgement
which awaits them is well deserved.'

7. falsehood: the meaning of the Greek word is 'lie'; occasionally,
but rarely, it is found in classical Greek meaning 'deceit', 'fraud'.
In biblical Greek (along with its cognates) it means 'unreliable
conduct' and is used, e.g., of fraud and stealing (Hos. 7:1; Jer.
6:13, etc.). ('To do falsehood' is to practise deception, in word or
deed.) The word then comes to have the semantic range of its
Hebrew equivalents (especially *kazabh* = 'disappoint', 'fail'. 'prove
unreliable', e.g. Isa. 58:11 (of a spring), and to mean 'unreliability',
'perfidiousness'. The masculine *pseustēs* means, not only a liar, but
an unreliable, perfidious, faithless person; Cf. 1:24.

9. What then? Are we Jews any better off? Both punctuation
and translation of these words have caused great difficulty. The
main problem centres on the meaning of the verb, whether middle
or passive. If middle, then its normal meaning is 'to put forward as
a defence or excuse'. 'What then do we (i.e. the Jews) plead in
defence?' makes excellent sense by itself, but the following answer
'by no means', 'absolutely not' (*omnino non*), does not suit the
question.

RV mg. has: 'What then? Do we excuse ourselves?' But it is
doubtful if the verb can be so construed without the object it
naturally takes.

Another solution is to give the middle an active force (cf. Vulgate:
praecellimus eos), but we have then to ask why St Paul uses the
middle in such a way without precedent? We may then, however,
render: 'Have we then any advantage over them?' This would then
be parallel to 3:1: thus *NEB*: 'Are we Jews any better off?' If we
take the *ti oun* as short for 'What then shall we say?' (see *Introduction*,
p. 14f.), we can render: 'What then shall we say? We have the
advantage of them? Absolutely not; for our indictment was that
Jews and Greeks all are under sin . . .' Grammatically the least
unsatisfactory solution is to take the verb as a passive (see MM s.v.,
citing (from Wettstein) Plut. 11, p. 1038c), as *RV* (cf. *NEB mg.*)
'Are we in worse case than they?' (lit., 'Are we excelled?') As the
various readings show, scribes found difficulty with this verb: D*

G etc., Or. Ambst., substitute *prokatechomen perisson* ('What advantage do we have over (the Gentiles)?) where it is the meaning 'Are
we any better off?' which is favoured.

It is possible to connect the interrogative with the verb in either
sense if the *ti* ('what') is taken in the biblical Greek sense of *num*
(asking a rhetorical question expecting an emphatic 'absolutely not'
which the question gets). (For this construction and use of the
interrogative, see the present author's *Aramaic Approach*[3],
pp. 121ff.) Paul asks: 'Are we Jews then really outdone by the
Gentiles?' To which the answer is: 'Absolutely not . . .' *NEB mg.*
takes the words *ou pantōs* in the sense of 'not in all respects' (see
also Cranfield, p. 190), but this meaning is questioned (B-D, § 433,
Moule *Idiom Book*, p. 168). See further, O. Olivieri, 'Quid ergo
amplius Iudaeo est?', *Bib.*, x (1929), pp. 31ff.; and F. C. Synge,
'The Meaning of Proechometha in Rom. 3:9', in *ET* LXXXI
(1969–70), p. 351.

I have already charged: *mg.* 'we', i.e. Paul, referring to the comprehensive 'charge' or indictment of human guilt which he has brought
in 1:18–2:29 against *both* Jews and Gentiles.

10–18. This long *catena* of quotations which clinches the argument
of this section is a familiar rabbinical practice. 'A favourite method
was that which derived its name from the stringing together of beads
(*Charaz*), when a preacher, having quoted a passage or section from
the Pentateuch, strung on to it another and like-sounding, or really
similar, from the Prophets and the Hagiographa' (A. Edersheim,
Life and Times of Jesus the Messiah (1959), I, p. 449). The first
quotation, as we can gather from this instance, need not come from
the Pentateuch: the present *catena* is made up as follows: Ps. 14:1–3
(verse 1 freely quoted, 2, abridged, 3, exactly, cf. also Ps. 53:1ff.),
Ps. 5:9, exactly, Ec. 7:20; Ps. 140:3, exactly, 10:7, freely; Isa. 59:7,
8, abridged; Ps. 36:1, exactly. The quotations are from the LXX. In
the first quotation Paul himself introduces the words, 'There is no
righteous man' (LXX: 'There is none who does good'), since they
represent an essential part of the argument.

19. whatever the law says: The 'law' can refer to the whole *OT*
revelation (cf. W. G. Kümmel, 'Jesus und der jüdische Traditions-
gedanke', in *ZNTW*, XXXIII (1934), pp. 111ff.), and the reference
here is to the composite quotation in the previous verses. It applies
first to the Jews, but Paul has already argued that the Gentiles stand
under the same condemnation, so that he can now conclude that
the whole of mankind ('the whole world') stands condemned before
the bar of God.

20. through the law comes knowledge of sin: 'clear knowledge'
(SH), 'recognition of sin'. See below on 10:2. The idea seems to be

a characteristically Pauline one: it is worked out more fully by St
Paul at 7:7ff.

THE NEW GOSPEL 3:21–8:39

EXPOSITION OF JUSTIFICATION BY FAITH

3:21–26

These verses might almost be described as the *locus classicus* for St
Paul's 'great thesis'. He returns more than once to the theme (5:1ff.,
8:1ff., 10:1ff.) in the same, but also in other, terms (at 5:1 he
speaks of 'peace' with God, and of 'reconciliation' (5:10) rather than
'justification').

The thesis is developed against its anthithesis, viz. the rabbinical
doctrine of 'justification by works'. A basic assumption of contemporary rabbinical Judaism was that a man could be 'justified', i.e.,
acquitted before the Judgement Seat of God, on the grounds of his
performance of works of the Law. This is categorically denied at
verse 20: 'For no human being will be justified in his sight by works
of the law . . .' (For a summary of the Jewish doctrine, see H. St. J.
Thackeray, *The Relation of St. Paul to Contemporary Jewish Thought*
pp. 8off.) Now (St Paul argues, verse 21) a 'righteousness' has been
manifested on the grounds, not of works, but of faith in Jesus
Christ.

The basic principle of 'justification' or 'righteousness' by faith alone
is set out in verses 21–23, where Paul is again at pains to underline
the universal application of his Gospel (verse 22) and in terms which
illustrate, in different ways, the nature of such 'righteousness'.

The supreme object of 'justifying faith' is defined at verses 24ff.
It is the Person of Christ crucified as a means of propitiation or
expiation, by whose blood God's wrath is averted, and his mercy
dispensed in a total remission of past sin.

In these verses which follow verse 23 St Paul's thought moves
forward, not in any logical sequence of argument, but in a series of
images or pictures—from the *law courts*, the *slave-market* (redemption), and then the *altar*. They are all designed or selected to give
expression to the Christian's experience of the 'liberation', the
'release' of 'absolution' through faith—it is like a guilty man being
pronounced 'innocent', a slave 'emancipated', a sinner 'redeemed'
by the sacrificial blood of the victim, slain on the altar. It is a
fruitless task pressing the metaphors in an endeavour to elaborate,
out of these, theories of the atonement. Paul thinks in 'film-strips',

not in metaphysical propositions. On this whole section, see further, J. Reumann, 'The Gospel of Righteousness of God: Pauline Interpretation in Rom. 3:21–31', *Interpretation*, XX (1966), pp. 432–52; E. Käsemann, 'Zum Verständnis von Röm. 3:24–26' in *ZNTW*, XLIII (1950–1), pp. 150–4. A number of scholars have detected the presence of a pre-Pauline confession in these verses (possibly connected with the celebration of the Eucharist); see Bultmann, 'Neueste Paulusforschung', *Theol. Rundschau*, VIII (1936), pp. 1–22; also Reumann and Käsemann, *op. cit.*

21. the righteousness of God: see the note on 1:17. Here equivalent to (divine) acquittal; cf. verse 24, and Gal. 3:11. But while the meaning 'acquittal' (virtually 'imputed righteousness') is indicated by the context, this need not exclude the wider meanings of *dikaiosynē theou*, e.g., of 'right relations under the (new) covenant', i.e., as discussed above, pp. 32, 36, n. 2. See further Ziesler, *op. cit.*, pp. 190f.

apart from law: i.e. independently of the performance of any legal 'works'.

although the law and the prophets bear witness: again and again Paul is at pains to emphasise that the Gospel was a development, foreseen and provided for in the *OT*; cf. 1:2, 3:21, the whole of chapter 4, 9:25ff., 10:16ff., 11:1ff., 15:8ff., 16:26, etc.

22. through faith in Jesus Christ: (objective genitive). It is the believer's faith in Christ which is the ground of the newly manifested righteousness. For an alternative, but less acceptable, interpretation, see SH, *ad loc.*

For there is no distinction: looking back to the argument of 2:1–16, and repeating the conclusion of the previous argument.

23. fall short: lit. 'be short of', 'be in want of' (cf. the use at Lk. 15:14), and therefore virtually 'have lost'. The middle form of the verb may have a special force here: man has not only lost the divine glory he once possessed, but he knows his loss.

the glory of God: The word for 'glory' (*doxa*) has undergone a remarkable change of meaning in biblical Greek. In classical Greek it means 'opinion'; in biblical Greek it means the divine brightness or 'glory' which radiated from the Presence of God (e.g., on Mt. Sinai (Exod. 24:16), in the Pillar of Cloud (Exod. 16:10), in the Tabernacle (Exod. 40:34) or Temple (1 Kg. 8:11)). According to rabbinical tradition, it also shone on the face of Adam before the Fall, but, along with the divine image, was withdrawn at the Fall. The 'glory' in this sense was only to be recovered when Adam's divine attributes were restored in messianic times (see L. Ginzberg, *Legends of the Jews*, V (Philadelphia, 1925) (Vol. V, notes to vols. I and II), p. 113 and IQS IV. 23 (cf. V. Taylor, *Names of Jesus* (1953),

p. 126, n. 8). It is sometimes mistakenly equated or confused with the divine image (cf. Dodd, *ad loc.*; Ginzberg, *loc. cit.*) Is it originally simply a poetic image for the divine favour? SH interpret it (with Lightfoot) to mean the divine perfection, 'the majesty or goodness of God as manifested to men' (Lightfoot on Col 1:11), but this seems a modern explanation.

At 2 C. 3:18ff., the 'glory' is restored to the believer by a reflection from the face of Jesus Christ; at 2 C. 4:4 the divine image is also mentioned; the Christian's recovery of the 'glory' and the renewal of the divine image come by faith in Christ, conceived as the Second Adam. See the present writer's article, 'The Pauline Doctrine of the Second Adam', *SJT*, VII (1954), pp. 170–9.

This highly poetic expression means virtually the same as the preceding 'all men have sinned': all men are in the state of fallen creatures separated from God, since they have lost the divine favour (and know this loss).

24. they are justified by his grace as a gift: here is the key verb to the Pauline doctrine. It means that men are freely acquitted by the grace of God, and by nothing else or less.

through the redemption which is in Christ Jesus: The word 'redemption' (*apolytrōsis*) means originally in biblical Greek the 'freeing', or 'liberation', of slaves or prisoners of war, generally effected by a ransom (*lytron*). For the verb, cf. Exod. 21:8 (release of a slave, Josephus, *Antiq.*, XIV. xiv. 1(371). The noun, which became established in Christian usage (see below), is found once only in biblical Greek at Dan. 4:34, of Nebuchadnezzar's 'liberation' or 'deliverance' from his madness. Though the attestation is so slight, we may take it as fairly certain that the word means, in general, 'deliverance' (from any form of oppression or evil). (Moffatt's rendering by 'ransom' is wrong: the abstract noun does not necessarily imply any reference to 'ransom'.) While there does not seem to be any precedent in Jewish Greek for the use of the noun in a religious sense, the verb (and its cognates) is especially employed of God's mighty acts of deliverance of his people, e.g. Dt. 7:8 (of the 'deliverance' from Egypt), Isa. 51:11 (from the Exile). The use of the noun (and verb) of the final 'deliverance' of mankind from the powers of sin and death appears to be a Christian development and usage: it is almost a *terminus technicus* in this sense in the Epistles (e.g., Rom. 8:23; Heb. 9:15; Eph. 1:7, 4:30; Col. 1:14). See further, K. Wennemer, '*Apolytrosis* Röm. 3:24–25a', *Studiorum Paulinorum Congressus*, 1961, I (Rome, 1963), pp. 283–8; E. Käsemann, 'Zum Verständnis vom Röm. 3:24–26', *ZNTW*, XLIII (1950), pp. 150–4.

25. whom God put forward: the verb used here is susceptible of

two alternative interpretations: (a) (*whom God*) '*proposed to himself,
purposed, designed*', and so 'ordained' (or 'foreordained')—as, e.g.
Orig., Syr^vg. This is the most natural (and more usual) sense. The
idea is also a Pauline one; e.g. 9.11 speaks of the divine 'purpose
of election' (*prothesis*); cf. further Eph. 3:11, 2 Tim. 1:9. It is true
that none of these passages refers to the *death* of Christ, but they
nevertheless furnish close enough parallels for this meaning here.
(b) '(*whom God*) *made a public show of*'. For this meaning, cf. 4
Mac. 8:12 where the word is used to signify the display of the Syrian
instruments of torture produced to intimidate the faithful Jews. In
favour of this sense are the terms in the context denoting 'publicity',
verses 21, 25, 26. Cf. also Gal. 3:1: Christ is 'placarded' on the
cross, i.e. a public exhibition is made of him. Is it possible that
Paul meant to leave both possibilities open?

as an expiation by his blood: does 'expiation' do justice to the word
here used (*hilastērion*)? Older exegetes interpret by 'propitiation';
more recently it has been argued that ideas of propitiation are foreign
to biblical thought, and that we should understand these words
solely in terms of expiation. The main exegetical issue, therefore,
is whether we interpret as 'expiation', without implying
'propitiation' of the divine anger. The linguistic evidence seems to
favour 'propitiation'; the closest parallel is 4 Mac. 17:22: '. . .
through the blood of these righteous men and the propitiation of
their death' (*dia . . . hilastēriou thanatou autōn*), lit. 'their
propitiatory death'), the divine Providence delivered Israel . . .' (See
the discussions of Dodd and Manson; *JTS*, XXXII (1931), pp. 352ff.,
XLVI (1945), pp. 1ff.; Leon Morris, *The Apostolic Preaching of the
Cross* (1955), pp. 125ff., and in *ET*, LXII (1950–1), pp. 227ff.; T.
C. G. Thornton, 'Propitiation or Expiation', *ET*, LXXX (1968–9),
pp. 53ff.; G. Fitzer, 'Der Ort der Versöhnung nach Paulus. Zu der
Frage des "Sühnopfers Jesu"', *TZ*, XXII (1966) pp. 161–83. Cf. also
C. H. Talbert, 'A Non-Pauline Fragment at Rom. 3:24–26?', *JBL*,
LXXXV (1966), pp. 287–96, and further, S. Lyonnet and L.
Sabourin, *Sin, Redemption and Sacrifice, A Biblical and Patristic
Study*, Analecta Biblica, 48 (Rome, 1970).)

The word *hilastērion* may be taken in several ways: (a) As an
adjective agreeing with some noun understood (e.g. *thyma*, 'as a
propitatory sacrifice'); cf. Josephus, *Ant.*, XVI.vii.1 (182), of the
propitiatory memorial (*hilastērion mnēma*) which Herod the Great
set up outside the tomb of David after he had robbed it of 3,000
talents of silver; it was intended to be a kind of 'lightning conductor'
for the divine anger. For a parallel to this expression, see B. P.
Grenfell and A. S. Hunt, *The Fayûm Towns and their Papyri*
(Oxford, 1900), p. 313 (no. 337). (b) As an adjective agreeing with

the previous relative: 'Whom (Christ) God set forth as propitiatory, endued with propitiatory power': so Denney, in *EGT*, II, p. 611. (c) As a masculine noun in apposition to the previous relative, 'propitiator', and this is how the Reformers tended to interpret it, e.g. Melanchthon ('propitiator'); Erasmus ('reconciler'); Cranmer ('the obtainer of mercy'); Purvey ('forgiver'); and, even earlier, Wyclif ('an helpere'). (d) As a neuter noun, the word is applied to any propitiatory offering or to the altar itself where such offerings were made. (e) Above all, in biblical Greek it is employed to designate the 'mercy seat' in the Holy of Holies, the golden plate above the Ark, on which, annually, on the Day of Atonement, the High Priest sprinkled the sacrificial blood to 'atone for' the nation's sins. While for non-Jewish hellenistic readers the first meaning which would probably occur would be that of 'propitiatory offering', for Jews it would tend to be taken as 'the Mercy Seat'. We need not assume that these different possible interpretations are mutually exclusive.

A further point has been well brought out by T. W. Manson (*JTS*, XLVI (1945), pp. 4ff.). If we adopt the interpretation 'Mercy Seat' (or 'propitiatory offering'), and combine it with the rendering 'displayed', a new and quite startling idea is being presented, especially if Day of Atonement associations are in the Apostle's mind. The culminating moment of the Day of Atonement liturgy is the entry of the High Priest alone into the Holy of Holies. No one except the High Priest was ever permitted to see the Holy of Holies or the *hilastērion*; he went in on behalf of the people. The whole transaction was wrapped in mystery, and carried out in great secrecy. The startling thing in this verse is that Paul here speaks of the public display of the *hilastērion*; it is no longer simply a piece of Temple furniture hidden behind the Veil to which only the High Priest had access. This divinely appointed *hilastērion*, Christ, in his Death (or through his blood) has been brought out into the open, and all men can go, by faith, directly into this Holy of Holies. 'Paul's application of Day of Atonement ideas to the Gospel has, as its first fruits, the new and startling notion of the display of the *hilastērion*. It is no longer hidden behind the veil; it is brought out into the open for all to see. The Mercy Seat is no longer kept in the sacred seclusion of the most holy place; it is brought out into the midst of the rough and tumble of the world and set up before the eyes of hostile, contemptuous, or indifferent crowds.' (*loc. cit.*, p. 5). This is a valuable insight, and since the ritual of the Day of Atonement refers specifically to *peccata ignorantiae* (the 'secret faults' of the Psalmist, Ps. 19:12) it includes this category of sin in the Christian gospel of the 'atonement'. On the other hand, the fact

that Day of Atonement ideas are restricted to *peccata ignorantiae* is
a reason for extending the Christian 'atonement' to embrace all
manner of *peccata*, and not just a single category.

to be received by faith: The phrase here which is simply 'by
(through) faith' is to be taken closely with *hilastērion*, and this is
well brought out in the *RSV*. 'It (the phrase) stands here to show
that the benefits dispensed from the *hilastērion* are appropriated by
believers.' (Manson, *loc. cit.*)

by his blood: it seems most natural to take this phrase along with
'by faith'; it is our faith in the sacrifice of Christ which atones.
Most commentators, however, prefer to take these words in close
connection with *hilastērion*. They make precise the sense in which
St Paul speaks of Jesus as a *hilastērion*: it is above all the dying
Jesus, Christ crucified; cf. SH: 'the shedding and sprinkling of the
blood is a principal idea, not secondary'.

This was to show God's righteousness: the divine 'justice', or
'righteousness', required satisfaction, and this had to be demon-
strated to the whole world; cf. W. G. Kümmel, '*Paresis* and *Endeixis*: a Contribution to the Pauline Doctrine of Justification', *Journ.
for Theol. and the Church*, III (1967), pp. 1–13. Cf. also S. Lyonnet,
'Notes sur l'exégèse de l'Épître aux Romains', *Bib.*, XXXVIII (1957),
pp. 40ff.; H. Conzelmann, 'Current Problems in Pauline Research',
Interpretation (1968), pp. 177ff.

in his divine forbearance . . .: God had passed over (the original
word means 'connived at', 'ignored') past sins, not forgiven them,
but this he had done only in his long-suffering forbearance. In the
long run, a righteous God could not 'connive at' iniquity; and the
full weight of his righteous anger bore down upon Christ.

26. it was to prove: the death of Christ, as a divine 'act of
righteousness', proved that God is righteous yet merciful, for, in
the act of demonstrating that he is a just God, he also provides a
means by which the believer can be acquitted.

27. boasting: i.e. the Jew's boasting in his exclusive privileges
(cf. 2:17).

excluded: the verb implies that such boasting has been finally made
impossible: Moffatt: 'It is ruled out absolutely.' Boasting about
meritorious works is only possible in a system of legal works. When
faith, not works, constitutes the ground of 'righteousness', there is
no place for merit or pride.

On what principle?: i.e. under what method of ordering conduct?
Can it be that of *tôrāh*? The implied answer is 'No' (*NEB*, 'The
keeping of the law would not exclude it . . .') It is ruled out in the
'system' (*nomos*) of faith-righteousness, since all now depends on
the gracious will or mercy of God, available to faith.

on the principle of works: C. F. D. Moule ('Obligation in the Ethic of Paul', in *Church History and Interpretation: Studies presented to John Knox* (Cambridge, 1967), p. 393) distinguishes two different attitudes to, and uses of, *tôrāh*: the recognition that it is a revelation of the divine will, and the attempt to exploit it 'legalistically', to establish personal 'righteousness'. Cf. further SB, III, pp. 186ff. (esp. p. 188): 'Der Nomismus des rabbinischen Judentums hat auch den Glauben völlig in seine Fesseln geschlagen.'

28. For we hold: 'accordingly we hold'. The verse recapitulates and summarises the Pauline position. It expresses in positive form the negative formulation at 3:20, again emphasising the universal application of justification by faith: *any* human being is justified by faith.

30. since God is one: the central Hebrew tenet of the unity of God. There is only one God, and he is the God of the Gentiles as well as of the Jews. Hence he will acquit all impartially, Jew and Gentile, on the sole grounds of faith.

on the ground of their faith: cf. G. Friedrich, 'Das Gesetz des Glaubens, Röm. 3:27', *TZ*, X (1954), pp. 401–17.

31. Do we then overthrow the law by this faith? Paul is anxious to meet the possible objection that by such a doctrine he is doing away with the Law of Moses altogether. His reply is that, on the contrary, such a doctrine 'establishes' the Law. Either its deeper principles are being maintained, or we fulfil or make effective the provisions of the Law, i.e. produce obedience to it by our faith, and this he now proceeds to illustrate from the *OT* scriptures about Abraham.

The two verbs which are used here 'to overthrow' 'to establish', may correspond to two semitic verbs (*katargein* = Aram. *battel* (above, p. 54), *histanein* = *qayyem*), meaning 'to nullify', 'prove wrong', and 'uphold, vindicate, prove true, right'. Paul's doctrine of faith-righteousness does not prove Scripture wrong, rather it proves it to be true. Cf. D. Daube, *The New Testament and Rabbinic Judaism* (London, 1956), pp. 6of.; B. Gerhardsson, *Memory and Manuscript* (Uppsala, 1961), p. 207; Cranfield, p. 223.

On this section, see also G. Howard, 'Rom. 3:21–31 and the Inclusion of the Gentiles', *HThR*, LXIII (1970), pp. 223–33. On the relation of 3:31 to chapter 4, see Barrett, *ad loc.*

Additional Note on Rom. 3:25
The main theological debate, in recent years, on this verse has focussed on the meaning of *hilastērion*: does it mean or imply 'propitiation' of the wrath of God, or can its meaning be confined to 'means of expiation', without any thought of the propitiation of

an angry deity? The main protagonists of this latter view have been C. H. Dodd and T. W. Manson (see above), who conclude that *hilastērion* is the place or means of 'expiation', where or by which God shows his mercy to men.

This view has been challenged by Leon Morris, most notably in *The Apostolic Preaching of the Cross*. The verb *hilaskesthai* is used with propitiatory force in the *OT*; e.g. Moses' averting (propitiating) the wrath of God (Exod. 32:30ff.) by offering his life for the people; the red heifer as a propitiatory offering (Dt. 21:1–9); Aaron's offering of the incense to avert the wrath of God, shown in the plague which had broken out among the people (Num. 16:46–47). 'Such passages demonstrate that the word, even as used in the LXX, retained a certain association with the removal of anger', *ET* LXII (1950–1), pp. 230f.; 'the averting of anger seems to represent a stubborn substratum of meaning from which all the usages can be naturally explained . . .' (p. 231).

The context in Romans supports the sense of 'propitiation': both the immediate and remoter context (e.g., 1:18) are concerned with the wrath of God. 'The context demands the *hilastērion* should include an element of propitiation in its meaning, for St Paul has brought heavy artillery to bear in demonstrating that God's wrath and judgement are against the sinner, and while other expressions in verses 21–26 may be held to deal with the judgement aspect, there is nothing other than this word to express the averting of the wrath. Wrath has occupied such an important place in the argument leading up to this section that we are justified in looking for some expression indicative of its cancellation in the process which brings about salvation' (p. 232).

There is one further essential consideration in understanding the distinctive character of Christ's propitiatory offering of himself. Morris writes (*loc. cit.*): '. . . while the Old Testament is emphatic about the reality and seriousness of the wrath of God, the removal of that wrath is due in the last resort to God himself . . .'. It was God who 'put forward' Christ as *hilastērion*, not only to dispense mercy, but as 'a means of propitiation'. The nature of this 'propitiation' is further characterised by the words 'in (by) his blood', which most exegetes agree goes with *hilastērion*—it was Christ's death which was the propitiatory deed. All this was a demonstration of God's 'righteousness'. But, above all, the unique feature of the biblical idea of propitiation, without parallel in pagan religion, is that it is God who himself provides the means of propitiation and expiation. The saving deed which at once was a manifestation of the divine anger was, at the same time, an expression of the divine love and forgiveness: the very wrath of God

visited on Christ for the sins of mankind was the expression of his
saving love.

All this, in Paul, is expressed in the vivid language of figure and
metaphor—the language of pictures, images, and poetry—'redemption', or 'emancipation', recalling the slave-market, 'justification'
the court-room, and *hilastērion* the altar. But it is the classic language
of the religious consciousness; and it is the only language which can
communicate the realities of divine justice and love. It is only in
poetry and the language of poetry that an adequate medium exists
for these unseen realities of the spirit; nowhere, for instance, is
Paul's Gospel more adequately conveyed than in Augustus
Toplady's 'Rock of Ages', much of its imagery borrowed from
Romans.

THE CASE OF ABRAHAM

4:1–25

One of the main purposes of this chapter is to provide scriptural
support for the doctrine of justification by faith (cf. Bultmann,
Theology, 1, p. 280). For Paul's opponents, Abraham was the
supreme exemplar of justification by works, the stronghold of the
Jewish position; e.g. Gen. 26:4ff. gave support to the doctrine
that the blessing on Abraham and his seed ('I will multiply your
descendants . . .') was a reward for Abraham's 'law-righteousness'
(cf. also Sir. 44:20ff. and Dodd, *in loc.*; see further below, on verse
2). To counter this Paul quotes first Gen. 15:6: 'Now Abraham
believed (*episteusen*) in God, and it was credited to him for righteousness.' Abraham's faith, not his works, constituted the grounds for
his 'justification'. The argument is further reinforced by Ps. 32:1–2
(verses 7–8).[1]

This whole chapter is best understood as an apologetic midrash

---

[1]For a discussion, see U. Wilcken, 'Die Rechtfertigung Abrahams nach
Röm. 4': *Stud. zur Theol, der alttest. Überlieferungen.* (Von Rad *Festschrift*),
Neukirchen, 1961), pp. 111–27. For a splendidly lucid exposition, W.
Neil, 'God's Promises are Sure: Rom. 4:21', *ET*, LXIX (1957–8), pp. 146ff.
Further, G. Klein, 'Heil und Geschichte nach Röm. 4', *NTS*, XIII
(1966–7), pp. 43–7; L. Goppelt, 'Paulus und die Heilsgeschichte:
Schlussfolgerungen aus Röm. 4 und 1 Kor. 10:1–3', ibid., pp. 31–42; E.
Käsemann, *Paulinische Perspektiven* (Tübingen, 1969), p. 173 (Eng. trans.
Perspectives on Paul (London, 1971), pp. 79ff.; N. A. Dahl, 'The Story
of Abraham in Luke-Acts', in *Studies in Luke-Acts: Essays presented in
honour of Paul Schubert*, ed. L. E. Keck and J. L. Martyn (London, 1968),
pp. 139–58.

on Gen. 15:6, Ps. 32:1–2 (extended to include, at vv. 17–18, Gen. 17:5), with the key word 'credited' (LXX *elogisthē*, 'God credited it to him for righteousness' (MT); for the passive so used, see above, p. 27). The verb *logizomai* is one of the favourite words of Paul: it occurs 29 times (apart from *OT* quotations) in Paul, 11 times here in Rom. 4 alone, and only 6 times elsewhere in the *NT*. It is a 'metaphor from accounts' (SH), implying a 'setting down', here 'on the credit side'; for a study of this metaphorical use in Paul, see especially W. H. Griffith Thomas 'Apostolic Arithmetic: a Pauline Word-Study', in *ET* XVII (1905–6), pp. 211–14. The two *OT* verses are then linked by the rabbinical *gezera shawa* rule of exegesis, according to which the use of identical words in different quotations justifies interpreting one verse (e.g. here, Gen. 15:6) in the light of another (Ps. 32:1–2, LXX). See J. Jeremias, *op. cit.*, pp. 149ff. (above, p. 15). The result is that it is on the grounds of his faith that God credited Abraham with 'righteousness', or, more correctly, 'with a view to righteousness' (see below, 68); and 'the man is blessed (Ps. 32:1–2)' whose sin the Lord does not 'set down' as a debt against him. It is 'faith', not legal works, which 'justifies', i.e., sets right with God and his sin no longer 'reckoned'.

The midrash may thus be described as an elaboration of the metaphor from 'the arithmetic of commerce', when God's arithmetic is the key to salvation: without this divine credit we are bankrupts before God; and no amount of 'good works' can help us. (The figure of speech is also a familiar one in the teaching of Jesus; cf. Mt. 6:12, 14; 18:23ff.).

Verses 9–12 seek to establish that, since this justification of Abraham by faith was prior to his circumcision, it was intended for the uncircumcised: 13–15 argues further that the blessing on Abraham and his seed was for all who believe, circumcised or uncircumcised, and was not dependent on Law, but on faith. Righteousness likewise is by faith, as Scripture proves in Abraham's case (22–5).

1. What then shall we say about Abraham, our forefather according to the flesh? This verse is a notorious *crux*. The *RSV* text follows the reading of only one ms. (B), which omits altogether the word which creates all the difficulty, viz. *heurēkenai* (lit. 'found' or 'gained'). The omission, however, may have been purely accidental, and the more difficult reading (with 'found') is to be preferred. *RSV mg.* ('was gained by') is a somewhat free rendering of the more difficult reading; the text reads literally: 'What then shall we say Abraham, our forefather after the flesh, has found (has gained)?' We may complete the sense by understanding 'by his law-righteousness'. Alternatively, we may connect the verb 'found' with the words 'according to the flesh', and render: 'What then shall we say Abraham our forefather has found (gained) *according to the flesh*, i.e. by his natural powers, and so by the performance of works of the law, and not through the grace of God?' None of these translations seems ideally suitable in the context.

It has been argued (cf. Michel, *ad loc.*) that the words 'What then has Abraham . . . *found*' are an allusion to Gen. 18:3, where Abraham asked God if he had found favour (grace) in God's sight. The answer then to the question was: 'Favour (grace), *not* justification by works.' Textual emendations have also been proposed, e.g., Michel, p. 115, n. 1, R. R. Williams, *ET*, LXIII (1951-2), pp. 91ff.

An alternative exegesis to these traditionally favoured would be to give the *heurēkenai* an Archimedian sense: 'What then shall we say Abraham *discovered*?' Legends about Abraham's 'invention' (*heurēsis*) are mentioned in Eusebius's *Praeparatio Evangelica* (ed. Gifford, Oxford, 1903, I, 419a) and in Josephus, *Ant.* I. viii, 2 (167ff.), the first attributed to Alexander Polyhistor (80–40 B.C.), and the second also probably from the same source. For Josephus, Abraham taught the Egyptians 'arithmetic' as well as 'astronomy'; for Eusebius's Polyhistor, Abraham, like the Babylonians, had himself discovered (*heurēkenai*) 'astronomy, etc.', and introduced it to the Egyptian priests during his sojourn in Heliopolis.

Such Abrahamite legends must have been well known in Rome in Paul's time. Is Paul here making subtle use of the Josephan/Polyhistor legend of Abraham as the 'inventor' of arithmetic, in introducing his midrash on Gen. 15:6, Ps. 32:1–2? That the key term in its exposition is *logizomai*, 'to reckon, count' used with reference to Abraham, the 'inventor' of arithmetic, would perhaps be appreciated by the Jewish merchants and bankers among Paul's Roman readers. It could, of course, be no more than an odd coincidence.

2. if Abraham was justified by works: the rabbinical doctrine largely based on Gen. 26:5; cf. Sir. 44:20ff. Cf. also Jub. XXIII. 10, B.T. Yoma, 28b, etc.

he has something to boast about: according to Jewish tradition, Abraham had cause to 'glory' both before men and God (cf. Jub. XXIV. 11). At first Paul seems here to be conceding the Jewish case. Is he, in so doing, hinting at 'justification by works' as Abraham's 'discovery', an idea only to be immediately rejected, '. . . but not before God'. For what does the Scripture say? "Abraham believed God, and it was reckoned (counted) to him as righteousness." Could there be an allusion to Sir. 44:19–20?

Great Abraham was the father of many nations;

no one has ever been found (*heurethē*) equal to him in fame
   (*doxa*).
He kept the Law of the Most High; . . .
and, when he was tested, he proved (*heurethē*) faithful. (*NEB*)

3. Abraham believed God . . .: Gen. 15:6. The closest parallel
is 1 Mac. 2:52, where, however, Abraham's 'faith' is his constancy
under trial, and it is this which is 'imputed to him for righteousness'.
In the original Hebrew, it was Abraham's willingness to believe the
promise he had just received, of which God approved. 'And he
brought him outside, and said, "Look toward heaven, and number
the stars, if you are able to number them." Then he said unto him,
So shall your descendants be' (Gen. 15:5). (St Paul takes up the
thought of the promise at verses 11ff.) Among the rabbis, Abraham's
faith was included among his good works and took a high place
there; St Paul sets it in antithesis to 'good works' as the ground of
salvation, and declares it was the ground of Abraham's 'righteousness' and is the sole ground of all 'righteousness'.

it was reckoned to him as righteousness: The view that Abraham's
'faith' was 'reckoned to him' as *equivalent* to 'righteousness' is less
convincing than to take 'for righteousness' as meaning that Abraham's faith was counted to his credit 'with a view to the receiving
of righteousness'. (Cf. for this use of *eis* ('for'), Rom. 1:16, 3:22,
10:10.)

4. Now to one who works: a simple analogy from daily life: the
worker is paid his wages as his due, not by grace and favour.

5. to one who does not work: the analogy has already broken
down, like so many of Paul's figures; the 'one who does not work
. . .' is the believer who does not rely on good works for salvation,
but simply trusts in the God who acquits not only the just but also
the impious, the ungodly.

6. David pronounces a blessing . . .: neither this rendering nor
that of the *NEB* ('David speaks of the happiness of the man,
etc.') is strictly correct. The Greek word 'blessing' does not mean
'blessedness' (or 'happiness') here, but 'the being pronounced
blessed by God'. Therefore we should render 'David mentions the
blessing (by God) of the man . . .'

7–8. It was good rabbinical practice to support a quotation from
the Pentateuch by one from the Psalms (or Hagiographa): here the
Psalm quotation both strengthens and further explicates the nature
of the 'righteousness' which is imputed by God on the basis of
faith. It includes an exculpation of past acts of unrighteousness, a
'covering' of sins (*NEB* 'whose sins are buried away').

Abraham the Father of all who, like Abraham, are justified by Faith
4:9–12

9. St Paul is anxious to establish the point that the divine pronounce-
ment of blessing which Abraham and his seed received was not just
confined to the Jewish race (the 'circumcision'), but was upon all,
Gentile and Jew alike, *whether circumcised or not*, who professed a
faith like Abraham's.

10. To establish this, St Paul appeals to the historical fact that
God's recognition of Abraham's faith preceded in point of time
Abraham's circumcision (the rabbis reckoned on an interval of
twenty-nine years, between Gen. 15:6 and Gen. 17:11 (Abraham's
circumcision). Faith-righteousness took priority over circumcision.

**11. He received circumcision as a sign or seal of the righteous-
ness . . .:** lit. 'he received a sign consisting of circumcision' (gen. of
apposition, definition or identity) 'as a seal of his faith-righteousness,
which he received while still uncircumcised.' According to Gen.
17:11, circumcision was a 'sign of the covenant' (*sēmeion diathēkēs*);
the Targums describe it as 'Abraham's seal'. In the latter, the idea
of belonging to Abraham seems prominent: in Romans the idea is
rather that of a seal which legitimises. (Cf. J. Bonsirven, *Le Judaîsme
Palestinien au temps de Jésus Christ*, I (Paris, 1934), p. 179, for the
'circumcision of the heart.)

without being circumcised: lit. 'all who believe "under" (*dia*, 'in
a state of') uncircumcision' (*dia* of attendant circumstances); cf.
2:27.

12. who are not merely circumcised . . .: Paul is anxious above
all to avoid giving the impression that Abraham was the father of
the circumcised Jew who held that justification was by works. The
category of Jew completely excluded here is that of those who are
circumcised and rely on justification by works of the law alone. It
was just this group which exclusively claimed Abraham for their
father. Cf. further, L. Cerfaux, 'Abraham "père en circoncision"
des Gentils', *Recueil Lucien Cerfaux*, II (Gembloux, 1954), pp. 333ff.

Law and Promise **4:13–17**

In verse 13, St Paul turns to the divine promises made to Abraham
(Gen. 15:5, 17:5, 22:17) summarised in verse 13b: 'The promise to
Abraham and his descendants that they should inherit the world.'
On the 'seed of Abraham', cf. M. Colacci, 'Il *Semen Abrahae* nel
Nuovo Testamento', *Bib.*, XXI (1940), pp. 19ff. From the idea of
the blessing on Abraham preceding his circumcision, Paul moves,
by inference, to the wider idea that, therefore, the promise to

Abraham (so closely related to the Blessing) was not given under a dispensation of Law, but under one where righteousness was a gift to Faith, not a reward of legal works. This promise was not given under any legal system, but under that of faith-righteousness. The Law is embraced in the Promise. Had the Law, in current rabbinical Judaism, come to eclipse the thought of the Promise and of the Covenant? Cf. SB, III, pp. 188ff.

The content of the promise is not exactly identical with anything in Scripture. It is not said in so many words to be the possession of the promised Land (Gen. 12:7, 13:14ff., Exod. 6:8, etc.), but it is clearly connected with the Promise in Gen. 15, trust in which called down the divine blessing on Abraham—viz. that he should have a son and descendants innumerable as the stars. The words have also for Paul messianic overtones; the promise was, that through one of these descendants the whole earth would be blessed, and through him Abraham's true seed would enjoy world-wide dominion.

14. adherents of the law: resembles a rabbinical phrase, *benē tôrāh*, 'children of the Law', 'Torah-ites'; SH: 'dependants of law', 'vassals of a legal system'. If it is the group of 'Torah-ites' alone who are the heirs (ultimately of Israel's future messianic kingdom), then clearly the faith of Abraham has been made null and void, and the promise also cancelled. It has likewise been made of no effect.

15. For the law brings wrath: this verse reads like an interpolation. All that the law (i.e. human legalism) produces, or brings down on itself, is the wrath of God, his condemnation—not salvation. Where law (i.e. human legalism) does not exist, then transgression of law cannot exist; in such an ideal state there can only be the promise fulfilled in the Kingdom of God.

16. That is why it depends on faith: lit. 'for this reason it is from faith'. Some supply 'all things are' before 'from faith'.

The style is 'telegraphic': cf. SH: 'In his rapid and vigorous reasoning St Paul contents himself with a few bold strokes, which he leaves it to the reader to fill out.' Some supply, instead of 'all things', 'the inheritance is' (from verse 14) or 'the promise is' (from verse 13). But St Paul leaves us with a kind of blank cheque which we can fill out from the context, e.g. 'the divine plan took its start from faith . . .'

may rest on grace: justification had to be by faith and pure grace, since the only alternative system—justification by works—has been shown by Paul to have broken down completely.

father of us all: cf. SB, III, pp. 185, 211.

The Faith of Abraham and the Birth of Isaac as a Type of the Resurrection 4:17–25

These verses are a further exposition of Gen. 15:6ff., where God promises Abraham a son and that his descendants would be as numerous as the stars. At the time of this promise Abraham was childless and Sarah barren. Such a promise made a great demand on Abraham's faith; it was to believe in a God who can make the dead live and call into existence things that did not previously exist. This faith of Abraham was a type of Christian faith in the God who raised up Christ from the dead.

17. in the presence of the God in whom he believed: lit. 'in the presence of Whom he believed (namely) the God Who gives life to the dead . . .' The antecedent of the relative is attracted within the relative clause (cf. SH).

The commonest explanation takes these words as describing the posture in which Abraham is represented as holding colloquy with God (Gen. 17:1ff.) (so SH). The words are usually, therefore, taken with the preceding verse; but, however they are construed, the connection is not very clear. *RSV* takes them after the word 'descendants' (verse 16), the words following, 'not only . . . nations', being a long parenthesis.

Alternatively we may understand them as closely following the quotation: 'Abraham is the father of many nations before the God in whom he believed . . .' 'Abraham is the father of Jewish and Gentile Christians, not in virtue of any human relationship with them, but *before God* . . .', i.e. in the eyes of God. Cf. Barrett, Cranfield, *in loc.*

The claim in verse 16 (end) that Abraham was 'the father of us all', so as to become 'the father of many nations' (17a) (thus including Gentile Christians in Rome among the descendants of Abraham) is one which was already a commonplace in contemporary Judaism. It was based on the meaning of the name 'Abraham' given at Gen. 17:5.[1] Cf. also Sir. 44:19, SB, Bd. III, p. 211 (Abraham is 'the father of proselytes and of all men'.) Probably just as well known in the synagogues of St Paul's day was the thought that God is 'He who restores the dead to life' (SB, III, p. 212, from the

---

[1]Cf. G. J. Brooke, *Exegesis at Qumran, 4 Q Florilegium in its Jewish Context*, Sheffield, 1985, Journal for the Study of the Old Testament, Supplement Series 29, pp. 20f.: '. . . the rabbis took Abraham's name-change as the biblical rationale for the use of notariqon in exegesis, a method whereby words are broken up and each letter or syllable is treated as an abbreviation: ". . . THOU SHALT BE AB HAMON, the father of a multitude of nations . . .".' Cf. ibid., p. 61.

Second Benediction of the Shemoneh Esreh (the Eighteen Benedictions).[1] Paul brings these two ideas together in his exposition of the faith of Abraham: Abraham believed the divine promise that he would become the father of many nations, but he believed also in this singular attribute of his deity, one about which he himself entertained doubts (Gen. 17:17), namely, God's power to work miracles, to quicken the dead womb of Sarah, when he himself was old and impotent. God was, however, Paul states, able to revivify the dead, and create afresh out of nothing (cf. 2 Mac. 7:28). This was the quality of Abraham's faith, belief in the impossible, which God can make possible—applied at v. 24 to the central Christian belief in the Resurrection of Jesus.

18. In hope he believed against hope: Against or beyond all human hope, he, nevertheless, believed and hoped on.

that he should become: This should probably be understood as '. . . with the result that he became the 'father of many nations'. It was not so much that his faith enabled him to become the 'father of many nations', as that the consequences of Abraham's extraordinary faith, his belief in the Lord who can make the impossible happen, was, so to speak, rewarded and crowned by the fulfilment of the Promise. The infinitive construction could be understood (as in *RSV*) in a final sense, i.e. he believed 'in order to become . . .' but this seems less natural in this context.

the father of many nations: Should the many (*polloi*) be understood here in an inclusive sense, i.e. virtually 'the father of all nations'? See the note on 5:15.

so shall your descendants be: Paul links Gen. 17:5 with 15:5, thus giving in summary scriptural form the content of the Promise. The ms. G adds 'as the stars of heaven or the sands of the sea', clearly an explication and expansion of 15:5. In the Pauline text the *houtōs*, 'thus', refers to the 'many nations'.

19. He did not weaken in faith . . .: lit. 'Abraham did not fall ill with respect to his faith'. According to rabbinical tradition, Abraham did fall ill in connection with his circumcision. See L. Ginzberg, *Legends of the Jews*, Vol. I, p. 240 (Vol. v, n. 127). Is Paul deliberately contrasting the robustness of Abraham's condition when his faith was reckoned to him for righteousness with his weakness at the time of his circumcision?

20. but he grew strong in his faith: Cf. Ac. 9, 19, 22: Saul, after his conversion and baptism 'took food and was strengthened'

---

[1]See J. Bowker, *The Targums and Rabbinic Literature: An Introduction to Jewish Interpretation of Scripture*, Cambridge, 1969, p. 68, n.3. Parts of the Shemoneh Esreh are certainly pre-Pauline; and as this formed the chief prayer in the daily synagogue services, must have been familiar in Rome.

(*enischysen* is ingressive aorist) (*NEB* 'his strength returned'.) At
verse 22, '. . . Paul increased all the more in strength' (*enedyna-
mouto*), the reference is still to Saul's recovery of his bodily strength,
but there is more than a suggestion of his restored powers of mind
and spirit as well as body (*NEB* '. . . grew more and more forceful').
The same verb is deliberately selected to emphasise the increasing
'robustness' of Abraham's faith, continuing the earlier figure of
speech, 'he did not fall ill with respect to his faith (as he did when
he was circumcised).

when he considered his own body: *NEB* renders 'Without any
weakening of faith he contemplated his own body, as good as dead
etc.' A variant text reads 'he did not contemplate (*ou katenoēsen* TR,
D G etc.) his own body.' Both readings make sense (cf. Cranfield).
The verb *katanoein* is used in biblical Greek for Hebrew *hibbiṭ*
(*nabaṭ*) 'to pay attention to', and this meaning suits the context
admirably here, with the preceding negative: Abraham did not
weaken in faith, and 'paid no attention to his own body . . .'.

as good as dead: *nenekrōmenon* = Hebrew *mēth* in the sense of
sexually impotent: see SB, III, p. 215, IV, p. 751: for the opposite
'alive' as a term for high sexual potency, Exod. 1:19, and the use
of *ḥayyah* in modern Hebrew for a woman in childbirth. Cf. A. R.
Johnson, 'Jonah II 3–10: A Study in Cultic Phantasy' in *Studies in
Old Testament Prophecy*, *Festschrift* T. H. Robinson, Edinburgh,
1950, p. 98.

21. what he had promised: The verb (*epangellesthai*) corresponding to the noun for 'promise' (*epangelia*) is always used in
classical Greek for spontaneous promises; the other common verb
'to promise' (*hypichneisthai*) is used of pledges given under contract.
The divine promise was a spontaneous act of God.

22. closes the argument with the scriptural conclusion, Gen. 15:6.

23–24. were written not for his sake alone: the conclusion is
now applied to the present-day faith of the Christian: Gen. 15:6 was
not just written to preserve the glorious memory of Abraham and
his story (Sir. 44:19ff.; Heb. 11:8ff.): these words were also written
on our account who believe in the same active Creator God capable
of performing such miracles as the awakening of life out of death;
and this is evidenced by the Resurrection of Christ.

25. who was put to death for our trespasses: the closing words
have been thought to derive from some early Christian hymn or
confession: the Hebrew-type parallelism has been noted (cf. Dodd,
p. 70): 'was put to death' is literally 'was surrendered up' (i.e., to
crucifixion), a stereotyped Passion term (e.g. 1 C. 11:23; Rom. 8:32;
Gal. 2:20; Eph. 5:2).

The term 'justification' (*dikaiōsis*) occurs once only again in the

NT at Rom. 5:18. The neat parallelism appears to produce the doctrine of justification through the Resurrection, whereas elsewhere the Pauline doctrine is of justification, etc., on the grounds of Christ's propitiatory death. It seems unnecessary to suggest a pre-Pauline doctrine of justification in this embedded fragment; Death and Resurrection cannot be separated in Pauline theology.

LIFE IN CHRIST

5:1–21

Chapter 5 marks the transition from the thesis of Justification to that of the spiritual life of the Christian believer ('life in the spirit' or 'life in Christ'); 8–11 are the transition verses. Verses 12–21—Christ and the Second Adam—constitute a kind of 'bridge' between the first part of Romans ('justification by faith') and the second part ('sanctification' or the 'spiritual life' in Christ, i.e., in the Body of Christ, the Second Adam).

Justification and Salvation 5:1–11

Transition from doctrine of justification *sola fide* to Pauline teaching on the Christian life: life in the spirit (spiritual life) = *eternal* life, i.e. *en Christō*, life *in the Body of Christ*, the Second Adam.

Verses 1–11 recapitulate and develop further the Pauline doctrine of justification. This is a new state of 'reconciliation' with God which Christians now enjoy; the causes of hostility between them and God have been removed. Through Christ they have entered, by faith, into the state of grace in which they now stand. It is a state full of hope in which they should rejoice—the hope of again sharing in the divine glory. We can even exult in present sufferings, for they are productive of patience, and patience produces fortitude, fortitude character, and character hope—which is not an illusory hope, since even now we have the experience of the love of God being poured out into our hearts through our participation in the Holy Spirit. If, while we were enemies of God, we were reconciled to him by his Son, *a fortiori* we shall be saved by his life, and glory in God through Christ by whom we have obtained reconciliation with God. Cf. N. A. Dahl, *Stud. Theol.*, v (1951), pp. 37ff.

1. we have peace with God: *mg.* 'let us . . .' The textual evidence is overwhelmingly in favour of the subjunctive, 'let us'. On the other hand, 'let us have peace' seems to imply that a man who has been justified may thereafter choose whether or not he will be at peace with God, and this seems un-Pauline. The indicatives in the

context also favour the present tense: in the next verse Paul says
'we have gained our access', 'we now stand', and in verses 10
and 11 'we were reconciled', 'we have been reconciled'. Exegesis,
therefore, points to 'we have'. C. K. Barrett writes: 'He (St Paul)
is not urging his readers to do and be what as Christians they ought
to do and be, but reminding them of the facts on which all their
doing and being rest.'

We could render: 'let us *enjoy* our state of peace with God',
without introducing any un-Pauline thought; this is a meaning well
attested for *echō* (= 'possess, enjoy'), and this may be the force of
the subjunctive. *NEB* renders 'Let us continue to be at peace . . .'
On the whole, however, *echomen*, the present tense, is preferable.

We may explain the subjunctive, *echōmen*, as an itacism, or as
resulting from assimilation to the later subjunctive, 'let us rejoice'
(*kauchōmetha*).

peace has the same meaning as 'reconciliation' at verse 11. It is a
state of 'peace' through the removal of God's wrath towards man.

2. Through him we have obtained access: the word translated
'access' means 'introduction', and it has been claimed that the idea
is that of introduction to the presence-chamber of a royal personage.
(Cf. Xenophon, *Cyr.* VII, v.45.) 'The rendering "access" is inadequate, as it leaves out of sight the fact that we do not come in our
own strength, but need an "introducer"—Christ' (SH). We need
not limit the meaning to 'introduction' only, however: the word has
also a special religious connotation describing the solemn 'approach'
(e.g. as at festivals) to deity (cf. Herod. ii. 58). The word is found
in a similar sense at Eph. 2:18, 3:12 (of 'approach' to God the
Father). This seems preferable to the assuming of the (rare) meaning
'landing-stage', and the intention by the writer to suggest a nautical
metaphor—'grace' being pictured as a 'haven' (cf. MM, s.v.). Some
mss. add 'by faith', but the best authorities omit.

this grace in which we stand: i.e. the condition of those who now
enjoy the divine favour. Note a possible word-play 'we have
obtained' (*eschēkomen*), '. . . in which we stand' (*hestēkomen*).

we rejoice in our hope: for this Pauline idea, cf. J. M. Bover,
'Gloriamur in Spe', *Bib.*, XXII (1941), pp. 41ff. The tense may be
indicative or subjunctive: thus *NEB* '. . . let us exult in the hope
of the divine splendour . . .' See also v:3 and the note on *kauchasthai*
at 2:17.

glory of God: see note on 3:23.

3. endurance: not merely the passive quality, but the virtue of
fortitude.

4. character: the word means literally the state of being proved
and tested. Hence 'tried' or 'approved' character.

produces hope: cf. Jas 1:12: 'Blessed is the man who endures trial, for when he has stood the test he will receive the crown of life which God has promised to those who love him.' Proven Christian character is our only ground for hope of final salvation and everlasting life.

5. does not disappoint us: lit. 'does not put us to shame by proving illusory'. There is an allusion to Isa. 28:16 (LXX), cited at 9:33. **God's love has been poured into our hearts . . .:** not our love to God, but, as is clear from verses 6ff., God's love for us. 'The idea of spiritual refreshment and encouragement is usually conveyed in the East through the metaphor of *watering*. St Paul seems to have had in his mind Isa. 44:3: 'I will pour water upon him that is thirsty, and streams upon the dry ground; I will *pour My Spirit* upon thy seed', etc. (SH). Our hearts are refreshed by God's love to us, and this is the experience of his Spirit.

which has been given to us: the Christian believer becomes the recipient of the gift of the Holy Spirit from his baptism and the experience of the Spirit in this life is an 'earnest' of its full enjoyment. Cf. 2 C. 1:22. See further, M. Dibelius, 'Vier Worte des Römerbriefes: 5:5, 12; 8:10; 1:30', *Symbolae Biblicae Upsalienses*, III (1944), pp. 3–17.

6. While we were yet helpless, at the right time Christ died for the ungodly. There appears to be textual corruption in this verse, and it is doubtful if the *RSV* (following the same traditional reading as the *AV*), has rendered the true text. There are two main difficulties: (a) *grammatical*: the subject of the main verb is in an unnatural position (within the subordinate clause); (b) *textual*: the *eti* 'yet (helpless)', repeated at *eti kata kairon* ('yet/still at the right time'), even if we give it different meanings (cf. Cranfield, p. 263, n. 5) is still, to say the least, stylistically awkward. Some inferior mss. omit it, but this looks like an attempt at amelioration of the difficulty, and the grammatical problem remains. 'Western' authorities, with Latin support (D^b F G it. vg. Iren.^lat.) read 'For to what purpose (*eis ti gar* for *eti*) did Christ, while we were yet helpless, die at the right time for the ungodly?' Cf. J. Hugh Michael, *JTS*, XXXIX (1938), p. 152 (see above, p. 35). Vaticanus (B) alone has for the first *eti* the reading *ei ge*, and this makes good sense, and is the preferred reading of SH; the verse is then to be read closely with the preceding verse: '(. . . because God's love has been poured into our hearts . . .) since, in very truth, while we were yet helpless, at the right time Christ died for the ungodly.' The singularity of the reading, however, suggests that it, again, is a skilful amelioration of the scribe of Vaticanus. The 'Western' reading is preferred by Michael on the grounds that it explains the reading *eti gar* better

than *ei ge* (*loc. cit.*); *eis ti* seems to be confined to biblical Greek
where it corresponds to Heb. *lammah* (Aram. *lema*); e.g., Jg. 13:18,
15:10 (LXX) (the more usual LXX equivalent is *hina ti*); it occurs at
Mk 14:4 (= Mt. 26:8) and Mt. 14:31. Cf. A. T. Robertson,
Grammar of the Greek New Testament (1914), p. 739 (Ac. 19:3 is
doubtful). Another instance is Mk 15:34. See further, N. Turner,
Grammar of NT Greek (J. H. Moulton *et al.*), III (Edinburgh, 1963),
pp. 266ff. The answer to the question: 'To what purpose . . .' is
given at verse 8: it is in this way (by Christ's death, not for the
good but for the bad) that God 'commends his love to us'. On the
whole, this does seem the least unsatisfactory solution. Under what
circumstances giving one's life for another was commendable was a
subject discussed in hellenistic as well as Jewish circles. See Michel,
p. 134. For the rabbinical *a fortiori* argument in 7–9, SB, III,
pp. 223f.

helpless: lit. 'weak'; but it is rather moral weakness which is meant
than weakness of faith: the parallel at verse 8 is 'sinners'. The
adjective may also convey the sense of human frailty (cf. Ps. 6:3
(LXX), Wis. 9:5), but it is here rather the 'weakness' of the wicked:
the adjective is rare in this sense, but the meaning is attested for
the noun, e.g. 1 Clem. XXXVI, 1, Hermas, *Mand.*, IV. III. 4.

9. much more shall we be saved: as Dodd points out, the 'much
more' here (= *a fortiori*) has great significance. 'It shows that, in
spite of the emphasis which Paul felt he must lay upon justification
(partly because it was at this point he had to meet opposition), he
found the real centre of his religion in the new kind of life which
followed upon justification. It was life 'in Christ' or 'in the spirit';
life in the love of God as mediated to us by 'the Lord the Spirit'
(*ad loc.*).

10. reconciled: in keeping with the idea of 'peace' with God
(5:1), St Paul introduces the conception of reconciliation (the noun
at verse 11). Cf. 2 C. 5:18, 19—the only other passage where the
verb occurs in this connection.

Adam and Christ 5:12–21

Behind these verses lies the Pauline doctrine of Christ as the Second
Adam. They are to be supplemented by 1 C. 15:35–49, where Christ
is described as 'the last Adam', in contrast to 'the first Adam' (verse
45) (the actual term '*second* Adam' is not Pauline). (See the present
writer's article on the subject in *SJT*, VII (1954), pp. 170ff., for an
exposition of the Corinthian passage.) In our passage St Paul works
out his doctrine of redemption (or justification) in terms of this
Adam-Christ typology: at 1 C. 15:45 he employs it in expounding

his doctrine of the Resurrection. Christ as 'the Second Adam' is a key conception for St Paul; it is closely related to his doctrine of the 'new creation' (Gal. 6:15; 2 C. 5:17), of Christ as the 'image (of God)' (2 C. 4:4, Col. 1:15), and of the reconciliation of Jew and Gentile in a new humanity (the second Adam) (Eph. 2:15, cf. 4:24).[1]

The literary structure of verses 12–21 is striking (see Bonsirven, *op. cit.*). Verse 12 has a chiastic arrangement a b b a:·

(a) . . . sin came into the world through one man
(b) and death through sin . . .
(b) so death spread to all men
(a) because all men sinned.

The passage also exhibits a Hebrew-type parallelism; and the 'telegraphic' or 'shorthand' rhetorical style makes it virtually a poetic composition, an 'Adam-Christ poem'. Note especially verses 16–18, below, p. 83f. The repeated *houtōs kai*, 'so also', at verse 18, 19, 21, continuing the correlative structure begun at verse 12, makes an effective balanced contrast between the two 'Adams'—'(just) as . . ., thus, in turn . . .'. The question and answer style of verses 13–14 (below p. 82) recalls the Jewish diatribe, modelled, no doubt, on its Stoic counterpart (above, pp. 14, 39).

As was pointed out above, Paul further prepares the way by this doctrine of a 'new humanity' for his exposition of the 'life' in Christ (i.e., in the second Adam).

Sin entered the world by Adam and through sin death, which passed to all sinful men. (Even before the giving of the Law there was sin, for death was on the throne from Adam to Moses.) God's act of grace in Christ, however, was unlike Adam's act of disobedience: all men died through the one and all men have grace

---

[1]See especially W. D. Davies, *Paul and Rabbinic Judaism*, pp. 31ff.; J. Bonsirven, *Exégèse Rabbinique et Exégèse Paulinienne* (Paris, 1939), pp. 269ff.; R. Bultmann, 'Adam und Christus nach Röm. 5', *ZNTW*, L (1959), pp. 145–65; J. Murray, *The Imputation of Adam's Sin* (Grand Rapids, 1959); K. Barth, *Christ and Adam: Man and Humanity, in Rom. 5. (SJT Occas. Papers 5)* (1956). On the literary form of Rom. 5, see H. Müller, 'Der rabbinische qal-wa-homer-Schluss in paulin. Typologie. Zur Adam-Christustypologie in Röm. 5', *ZNTW*, LVIII (1967), pp. 73–92; Felice Montagnini, *Rom. 5:12–14 alla luce del dialogo rabbinico* (Brescia, 1971); A. Vitti, 'Rom. 5:12–21', *Bib.*, VII (1926), pp. 132ff.; J. M. Bover, 'La justificación en Rom. 5, 16–19', *Estudios Eclesiásticos*, XIX (1945), pp. 355ff.; F. W. Danker, 'Romans v. 12. Sin under Law', *NTS* XIV (1967–8), pp. 424–39; R. Scroggs, *The Last Adam* (Philadelphia, 1966). For a summary of the history of interpretation, see C. E. B. Cranfield, 'On Some of the Problems in the Interpretation of Romans 5:12', *SJT*, XXII (1969), pp. 324ff.

richly bestowed on them through the other: judgement came by
one: but acquittal by the other. Death reigns under Adam; all men
reign in eternal life through Christ and unto a righteousness leading
to life. By one act of disobedience all were made sinners: by one
act of obedience all men become righteous. (The purpose of the
Law was to bring grace and life for death.)

12. **Therefore as sin came into the world . . .:** This verse has
proved a *crux interpretum*; for a useful bibliography of studies on it,
see E. Brandenburger, *Adam und Christus* (Neukirchen, 1962). See
also A. J. M. Wedderburn, 'The Theological Structure of Romans
V:12', *NTS*, XIX (1972–3), pp. 339–54 (also contains useful modern
bibliographical material). For background, in style and ideas, cf.
Wis. 2:24. 'Now then', 'accordingly', 'it follows from all this' (in
referring back to the general sense of vv. 1–11). Michel (*ad loc.*)
comments: 'So much has been claimed for Jesus Christ that he may
justifiably be seen as the beginner of a new mankind. He cannot,
therefore, be compared with any one within the salvation-history of
Israel, like Abraham or Moses, but can only be set over against the
one who began the old mankind.' While Paul is undoubtedly
thinking of Adam as an historical individual, he is also assuming
that Adam (= *homo*) is also the head and inclusive representative of
the human race. Cf. H. W. Robinson, *The Cross of the Servant*
(1926), and 'The Hebrew Conception of Corporate Personality', in
Werden und Wesen des Alten Testaments (Beitrag zur ZAW 66, ed. J.
Hempel (1936), pp. 49–62): '. . . the whole group, including its
past, present and future members might function as a single individual through any one of those members conceived as representative of it' (p. 49). Cf. also A. R. Johnson, *The One and the Many
in the Israelite Conception of God* (Oxford, 1942), and also T. W.
Manson, *Studies in the Gospels and Epistles* (Manchester, 1962),
p. 142, n. 1. For an example, cf. Gen. 34:30.
world: in the sense of the entire human race.
through one man . . .: Paul assumes current rabbinical teaching.
Adam's Fall involved all his descendants; for this reason he can say
that in 'one man' all men die.
and so death spread to all men because all men sinned: so all
English versions (following the main exegetical tradition of this
verse); consult SH for the usual exposition. If so construed, then
the correlative to the 'as' clause ('as (*hōsper*) sin came into the world
. . .') is postponed till verse 19, where it is resumed and completed:
'For as by one man's disobedience . . .' Cf. Cranfield, who takes
18b as the delayed apodosis. This exegesis is supported by the main
verb 'spread (to all men)', i.e. was transmitted (from Adam) to all
men.

The main difficulty with this understanding of the verse is then the following clause, '*because* all men sinned', since we are then involved in the contradictory proposition that, while death is traced back to Adam's transgression, and thence was transmitted to all men, at the same time it came to all men '*because* all men sinned'. Cf. especially M. Dibelius, 'Vier Worte des Römerbriefes', *Symbolae Biblicae Upsalienses*, III (1944), pp. 7–8.

Alternative explanations of the 'because' (*eph hō*) clause are given to avoid this contradiction; e.g., that we should understand the words to mean 'in whom' (i.e. in Adam) all men sinned', but the antecedent is too remote for this to be grammatically defensible. Origen and Augustine rendered 'in which', i.e. in death, but this is meaningless. Cf. the modern suggestion of E. Stauffer, *Neutestamentliche Theologie* (Stuttgart, 1941), pp. 248ff., n. 176; 'in the direction of which (i.e., death) all men sinned'; Stauffer compares 2 Tim. 2:14 for this use of the preposition.[1] Such an understanding of the words, is, however, strained and artificial. The *eph hō* means *propterea quod* (e.g., 2 C. 5:4, Phil. 3:12), or *quapropter* (see further below, pp. 81f.).

More recently an alternative exegesis has been offered by Professor C. K. Barrett (*ad loc.*), which takes the 'and so' clause in the sense of 'thus also', and makes it the correlative of the 'as sin came', and so on. Cf. below, note on 11:30–31. With this exegesis the verb (*diēlthen*) would require to be rendered literally 'came', or possibly 'came severally', 'to all men, because all men sinned'. Barrett writes (p. 111): 'So far Paul has been describing the historical events (as he would deem them) of Adam's career, and established that he was responsible for the entry of sin and death into the world, at least as far as his own person was concerned. But once the connection between sin and death has been established, Paul moves onward: 'So also death came to all men, because they all sinned.' That is, all men sin (cf. iii:23), and all men die because they sin; but Paul does not add here that they sin, or that they die, because they are physically descended from Adam. Nowhere, even in verse 19, does Paul teach the direct seminal identity between Adam and his descendants which seems to be implied in the nearly contemporary 4 Ezra (especially iii:7, 21).' By 'seminal identity' Barrett appears to mean the natural involvement of all men in Adam's sin and its consequences by *physical* descent from Adam, i.e. their natural inheritance of sin and death, apart from their own personal

---

[1] I have not been able to trace this note in the English edition. For other similar interpretations, see J. Cambier, 'Péchés des Hommes et Péché d'Adam en Rom. V:12', *NTS* XI (1964–5), pp. 242ff.

responsibility. (Cf. St Augustine's belief that original sin was transmitted in the act of concupiscence.)

There appear to have been *two* doctrines about the origins of
sin current in contemporary Judaism. The first is that of natural
involvement in Adam's sin and its consequence, death; it is
represented especially by the Jewish doctrine of the 'evil tendency
(impulse)' (*yētzer hārâ*') inherent in human nature. Cf. 2 Esd. 3:7:
Adam sinned and God condemned him *and his offspring* to death;
cf. also Sir. 25:24:

> From a woman sin had its beginning,
> And because of her we all die.

On the other hand, the doctrine of individual responsibility, based
on Ezek. 18:20, is found, e.g., in the Talmud (T. B. Shabb. 55a),
side by side with this possibly more popular, more primitive view.
Edersheim (*Life and Times of Jesus the Messiah*, I, p. 166, n. 3)
argues that Jewish teaching, while admitting both—mutually
exclusive—views, tended on the whole to favour the first (the
connection between death and the fall). See further, Cambier, *op.
cit.*, pp. 219ff.

On Barrett's interpretation, Paul takes the Ezekiel position. If
this is so, however, how are we to understand verse 19 or verse 15?
'Many' (i.e. 'all'; see below) 'died through one man's trespass',
which assumes original or inherited sin.

There is no doubt that in verses 19 and 15 Paul takes the popular,
primitive viewpoint—death came through Adam's sin (original sin).
This is also the most natural interpretation of verse 12. Is it possible
that at verse 12 Paul is making room for both doctrines? Cf. Wedderburn, *op. cit.*

The verb in 12c (*eisēlthen*: 'came into', 'entered') should perhaps
be given greater emphasis; through the first man, sin forced its way
into mankind as through an opened door (cf. K. Heim, *Weltschöp-
fung und Weltende* (1952), p. 142). Adam's trespass was the *beginning*
of sin and death among mankind: but this does not carry with it
the *necessary* implication that, therefore, Adam's trespass was *the*
cause of sin and death in the world. In this respect, every man is
his own Adam (2 Bar. liv. 19), though bound by ties of heredity
and descent from 'the first Adam (*homo*, 'man')'. Cf. Cambier, *op.
cit.*, p. 254.

A similar position is maintained by S. Lyonnet, 'Le sens de *eph
hō* en Rom. 5:12 et l'exégèse des Pères grecs',[1] on the grounds that

---

[1]*Bib.* XXXVI (1955), pp. 452ff.: '. . . les hommes n'encourent la mort éternelle de l'enfer qu'à la condition d'avoir eux-mêmes péché gravement:
condition nécessaire, sans doute, mais dont Paul affirme, selon l'exégèse

eph hō does not mean 'because' in this context: 'la locution désigne une *condition remplie*.' As is clear from Lyonnet's argumentation, the suggestion goes back to J. H. Moulton, *Prolegomena* (*Grammar of NT Greek, I*), p. 107, where *eph hō* is rendered: 'in view of the fact that'.

Blass and Debrunner seem in doubt what precise meaning, other than 'because', to give to *eph hō*—even when the grounds given are a fulfilled condition (B-D, §235 (2)). Since Lyonnet showed, however, quite conclusively, that *eph hō* could also mean *quapropter, en suite de quoi* (depending on the context),[1] this alternative understanding could be original at Rom. 5:12, where it does make good sense in the context. 'Death passed from Adam to all men, *wherefore, from which it follows*, that all men, like Adam, sinned.' This exegesis is supported by verses 13 and 14; 13a asserts that sin was in the world before the (Law of Moses); 13b raises the objection to this proposition: 'But sin is not imputed where there is no Law', i.e. in the period where there was no Law, there could be no sin. Verse 14: '*But* death reigned supreme from Adam to Moses . . .' incontrovertible proof of the presence of sin in this period.

On this exegesis, Paul adheres to the traditional and popular Jewish view which traces 'death' to the original sin of Adam.

13-14. The connecting links of the argument require to be supplied. Paul is arguing (with himself or with an imaginary opponent) in the style of the Stoic diatribe (cf. above, pp. 14, 39, 78). '(Death came to all men, wherefore all sinned.) Yes, (I tell you, *gar*) until the giving of the Law (of Moses) there *was* sin in the world, though you might argue that where there was no Law there could not have been any sin. But sin cannot be imputed (and therefore punished)—you will go on to object—where there is no

---

grecque, qu'elle a été de fait remplie. Et cependant, d'après la même exégèse, c'est le péché d'Adam qui cause cette universelle damnation du genre humain . . . Aucune antinomie, parce que la causalité des péchés personnels est secondaire par rapport à celle du péché d'Adam, subordonnée à elle: la puissance du péché introduite dans le monde par Adam produit son effet de mort éternelle à travers les péchés personnels, qui ratifient en quelque sorte la révolte d'Adam; elle ne produit même cet effet dans sa plénitude qu'à travers eux.'

[1] *ibid.*, p. 438, *Diodorus Sic.* XIX. 98: '. . . from its centre (the Dead Sea) each year, it sends forth a mass of solid asphalt, sometimes more than three plethra (300 feet) in area, sometimes . . . less. That is why (*eph hō de*) the barbarians who live near are accustomed to call the larger mass a bull, and the smaller one a calf . . .'. Cf. also, J. Meyendorff, '*Eph hō* (Rom. 5:12) chez Cyrille d'Alexandrie et Théodoret', *Stud. Patrist.*, IV (*TU* 79), Berlin, 1961, pp. 157-61.

Law. Be that as it may (*alla*), death did hold sway from Adam to Moses (as it did from Moses onwards) even over those whose sin was not exactly like the transgression of Adam—who is the type of the One to Come (the second Adam).'

13. is not counted: a book-keeping term: 'is not entered in the ledger against'. Cf. Phm. 18. (The inferior imperfect reading, 'was not counted', is clearly a mistaken correction to the tenses of the context.) See above, p. 65f.

14. whose sins were not like the transgression of Adam: Hos. 6:7 (MT) uses the same word of Adam's 'transgressing', or breaking his 'covenant' with God. Cf. Gen. 2:17: Adam disobeyed an *expressed* command of God. Presumably the other forms of 'sin' are of a lesser kind?

15. if many died . . . abounded for many: 'Many' is used here in the inclusive sense of its Hebrew equivalent, and should really be rendered by 'all' to avoid all possibility of misunderstanding. Cf. J. Jeremias, *The Eucharistic Words of Jesus* (London, 1966) on Mk 14:24, pp. 179ff.: 'While "many" in Greek (as in English) stands in opposition to "all", and therefore has the exclusive sense ("many but *not* all") Hebrew *rabbim* can have the inclusive sense ("*the whole, comprising many individuals*")'. E.g., Isa. 53:12 ('. . . he bare the sins of many'.); 2 Esd. 8:3, Mk 14:24 (see R. H. Lightfoot, *The Gospel Message of St. Mark* (Oxford, 1950), p. 65). Cf. 5:12, 'all', 5:18, 'all men'. The point was noted by some of the early Fathers (see SH, *in loc.*). Richard Bentley pleaded for 'all' as a more accurate version: 'By this accurate version some hurtful mistakes about partial redemption and absolute reprobation had been happily prevented' (*Works*, ed. A. Dyce, III (1838), p. 244; cited in SH, p. 140). Cf. further, J. M. Bover, 'In Rom. 5:15: exegesis logica', *Bib.*, IV (1923), pp. 94ff.

grace . . . and the free gift may be explained as a hendiadys, i.e. 'the free gift of God in the grace . . .'; or 'the gracious gift of God . . .'. It seems more likely, however, that Paul is defining further that in which the divine 'grace' lay, viz. the free gift of righteousness; the 'free gift' is thus defined at verse 17. Some think that the expression 'the free gift in the grace' is to be taken as a unity, i.e. the free gift consisting of the grace of the one man Jesus Christ.

abounded . . .: Michel (p. 141, n. 1) suggests that an old rabbinical commonplace about the mercy of God vastly exceeding the penalties for Adam's sin lies behind this verse. Cf. 2 Esdr. 4:30.

for many: i.e. men in general (see note above).

16. Note the Hebrew-type parallelism and the compressed style (*Lehrstil* (Michel)): trespass—condemnation—free gift—justification. Moffatt renders: 'Nor is the free gift like the effect of the one man's sin'; lit., 'For the judgement (sentence) was pronounced upon one man, resulting in the condemnation (of all), but the gift of grace, following on many trespasses, had for its effect acquittal (for all)'.

17. death reigned: the same idea as above, at verse 14. By the transgression of the one man, death came to rule (*ebasileusen*, ingressive aorist), so *a fortiori* the recipients of the abundant grace etc. of the other will reign in life through the one man, Jesus Christ. We should expect the contrast to be 'death reigned': '(eternal) life reigned'; but Paul turns it round, so that it is the believers who reign in eternal life. For the idea of Christians as 'reigning', cf. 1 C. 4:8, Rev. 1:6, 20:4.

18. acquittal and life: lit. 'acquittal of life', i.e. leading to (eternal) life.

19. as by one man's disobedience: the same fundamental ideas as verse 18, expressed in synonymous terms: 'trespass' = 'disobedience'; 'act of righteousness' = 'obedience'; 'led to condemnation' = 'were made sinners'; 'leads to acquittal and life' = 'will be made righteous'.

many were made sinners: The verb here used has a legal connotation: *kathistanein*, means 'to appoint', 'to constitute', i.e., to bring into a certain class, category or state. Cf. Ac. 7:27, Lk. 12:14. The emphasis is not on their personal state of sinfulness (though that would follow) as on the category or class ('sinners') into which they have been placed by Adam's disobedience. Corresponding to this, as its polar opposite, is the category or state of 'righteousness' into which they have been brought by the obedience of one man, Christ: they are now in the category of the 'acquitted' (*dikaioi*).

20. Law came in, to increase the trespass: cf. 3:20, where it is said that it was through Law mankind 'attained a deepening awareness of' or 'came to a recognition of' sin. The sense here is not that the multiplication of trespasses is a primary purpose of law, but that it is a secondary consequence (the *hina* clause is ecbatic, or consequential).

came in rather than 'was given'. The Greek verb means literally 'came in' to the side of a state of things already existing. St Paul regarded Law as a "parenthesis" in the Divine plan: it did not begin until Moses, and it ended with Christ' (SH, *in loc.*).

21. repeats the idea of verses 14 and 17 in another variant form. Here it is not death which reigns, but 'sin-in-death', i.e. sin which has its inevitable outcome in death; and it is grace which reigns, but in a state of or under (*dia*) 'righteousness', which has as its consequence eternal life. And all this, as everything else in the

Christian life, is 'through Jesus Christ our Lord' (again 'under'
(*dia*), 'within the domain of').

THE CHRISTIAN LIFE AND FREEDOM FROM THE LAW
6:1–8:39

By his Adam-Christ typological poem at 5:12–21 St Paul has now
laid the foundation for his doctrine of Sanctification, or of the 'post-
Justification life in Christ' or 'life in the Spirit'—life 'in Christ'
being life in the new Man(kind). Thus we are introduced to the
second half of the 'great thesis' of Romans. Moreover, it is a life
which follows the rite of baptism, by which the believer is incorporated into the new Man(kind), so that 6:1f becomes a classic statement of Paul's baptismal theology; at the same time, running
through the whole of chapters 6 and 7 is the thesis of Christian
freedom—from sin and the Law. These three chapters set out, in
effect, a programme for Christian living, by a new Spirit-enabling
and ennobling faith in Christ, within the Body of Christ. As Brunner
remarks: 'The key to the ethics of the New Testament is contained
in . . . Romans vi, vii and the beginning of Romans viii.' (*The
Divine Imperative*, London, 1937, p. 586.)

For a discussion of 6:1–11, see especially G. Wagner, *Pauline
Baptism and the Pagan Mysteries* (Edinburgh, 1967); cf. also J. Knox,
in *Chapters in a Life of Paul* (London, 1954), pp. 141–59.

There are three main divisions in the section: (a) 6:1–7:6 deals
with the death of the old mankind (the 'old man' in corporate terms)
or the old selfhood (in terms of the individual) and the emergence
of the new self—a 'death' and 'resurrection' which Paul conceives
of as taking place through baptism. The new experience is further
illustrated by analogies from slavery (15–23) and marriage and
divorce (7:1–6); (b) 7:7–25 contains a psychological analysis of the
experience of salvation, the death of the old Adam and the emergence of the new. (This chapter is often regarded as autobiographical;
Paul is speaking, however, for every man, though his thought clearly
comes out of his own Christian experience. See further, below,
p. 94f.) (c) 8:1–39, is a closing section on this new life 'in Christ',
or a Spirit-filled (or Spirit-enabled) life.

Death of the Old Man 6:1–7:6

1. **Are we to continue in sin . . .:** or 'are we to persist in sinning,
that there might be more and more grace?' This seems a natural
enough consequence to draw from the principle laid down at verse

20 that, where sin increases, grace correspondingly increases, in 'geometric progression' ('abounded all the more').

2. By no means: a very strong denial. The idea is preposterous. See above, p. 54.

These verses serve as a transition to the main theme of this second part. The antinomian argument that one should become a persistent sinner in order to enjoy the grace of God more and more is rebutted by the statement that the baptised Christian is dead to sin.

3. Do you not know: cf. the similar phrase at 1:13.

The Pauline Doctrine of Baptism 6:3–11

Rom. 6:3–11 is the *locus classicus* for St. Paul's doctrine of baptism. The pattern of baptismal practice in the primitive Christian communities (e.g. in Acts) was the baptism of the catechumen by immersion (on his repentance and confession), accompanied by the laying on of hands and the gift of the Holy Spirit (cf. e.g. Ac. 2:38ff., 8:16ff.). Here Paul interprets the act of immersion in relation to the death of Christ (chapter 8 is concerned with the gift of the Spirit). Unlike the baptism of John the Baptist, Christian baptism for the remission of sins is integrally related to Christ's death for sins (cf., in addition to the present passage, 1 Jn 5:6 (cf. Jn 19:34), 1 Pet. 1:2, Heb. 10:22, 1 C. 6:11, Eph. 5:26, Tit. 3:5, etc.[1]

The primitive church practised two originally separate rites, Baptism and the Eucharist. The former owed its origin to John the Baptist, and in the Gospels follows repentance and confession, and symbolises a cleansing or remission of sin (Mk 1:4). (Josephus, *Ant.* XVIII. v. 2 (116–17) represents it as a ritual cleansing only.) The Eucharist was also a spiritual catharsis (Mt. 26:28), i.e., it too was a rite symbolising a spiritual cleansing and remission of sins. St Paul (or his *paradosis*) invested the rite of baptism with an even richer Christian content by linking it with the death of Christ as an atoning rite. Thus Baptism and Eucharist came to have the same doctrinal meaning.

3. all of us who have been baptised into Christ Jesus: in his baptism the Christian is plunged into the water—so, similarly, in our baptism, we are immersed 'into Jesus Christ'. The verb 'baptise' ('be baptised') is an intensive form of the verb *baptō* ('to dip'), and

[1]Cf. L. Fazekas, 'Taufe als Tod in Röm. 6:3ff.', *TZ* XXII (1966), pp. 305–18; R. Schnackenburg, *Das Heilsgeschehen bei der Taufe nach dem Apostel Paulus* (Münster, 1950); V. Iacono, 'La Palingenesia in S. Paolo e nell' ambiente pagano', *Bib.*, XV (1934), pp. 369ff.

means, literally, 'to plunge'. Both Josephus and Polybius employ the verb of a 'sinking' ship (e.g., Polyb. I, LI. 7).

into Christ Jesus: what are we to understand by 'baptism into Jesus Christ'? That it is no more than an abridgement of the regular formula about baptism 'into the name of Jesus Christ' (Ac. 8:16, 10:48, 19:5, cf. Mt. 28:19) seems unlikely (cf. Cranfield). Paul was familiar with this baptismal formula (cf. I C. 1:13, 15) and is certainly deliberately modelling his phraseology here on it: nevertheless, there is much more in his rephrasing of it here, and at the parallel verse at Gal. 3:27, than the familiar expression '(to be baptised) in the name of Jesus Christ' conveys. Older commentaries (consult SH for a classic presentation) describe this incorporation by baptism into Jesus Christ as Paul's doctrine of 'mystical union', defined (SH, p. 163) as 'really faith, the living apprehension of Christ'. This is all (it is claimed) which lies at the bottom of the language of identification and union. One cannot overestimate the value of such insights into the character (or one fundamental aspect of the character) of Pauline 'mysticism', but one may doubt if it does really get to the bottom of the language of 'identification and union'.

Nowadays it is recognised that one key to the Pauline meaning (and doctrine) lies in the understanding of 'Jesus Christ' here as *corporate* personality—the new 'redeemed, risen and glorified humanity of which he is the Head and inclusive Representative, i.e., the Body of Christ, or 'the second Adam'. To be baptised 'into' Jesus Christ is to be incorporated into the Body of Christ. The same expression occurs at I C. 10:1-2: 'I want you to know, brethren, that our fathers were all under the cloud, and all passed through the sea, and *all were baptised into Moses* in the cloud and in the sea . . .' (*RSV*, italics mine.) Here 'to be baptised into Moses' cannot mean 'mystical union' of the Israelite with Moses. It means simply to become a member of the Israelite community redeemed from Egyptian bondage, of which Moses was the head and inclusive representative. The expression here, therefore, 'baptised into Jesus Christ', is synonymous with that at I C. 12:13, 'For by one Spirit *we were all baptised into one body*—Jews or Greeks, slaves or free— and all were made to drink of one Spirit.' (italics mine.) The 'one body' is the Body of Christ. Cf. I C. 15:22. At Gal. 3:27 the emphasis is more on the individual as sharing in the 'new humanity' of Christ (cf. below on 13:12): but again doing so manifestly as a member of the Body of Christ.

The doctrine of baptism so expounded follows thus naturally and logically on the Adam-Christ typology at 5:12ff., which thus prepares the ground for Pauline baptismal teaching. On other uses of the Pauline 'into/in/with/through Christ' phraseology, see below on 8:1, 2.

were baptised into his death: The Greek Orthodox church gives symbolical presentation to this doctrine in the shape of its baptisteries: they are fashioned in the form of a tomb. The 'sacramental dying' of the Christian in baptism is further explained at verse 6 as the 'crucifixion' of the 'old Adam'; see further below.

4. We were buried therefore with him by baptism into death: this total 'immersion' was also a kind of 'burial', more accurately 'into his death', and these words may go closely with 'by baptism', though they can be construed with the main verb (cf. Col. 2:12).

by the glory of the Father: commentators take 'glory' here as practically synonymous with 'power', and it is true that the two words frequently go together, especially in doxologies (cf. the Lord's Prayer). But it is doubtful if we can understand here 'through' (i.e. 'by means of') 'the power of God the Father'. The preposition describes, rather, attendant circumstances—i.e. the accompaniment of a manifestation of the glorious power of God. *NEB*: 'in the splendour of the Father'.

newness of life: The new 'life after death' (post-baptismal life) is characterised (a) negatively, by a freedom from sin; it is a sinless life (vv. 2, 6, 7); (b) positively, by 'newness of life' or 'new life'; Paul means a life which has the quality of 'everlastingness', i.e. eternal life (vv. 5, 8, 11); verse 8 (life like Christ's), verse 11 (alive to God in Christ).

For an analogous expression to 'newness of life', cf. Rom. 7:6: 'new life of the Spirit'. Though the character of this new life is not here further specifically defined, beyond the fact that it is a new eternal life of righteousness, without sin, the further ethical content of this new post-baptismal life is indicated at Gal. 3:27: 'For as many of you as were baptised into Christ have put on Christ . . .': baptised Christians have 'put on', or 'been clothed with', Christ, i.e. have become 'new men' (cf. Col. 3:12; Eph. 4:24; cf. Rom. 13:14), members of the Body of Christ, where racial, national, and all other distinctions have been abolished. (Is it possible that, even at this early period, the rite of baptism included, after immersion, the donning of a new (white?) robe?) Col. 3:10ff. describes the life of the 'new man', and its main features seem to come from the character of Christ as the early Church envisaged it. (The main lineaments of a 'portrait' of Christ can be traced in this passage in Colossians.)

5. united with him in a death like his: 'united by growth', lit. 'planted together'. The word exactly expresses the process by which a graft becomes united with the life of a tree. So the Christian becomes 'grafted into' Christ. The verse may be interpreted 'united with a death like his', i.e. Christians share in the death of Christ by growing up into a sacrificial life like his life.

we shall certainly be united with him in a resurrection like his: lit., '(not only this) but we shall also be (united with him in the likeness) of his Resurrection.' For the construction, cf. Lk. 16:21.

6. our old self was crucified: lit. 'our old man': the expression occurs again at Col. 3:9; Eph. 4:22. Cf. Gal. 2:20: 'I have been crucified with Christ'. While *RSV* renders correctly, Paul also intends the phrase to refer to the 'old Adam' in all men.

sinful body: lit. 'body of sin': the genitive is more than adjectival; it means: '(the body) belonging to sin', 'under the dominion of sin'; 'belonging to' is the general sense, but the genitive has a special shade of meaning in different contexts; SH (cf. 7:24): 'this body which is given over to death'; Phil. 3:21: 'our body in its present degraded state'; Col. 2:11: 'the body which is the instrument of its carnal impulses'. So here: 'the body given over to sin'.

might be destroyed: 'should be "done away"', lit. 'annulled', 'cancelled out'. The verb is one specially appropriate in a legalistic context. Cf. verse 7.

7. freed from sin: lit. 'is acquitted from sin'; but the construction is a pregnant one: 'is acquitted, and so freed from sin and its consequences'; cf. E. Klaar, in *ZNTW*, LIX (1968), pp. 131–4. Are the aorists ingressive: 'he that takes death on himself' (cf. verse 6: 'has taken up his cross with (Christ)')?

Commentators are widely agreed that Paul is echoing, if not quoting, familiar rabbinical teaching: the sentence reads like a *halachah*. The idea that death ends all obligations under the Law is a familiar one among the rabbis. The idea that guilt is wiped out by death, and the sinner thereby freed from sin, is a widespread belief of the ancient world; cf. 1 Pet. 4:1.[1]

8. has been explained as coming from some early confession of faith. Cf. 2 Tim. 2:11. It seems more likely to have been a Pauline argument repeated by the author of 2 Timothy, who was no doubt familiar with the passage in Romans.

9. death no longer has dominion over him: the rabbis frequently represent man as under the absolute power of the Angel of Death.

10. once for all: Christ died to sin a death which is also 'final' so far as sinning is concerned (cf. verse 2); and this death of Christ was a unique event—single, singular, unrepeatable, possessing an

---

[1]See further, S. Lyonnet, 'Qui enim mortuus est, iustificatus est a peccato', *Verb. Dom.* (1964), pp. 17–21; R. Scroggs, in *NTS* x (1963–4), pp. 104–8. Cf. also, K. G. Kuhn, 'Röm. 6:7', *ZNTW*, xxx (1931), pp. 305–10.

unparalleled 'once-for-all' character. For this representation of Christ's death, cf. 1 Pet. 3:18; Heb. 9:12, 28.

11. dead to sin and alive to God: the Christian is 'dead and alive', but in a totally different sense from this familiar English phrase: 'dead', so far as sin is concerned; 'alive' with the new life of right living under God.

in Christ Jesus: cf. note above on verse 3. It is 'within' the Body of Christ we are truly alive, as members of the new human being. Cf., however, SH for the older interpretation of this verse as 'mystical union', 'in Christ', as living in an atmosphere we breathe (Christ in us). See further below, p. 107f.

The Analogy from Slavery: the Release from the Captivity of Sin and the New Captivity under Righteousness 6:12–23

12. passions: evil desires; cf. Rom. 7:7, Gal. 5:16. The old Adam 'lusts' to possess. The word is used here in a general sense; it includes both covetousness and lust.

13. your members . . . as instruments of righteousness: lit., 'weapons of righteousness'. It may have been from his own rabbinical teachers or from Stoic philosophers that St Paul derived the image of the 'limbs' or 'bodily members' as weapons in the warfare against evil, and for righteousness. For a list of such 'bodily members' and the use to which they can be put as 'weapons of wickedness', cf. Rom. 3:13–18. We are probably to think of the 'members' here, not just as bodily organs, but as all our human faculties and powers. Cf. Col. 3:5, where 'earthly members' refers to everything in man's life and existence, outward and inward, which is 'of the earth' or lower nature.[1]

14. sin will have no dominion is a kind of promise, corresponding to the command at verse 12 (Michel).

since you are not under law but under grace: Is 'Sin' here personified? It is no longer 'reigning over you' like the tyrant it is (verse 12, cf. 5:21): it will no longer have the mastery over you (*kyrieusei*) because you are no longer living in a dispensation of Law, i.e., on Paul's premises, in a life-situation where Sin, aggravated by Law, is lord, but where Grace prevails.

15–23 *Analogy from Slavery.* Cf. 1 C. 7:22. Cf. verse 1—neither

[1]See also E. Schweizer, 'Die Sünde in den Gliedern', in *Abraham unser Vater: Juden und Christen im Gespräch über die Bibel (Festschrift* O. Michel), ed. O. Betz, M. Hengel, P. Schmidt (Leiden-Köln, 1963), pp. 437–9 (*Arbeiten zur Geschichte des Spätjudentums und Urchristentums*, No. 5).

merely rhetorical questions, but here warding off misunderstanding. For the Jew, when the Law was not paramount sin was rampant.

16. slaves of the one whom you obey states an axiomatic position. If you offer yourselves to anyone as his slave, you are bound to obedience to that master.

The usual interpretation assumes that the two masters here are Sin and Obedience; at verse 18 they are Sin and Righteousness. This apparent illogicality has been resolved by arguing that 'obedience' here ('you are slaves . . . of obedience, which leads to righteousness') is a 'slip of the pen', or an inadvertence in dictating, for 'righteousness': 'it is certainly not felicitous to suggest that the master who is obeyed is Obedience!' (Dodd). Alternatively, it is argued that 'obedience' is here deliberately chosen in contrast to 'sin', this 'obedience' to which the Christian is enslaved being later defined as 'Righteousness'. Throughout this passage St Paul has a special kind of 'righteousness' in mind, the 'righteousness-by-faith', and this is or stems from obedience to Christ; so that the Christian convert yields his new loyalty to Christian obedience, which is Christian righteousness. Cf. C. K. Barrett (p. 131): 'Paul introduces this additional matter (the addition of slavery to 'obedience') because it is important to him to show that obedience has a place in the system of grace and faith.' A third alternative is the exegesis of Zahn *ad loc.* who takes the genitives *hamartias* and *hypakoēs* as adjectival, going with the previous *douloi*, (. . . you are slaves of the one whom you obey), either sinful—and that leads to death—or obedient—and that leads to righteousness (or (slaves) obedient to righteousness'.) The genitival phrases *hamartias eis thanaton* and *hypakoēs eis dikaiosynēn* may be paraphrased as adjectival, 'death-destined, sinful (slaves)' or '(slaves) obedient to righteousness.' Quite simply rendered: '. . . you are slaves of whomsoever you obey, either sinful (slaves), doomed to die, or obedient, righteous (slaves).'

17. the standard of teaching to which you were committed: St Paul here further defines in different terms the object to which Christians yield themselves (or are committed) in obedience. It is to a form of doctrine handed down to them. In fact, of course, obedience is yielded to the Person who is proclaimed by Christian teaching, but Paul can vary his figure by further defining the obedience we obey as the Christian Gospel. The choice of verb, 'committed', is significant; it is the regular word for 'tradition' (handing on) but, instead of saying we are to obey the doctrine 'transmitted to us', he says 'we are handed over to' it, recalling the other common use of this verb of being 'surrendered up to', 'made captive to'—in line with the figure of slavery: the Christian has been

delivered up captive to Christian doctrine.[1] Cf. *NEB* (1961) 'you
. . . have yielded whole-hearted obedience to the pattern of teaching
to which you were made subject . . .' (*mg. or* 'which was handed
on to you.')

Notice that this verse is a thanksgiving for past deliverance (from
sin) and present deliverance over to the Christian Gospel, which is
slavery to the true righteousness (verse 18).

**18. and, having been set free from sin, have become slaves of
righteousness:** The analogy may have been a commonplace of
Jewish as well as Greek moralists. Cf. Jn 8:34 '. . . everyone who
commits sin is a slave of sin.' (Was there an Aramaic saying with a
word-play on 'commit' and 'slave' (both '*bd*)?) Cf. SB, Bd. II,
pp. 523ff.

**19. I am speaking in human terms, because of your natural
limitations:** Cf. Gal. 1:11, 3:15; 1 C. 9:8; 15:32. Was the state of
the slave so degraded a condition that Paul had to apologise even
for using it as an analogy? Or is he apologising for specifying the
typical Gentile 'sin' as 'impurity' and 'lawlessness'? Probably the
expression here means little more than 'I am using an everyday
(human) analogy.' Paul adds 'because of your human (moral)
frailty'; and the reason for this addition is contained in the next
sentence—'for you were once subservient to impurity and lawlessness—you *were* the slaves of sinfulness, bound by it like any slave
in real life to his master.

20. you were free in regard to righteousness: i.e. at that time
you did not serve righteousness as your master. 'Righteousness' to
which as Christians we are 'enslaved' is, in its aspect as the pure
service of God, 'holiness' or 'sanctification'. For a definition of
'sanctification' (*hagiosmos*), 1 Th. 4:3f.

21. what return did you get: the question may end at 'get', and
the answer be '(things) of which you are now ashamed'. The return
or wages of the service of unrighteousness is shame and shame's
children. Their outcome is death, here for Paul, not only the consequence of evil-doing, but the final judgement of God upon it.

22. Emancipation **from sin** and enslavement to righteousness
means also that we have become God's slaves.

the return you get is sanctification . . .: *NEB* is closer to the

---

[1]See further, J. Kürzinger, '*Typos Didachēs* und der Sinn von Röm. 6:17ff.',
Bib., XXXIX (1958), pp. 156–76. Cf. also F. W. Beare, 'On the Interpret-
ation of Rom. 6:17', *NTS*, v (1958–9), pp. 206–10; C. H. Dodd, in *New
Testament Essays: Studies in Memory of T. W. Manson*, ed. A. J. B. Higgins
(Manchester, 1959), p. 108.

Greek: 'your gains are such as make for holiness, and the end is
eternal life'.

23. the wages of sin is death: though the word translated 'wages'
can be used in the general sense of 'reward', the figure here is
probably a military one, the reference being to the soldier's daily
pay, lit. 'provision-money'. (Cf. the use of the term at Lk. 3:14, 1
C. 9:7.) The contrasting term here rendered 'free gift' is also used
in the sense of a 'bounty' (*donativum*), cf. Michel, *ad loc.*, such as
was distributed to the army on the accession to the throne of a new
Emperor. Sin pays her mercenaries in the coin of death: the divine
bounty is everlasting life in Jesus Christ our Lord.

Cf. further, E. Käsemann, 'Römer 6:19-23', in *Exegetische
Versuche und Besinnungen*, I (Göttingen, 1960), pp. 263-6.

Does Paul's use of the analogy of slavery in this section perhaps
imply that a large number of slaves in Rome had been attracted to
Christianity by its 'liberation theology'?

The Law of Marriage 7:1-6

Verses 1-6 of chapter 7 develop a further analogy from the insti-
tution of marriage, illustrative of the Christian's emancipation from
sin and the law of Moses. Cf. J. D. M. Derrett, 'Fresh Light on
Rom. 7:1-4', *JJS*, xv (1964), pp. 97-108; C. L. Mitton, 'Rom. 7
reconsidered', *ET*, LXV (1953-4), pp. 78-81, 99-103, 132-5.

The general point of the analogy is clear; its details, like those of
the allegory of the Wild Olive at chapter 11, are not to be pressed.
A death has taken place which releases the Christian (= the wife
whose husband has died) from the Law, so that she can then be
legally united in marriage with another—namely her Risen Lord.

3. if she lives with another man: *NEB*: 'she consorts with another
man'. The usage is Hebraic, and means 'becomes wife to another
man' (lit. 'becomes the property of . . .', e.g., Dt. 24:2, Jg. 15:2,
etc.).

**4. Likewise, my brethren, you have died to the law through the
body of Christ:** the Christian believer has died with Christ—his
baptism is a kind of sacramental death—but will also live with him
(6:8, cf. 2 Tim. 2:11). This sacramental death is 'through the body
of Christ', i.e. through the death of Christ, into which all Christians
are baptised to become members of his body. Is Paul thinking of
the death of the 'old Adam', releasing the 'new man' (Eph. 2:15,
4:24; cf. Gal. 6:15) from any further obligation to the Law?
that you may belong to another: the figure of marriage is continued.
Release from the Law (and the old partner, the old Adam?) means

that the believer is free to contract a new union with his Risen Lord, and obtain new progeny through this fresh 'marriage'.

5. to bear fruit for death develops the idea of bearing of progeny (lit., 'fruit'). When life had no higher object than gratification of the senses ('while we were living in the flesh'; cf. Gal. 2:20), then our sinful passions (which the Law calls forth and aggravates) were active within us, to lead us into the kind of actions that ends in death ('our sinful passions . . . were at work in our members to bear fruit for death').

6. But now we are discharged from the law: the Law under which the old Adam was held down has become a dead letter. It is God we now serve (not sin or the obedience of the Law) in a new spiritual life, not in the old life of obedience to an external code.

A similar attitude to the hopelessness of the natural life, even with the Law, is found at 2 Esd. 3:20–22, cf. 9:36. But Paul takes a step further than this author; for, whereas for the latter the Law never loses its glorious character, for Paul it has become a hindrance, even providing an impetus to sin. There seems little doubt that such an apparent depreciation of the Law arose in the course of controversy with Jewish opponents who could find nothing higher than the Law.

the old written code: not, of course, the written *tôrāh*, but the 'letter of the Law', i.e. its strait-laced interpretation. Cf. E. Käsemann, *Perspectives on Paul*, pp. 138ff.

Man's Spiritual Pilgrimage 7:7–25

The passage, verses 7–25, is generally regarded as autobiographical (cf. Phil. 3:3ff.); Paul speaks in these verses about himself in the first person. In general, this is true but, though it is indeed his own spiritual experience St Paul is recounting in these verses, it is equally clear that he intends us to understand them as a description of a typical human experience; it is for every man he is speaking in this famous passage; the 'I' in these verses is the unredeemed man. See further, W. Wrede, *Paul*, trans. E. Lummis (London, 1907), pp. 144ff. Wrede plays down the autobiographical emphasis, maintaining: 'The truth is, the soul-strivings of Luther have stood as model for the portrait of Paul' (p. 146).[1]

[1]Cf. further, H. Jonas, 'Philosophische Meditation über Paulus Römerbrief, Kap. 7', *Zeit und Geschichte: Dankesgabe an R. Bultmann* (Tübingen, 1964), pp. 557–70; H. Braun, 'Röm. 7:7–25 und das Selbstverständnis der Qumran Frommen' *in Gesammelte Studien zum Neuen Testament und seiner Umwelt* (Tübingen, 1962), E. Fuchs, 'Existentiale Interpretation von Röm.

The question whether Paul is describing the pre- or post-conversion state has received a variety of answers. Nygren takes the latter position, Dodd the former. A. M. Hunter compromises: '14–25 therefore depict not only the man under the law, but the Christian who slips back into a legalistic attitude towards God. The present tenses describe not merely a past experience, but one which is potentially ever present' (*Romans*, p. 74).[2] Dodd's position is that 'it would stultify his (Paul's) whole argument if he now confessed that, at the moment of writing, he was a 'miserable wretch, a prisoner to sin's law' (p. 108). It is a convincing point (verses 23, 24). Advocates of the pre-conversion view include Origen, Wesley, J. Weiss. Cf. further, Bultmann, 'Romans 7 and the Anthropology of St. Paul', in *Existence and Faith* (London, 1961), pp. 147–57.

The passage stands in close connection with the doctrine of chapter 6:1ff. representing further reflection on the Christian experience of salvation as consisting of the death of the old self and the emergence of the new self (dying with Christ to live with him); but this is now expressed in psychological terms, and as a typical human experience as well as the personal experience of the writer. Every man recapitulates in his own personal life the fall of Adam: he is beguiled (verse 11, cf. Gen. 3:13); the temptress is *hamartia*; and Sin in this passage, like the Law, is best thought of as personified, corresponding to the Serpent in the Genesis allegory (Gen. 3:13: 'the serpent beguiled me, and I ate'). The penalty is death.

This central proposition is worked out in relation to the characteristically Pauline idea about the part played by the Law, or law, in man's spiritual odyssey. While good in itself, the Law proved less a help to man's salvation than in fact a stumbling-block, so that it became in the end the instrument of his downfall; the only result of the Law for man's life was to intensify his sense of sin or guilt (cf. 3:20). From this personal tragedy, repeated in the case of every man—the Fall of Everyman—we are saved, not by the Law, but *dia Iēsou Christou* ('through Jesus Christ'), verse 25, the conclusion

---

7:7–12 und 21–22', *Glaube und Erfahrung* (Tübingen, 1965), pp. 364–401; J. M. Bover, 'Valor de los Terminos *Ley, Yo, Pecado* en Rom. 7', *Bib.*, V (1924), pp. 192ff.; W. G. Kümmel, 'Röm. VII und die Bekehrung des Paulus', *Untersuchungen zum Neuen Testament*, XVII (Leipzig, 1929). Cf. also D. J. Moo, 'Israel and Paul in Romans 7:7–12' in *NTS* XXXII (1986), pp. 122–35.

[2] Cf. also C. L. Mitton, 'Romans 7. Reconsidered', *ET*, LXV (1953–4), pp. 78ff., 99ff., 132ff. A survey of modern interpretations in O. Kuss, *Der Römerbrief* I (Regensburg, 1963), pp. 462–85, and K. Kertelge, in *ZNTW*, LXII (1971), pp. 105–14.

of the passage and the main theme to be developed in the following chapter.

For corresponding passages reflecting a similar despair in fulfilling the Law, cf. 2 Esd. 3:17–22; 7:45–48, 116–26. See F. C. Porter, *Journal of Religion*, VIII (1928), p. 60. Rom. 7 is actually a less drastic attitude to the Law than Ezek. 20: cf. Rom. 7:9–14 with Ezek. 20: 18–26.

The Problem of Indwelling Sin 7:7–12

7. What then are we to say? The Law is sinful? Heaven forbid! I would not have come to recognise sin except with the aid of the Law; for example, I would not have known what evil desires and inclinations were had the Law not said: 'You shall not covet'.

8. Sin seized its opportunity through the commandment to actualise all manner of wicked inclinations in me. Apart from the Law, I say, Sin is a dead thing.

9. Once, indeed, I lived apart from Law: but once the commandment came, it was Sin that came alive.

10. It was I who died, and the commandment that should have led to life proved, so far as I was concerned, not one to lead into life, but into death.

11. For Sin, seizing its opportunity through the commandment, deceived me, and through it, was the death of me.

12. So that the Law is holy, and the commandment holy and righteous and good.

7. **What then shall we say:** a transitional formula found, for example, at chapter 4:1, 6:1: in the present case it carries forward the argument by asking not only a rhetorical but a ridiculous question. Cf. also 8:31 and above, p. 14.

As we have seen earlier (above, p. 56) this idea that man came to know sin through the Law appears to be a distinctively Pauline thought; and here it is expounded and explained by an example. The meaning is that of personal knowledge or experience of evil desire rather than knowledge in any other sense; cf. G. B. Caird, *Principalities and Powers* (Oxford, 1956), p. 42, note 5. Cf. 2 C. 5:21, where the meaning appears to be, not 'him who knew not the meaning of sin', but 'him who had no personal acquaintance with sin'.

You shall not covet: 'If the Law had not said: "You shall not covet",' Paul argues, 'we should not have known what the nature of "covetousness" was'.

The word *epithymia* here, frequently rendered 'covetousness' is much wider in meaning, and broad enough to include all evil inclinations. Paul has probably in mind the 'evil inclination' of Jewish tradition or the 'evil heart' of 2 Esd. 3:20.

The prohibition in the Decalogue (e.g., Exod. 20:17) specifically refers to the desire to possess (a neighbour's wife, his servants, his land). The shortened form here and at 13:9 seems to be a case of brachylogy, i.e., an abridgement intended to recall the full text. All covetous desire (*pasan epithymian*, v. 8) is meant, but this necessarily includes sensual desires, and, in particular, sexual lust. The condemnation of illicit sexual behaviour is a central aspect of Pauline anthropology (e.g. Rom. 1:24, Gal. 5:19, cf. Col. 3:5), though not all students of Paul would agree with E. Lohmeyer that 'for Paul sensual desire (*sinnliche Begierde*) and especially sexual lust is the root of all sin'. ('Probleme Paulinischer Theologie', III, in *ZNTW.*, XXIX (1930), p. 34.)

In Philo's exposition of the Ten Commandments (see especially *Decal.*, 142ff., 150, 173) there is a similar description of the power of *epithymia*; in Philo it is closely linked with *hēdonē* (lit. 'pleasure'), and both together are regarded as the root of all evil. There was probably an ancient Jewish tradition which linked evil desire, sin and death, as at Gen. 3 (cf. Jas 1:15).

8. finding opportunity in the commandment: the word translated 'opportunity' here in the *RSV* means literally 'starting-point' (the corresponding verb means 'to make a start from' a place). The noun comes to be used in a military sense referring to a base of operations (Thucydides, I. XC.2). St Paul's meaning is that the Law, or rather this particular commandment of the Law, was, as it were, a kind of bridgehead into human nature for the invading forces of Sin. Paul's argument is that Sin is 'dead'—that is to say, 'powerless'— apart from the Law.

9. apart from the law: there was a time when he once lived apart from the Law; but, whenever the commandment came into his consciousness, then Sin sprang to life (ingressive aorist), with the result that, instead of the Law being dead, he now died, and the commandment whose intention had been to bring life (cf. Dt. 6:24f.) really proved to be a cause of the sinner's death.

10. the very commandment . . . proved to be death to me: The commandment which should have led to life proved in my experience to lead to death: literally, 'the commandment which should have led to life was found (*heurethē*) for me (leading) to death'. We have here probably a LXX expression: 'was found' corresponds to Hebrew *nimṣa* ('was found out to be', i.e. proved to be), cf. Mt. 1:18.

11. sin . . . deceived me: verse 11 is a kind of allegorising of the story of the Fall. Like Adam, Paul once lived in a time of innocence without benefit of Law; but the Law did come, as it did to Adam, in the form of a divine commandment. Sin then beguiled or tempted Paul, as the woman tempted Adam. (Note the verb 'deceived' (*exēpatēsen*), directly alluding to Gen. 3:13.) Cf. further 2 C. 11:3 and 1 Tim. 2:14. Dodd (pp. 105ff.) cites parallels from Philo and elsewhere, e.g. 2 Bar. 54:19. 'Each of us has been the Adam of his own soul'. Note that Eve or the serpent do not play any part in the Pauline analogy: in their place is the personified *Hamartia*, or 'Sin'.

Notice the close parallelism between verses 8 and 11. Both have the same main point—namely, the indictment of Sin which in this way makes use of the Law. Some commentaries give the impression that it was Paul's intention to attack the Law as calling forth 'evil desire'; in reality, as Gaugler emphasises (*ad loc.*), it is above all *hamartia* which is the object of Paul's attack in this chapter. As a spiritual reality, Sin may be said to have a Satanic or demonic character, because it uses a commandment of God's Law for its own ends (see further below).

12. the law is holy is finally the answer to the question of verse 7. Here Paul replies once and for all to his critics. So far as the Law is concerned, then it is holy, and its commandments are also holy, just, and good. It is not the Law or the commandment in itself that Paul indicts. For a similar statement about the Law, cf. verse 16 below, and 1 Tim. 1:8.

13. that which is good . . . bring death: Did something good then become the death of me? Absurd. But Sin did become the death of me in order that Sin, which brings death as a consequence of its activity, might be exposed for what it really is, since it operates in this way through that which is good. Sin, I say, produced my death in order that Sin might be shown up and proved to be the wicked thing it was through the commandment.

Notice the two purpose clauses—both parallel and both conveying the same sense. By 'that which is good', Paul here clearly means the Law (cf. verse 16 below, and parallels in rabbinical sources SB, 1, p. 809) in which the Law is the good *par excellence*.

14. the law is spiritual: the spiritual character of the Law is something of which we are fully aware (cf. 3:19). There is an alternative reading here, according to which the words were: 'for while I know (*oida men*) that the Law is spiritual . . . nevertheless I am "carnal", the purchased slave of sin.' (This is the preferred reading of Barth in his *Römerbrief*, following Zahn and others, and it is as early as St Jerome.) For a parallel to the latter phrase, cf. Jn. 8:34.

By 'spiritual' here as a description of the Law, Paul evidently means that the Law comes from the Spirit of God—that is to say, that it has something divine in it. He means much the same as he has said earlier at verse 12, when he described the Law as holy—that is, the Law is God's Law. The statement 'I am carnal' implies, not only that the personal 'I' is enclosed in a physical body, but that this embodiment of personality is in fact in possession of tendencies which are the opposite of spiritual—that is, away from, not towards God. Behind this is probably the rabbinical doctrine of the 'evil inclination' which for St Paul appears to reside in the flesh (see below)—that is to say, the physical being of man is so tainted. Paul possibly took this idea of 'carnal' or 'of flesh', a concept more fully developed in the next chapter, from the hellenistic Judaism of his period. (See further below, pp. 104f.) Cf. also P. Althaus, 'Zur Auslegung von Röm. 7:14ff.', *Theol. Ltzg.* LXXVII (1952), pp. 475–80.

For a fuller discussion of the meaning of the word 'carnal', see the note on 'flesh' in the following chapter.

sold under sin: St Paul has evidently the slave market here in mind. Sin is the slave-owner, or master to whose possession the human person is delivered by the flesh with its impulses and appetites.

15. I do not understand my own actions: 'I do not even acknowledge my own actions as mine' (*NEB*). It may be suggested that the meaning of the verb *ginōskō* here is that of 'know' in the biblical sense of 'choose'; see, for example, Philip Hyatt's note on Am. 3:2 in the revised *Peake's Commentary*. In that case, we ought perhaps to render it: 'I do not determine what I am about/am doing'; 'I do not determine my own actions'.

The verb here translated in the *AV* simply by 'do' refers to conduct and behaviour generally; it occurs at verses 15, 17, 18 and 20 in this chapter. It refers to the completed and overt action, acquired habit, and so can be used in general of 'conduct': 'I do not choose my conduct (behaviour)'.

For I do not do what I want, but I do the very thing I hate: similar analyses of this contradiction in human behaviour occur in hellenistic writers; the closest parallel is that of Ovid (*Metamorph.*, vii. 20f.: *video meliora, proboque; deteriora sequor*). Here St Paul is not, however, simply indicating a curious psychological situation that occurs occasionally in human conduct: what he is thinking of is the whole existence of man as being involved in a conflict between what he, in agreement with the demands of the Law, wills to do, and what in fact his actual behaviour is under the compulsion of Sin. One may compare the further hellenistic parallels in Epictetus (*Dissertations*, IV.1.72f.), but this conflict goes much deeper in Paul than in these hellenistic writers, since it is a conflict between the ideal of obedience to the Law and the actual reality of human nature as under the pressure of an occupying power, Sin (see below). Between these two, for Paul, there is a wide gulf.

16. the law is good: the ideal, the Law, is good enough. It is not the Law that is inadequate; it is our own natural human weakness overcome by sin.

17. So then it is no longer I that do it, but sin which dwells within me: Cf. Test. Sim. v:1. Is it possible that 'dwell' *enoikein* has here the sense of *katoikein*, 'possess', ('demon possession')? (Cf. Mt. 12:45 par., Rev. 2:13). (See Bauer, s.v., *katoikeō*.)

18. nothing good dwells within me: verse 18 repeats in other words this central Pauline idea where the term 'flesh' is applied to this aspect of human nature, left, as it were, to its own resources and devices. 'I can will what is right, but I cannot do it.'

19–20 repeat in parallel, but slightly different, ways these same leading thoughts. The will is present with me, but to accomplish the good is beyond me; and this is entirely due to that sin which dwells within me.

'It is difficult not to believe that the Apostle is there [Rom. 7] describing his experience as a Jew suffering under the *yêtzer ha-râ*' (W. D. Davies, *Paul and Rabbinic Judaism*, pp. 25ff.). While this familiar concept may well lie in the background of this chapter, it is nowhere explicitly mentioned. It is 'sin' which is the enemy, not the 'evil impulse'.

Paul's teaching in these verses (and in this chapter) can easily lead to misunderstanding. He appears to assume that Sin is a usurping force—personal, alive, and tyrannical—which exercises complete authority over human nature, indwells human nature (flesh); and Paul sees the human predicament in this light. Man is, as it were, caught up in this situation; he is an unwilling slave of this tyrannical force. James Denney has written (*Commentary on Romans*, pp. 641–2): 'That might be antinomian, or manichean, as well as evangelical. A true saint may say it in a moment of passion, but a sinner had better not make it a principle.' As Dr. J. S. Stewart has reminded us in an article entitled: 'On a Neglected Emphasis in New Testament Theology' (*SJT*, IV (1951), p. 293), this warning of James Denney is entirely salutary; but he goes on to add that when 'a saint, or for that matter a common sinner, says this thing in a moment of passion, "It is not I who do the deed but sin that dwells in me"—as though some outside force getting hold of him were ultimately responsible—it is at once much more biblical and much nearer to the mark objectively than any psychological re-interpretation which suggests that Romans 7 and the perpetual predicament there mirrored can be dealt with under some such formula as "the divided self".' What is really at issue here is the 'whole mystery of iniquity', and for St Paul this is not simply a conflict within the human self only, between a higher self and a lower self, between personal integrity or dishonour. What is at issue here is the conflict between forces of evil in which man is caught up and the opposing powers of the Kingdom of God.

There is little doubt that such an outlook implies some kind of 'dualism'; and it is impossible to deny a dualistic concept of the universe to Paul and his contemporaries. The closest parallels to Paul are now in the Qumran writings (see my *Scrolls and Christian Origins*, p. 134). In acknowledging this, it is important, at the same time, to recognise that Pauline (or Qumran) dualism is not of the philosophical or speculative kind, although it is a *cosmic* dualism, with philosophical and metaphysical presuppositions. But the latter are never examined or made explicit in a form of dualism which is best described as an *ethical dualism*, a dualism of experience, recognising the reality of good and evil in the human situation, and seeking to cope with them rather than speculate about them. If to 'objectify' evil in this way, thinking of it as somehow 'built into the Cosmos', is to surrender or compromise belief in the absolute sovereignty of God, it is a more down-to-earth assessment of the human condition—always provided it is not made grounds for indulgence in evil ('it is only human nature') or for pleas of 'diminished responsibility' by evil-doers.

We have, somehow, to retain our conviction about 'the mystery of iniquity' along with belief in human freedom and responsibility—and always to watch and pray to be delivered from the Evil One.

21. I find it to be a law: human nature has this kind of constitution. 'Law' here in the sense of 'principle'.

22. inmost self: the same expression again only at 2 C. 4:16 where, as the inner self which is daily 'renewed', it is contrasted with the 'outer man' that is perishing. The parallel with *nous* ('mind', verse 23) shows that it is of the 'higher (inner) self' Paul is thinking. Is this another expression for the 'new creation' (Gal. 6:15; 2 C. 5:17) or the 'new man' (Eph. 2:15; 4:24)?

23. members: *NEB* rightly paraphrases 'bodily members': it is 'the body' with its appetites Paul means.

Note the military metaphors, and cf. Jas 4:1; a law or principle in the body which is at war with (lit. 'campaigning against') the law of my mind and which brings me into captivity, etc.

law of my mind: Paul may again have the Stoic *lex naturalis* in mind. Cf. above on 2:14ff. This was also the 'Law of God' as much as the *tôrāh*. The ambiguous *nomos* is here used both for the higher

law (the law of the mind) and the lower 'law', or 'order', of sin
which resides in the 'bodily members'.

24. Wretched man that I am: cf. J. I. Packer, 'The "Wretched
Man" in Rom. 7', *Stud. Ev.*, II (1964), pp. 621–7.

this body of death: more than 'this mortal body'; *NEB*: 'this body
doomed to death', i.e. by the operation of the 'law of sin' (scarcely
as *NEB mg.*, 'doomed to this death').

25. Thanks be to God . . . Lord! The first sentence of this verse
does not really supply an answer to the question asked in verse 24.
That question is a rhetorical one, and the answer appears only to
be implied in verse 25. It is, in any case, supplied elsewhere in
Romans. The answer is, of course: 'God through his intervention
in Christ'. But all that we have in Paul is a thanksgiving which
assumes the deliverance described elsewhere in Romans. In these
circumstances, it is doubtful if *NEB*'s rendering of verse 25 is
legitimate, except as a free paraphrase. To the question asked in
verse 24 *NEB* replies: 'God alone, through Jesus Christ our Lord!
Thanks be to God!'

A problem may still be felt to remain here, so that the suggestion
of Michel may be welcomed by many, namely, that we should take
8:2 immediately after this thanksgiving in verse 25. It is possible
that there has been some dislocation in these verses. Verse 25b, for
instance, would come much more logically within the argument of
the previous verses if it followed immediately after verse 23. Chapter
8:1 would lead very naturally into verse 3.

The Spirit-enabled Life 8:1–39

In the last two chapters, St Paul has been more concerned with the
negative rather than with the positive aspects of salvation (freedom
from Sin, freedom *from* the Law), though at more than one point
the positive side has been mentioned (e.g., 5:18: 'absolution carrying
with it life'; 6:8 'we shall *live* with him'). In chapter 8, however, St
Paul goes on to expand the theme of 7:25 (salvation through Jesus
Christ), and to expound the more positive content of the Christian
life, which is a life lived *in Christ*, i.e. as a member of the Body of
Christ, by the power of the Spirit of God, the Holy Spirit, which
enables us to fulfil the demands of the Law, which under the old
system of frail and unaided human nature, man proved himself
incapable of doing.

In the traditional doctrinal scheme (cf., e.g., Ac. 19:6), Baptism,
introduced at 6:3, should be accompanied by the illapse of the
Spirit. Having dealt in chapters 6–7 with the fundamental aspects
of baptism as a 'death' and 'resurrection' of the believer within the

Body of Christ—i.e. a new life in Christ—chapter 8 now goes on to develop the theme of the spiritual endowment of the Christian in his baptism.

Note on 'Flesh', 'Body', 'Spirit'

The basic meaning of 'flesh' (Greek *sarx*; Hebrew *basar*) is the same in all languages. It denotes primarily the muscular tissue, the fleshy substance common to men and all living creatures; cf. J. A. T. Robinson, *The Body: a Study in Pauline Theology. Studies in Biblical Theology*, 5, (London, 1952); and also R. Bultmann, *Theology*, I, pp. 232ff.; R. Jewett, *Paul's Anthropological Terms: A Study of their Use in Conflict Settings* (Leiden, 1971). In Hebrew thought, *basar* stands for 'the whole life-substance of men or beasts as organized in corporeal form', cf. Robinson, *op. cit.*, p. 13.

In Hebrew thought and in its applications to man, the word *basar* or, in its Greek form, *sarx*, or *sōma* ('body'), came to denote, not just the physical body, but the whole human being, and in this it differed fundamentally from Greek ideas about the physical body (*sōma*), or its substance 'flesh' (*sarx*). As Robinson points out the '. . . most far-reaching of all the Greek antitheses, that between *body* and *soul*, is also foreign to the Hebrew. The Hellenic conception of man has been described as that of an angel in a slot-machine, a soul (the invisible, spiritual, essential ego) incarcerated in a frame of matter, from which it trusts eventually to be liberated. The body is non-essential to the personality: it is something which a man possesses, or, rather, is possessed by. "The Hebrew idea of the personality," on the other hand, wrote the late Dr. Wheeler Robinson in a sentence which has become famous, "is an animated body, and not an incarnated soul' (*The People and the Book*, ed. A. S. Peake (Oxford, 1925), p. 362)". Man does not *have* a body; he is a body. He is flesh-animated-by-soul, the whole conceived as a psychophysical unity: 'the body is the soul in its outward form' (J. Pedersen, *Israel*, (London, 1926), 171).' There is no suggestion that the soul is the essential personality, or that the soul (*nephesh*) is immortal while the flesh (*basar*) is mortal. The 'soul' does not survive a man: it simply goes out, draining away with the blood.' (*op. cit.*, p. 14).

A second important point of differentiation from Greek ideas, according to J. A. T. Robinson, is what he calls 'the principle of individuation' in Hebrew thought about the whole human personality. Greek thought, he contends, tended to see the *sōma* or body as that which sets off or isolates one man from another. The body is the most individual thing the soul possesses. In Hebrew thought the principle of individuation is not to be found in the outward appearance of the body; it is grounded solely on the individual responsibility of each man to God and the nature of the response each man makes to the demands of God; see Jer. 31:29f., and cf. Walter Eichrodt, *Man in the Old Testament*, Eng. trans. by K. and R. Gregor Smith (*Studies in Biblical Theology*, 4, London, 1951), pp. 9ff. and 23ff.; and J. A. T. Robinson, *op. cit.*, p. 15.

There is a further important aspect of this so-called principle of individuation. Hebrew thought, when it thinks of body or 'flesh', in this sense of the whole individual responsible to God, thinks, not only of the whole man as an isolated individual or unit, but the whole man as a social personality, just as in ancient tribal life, and especially the life of ancient Israel, there were no solitary individuals—the unit was the tribe or group. So in later Hebrew thought, man's only life is the life of a social being. Thus J. A. T. Robinson writes (p. 15): 'The flesh-body was not what partitioned a man off from his neighbour; it was rather what bound him in the bundle of life with all men and nature, so that he could never make his unique answer to God as an isolated individual, apart from his relation to his neighbour. The *basar* continued even in the age of greater religious individualism, to represent the fact that personality is essential social.'

Finally, 'flesh' comes especially to denote in the Old Testament weak mortal and perishable human nature; cf. especially Isa. 40:6–8: 'The voice said, Cry. And he said, What shall I cry? All flesh is grass, and all the goodliness thereof is as the flower of the field: The grass withereth, the flower fadeth: because the spirit of the Lord bloweth upon it. . . . The grass withereth, the flower fadeth: but the word of our God shall stand for ever' (*AV*). 'All flesh' denotes weak and perishable mortality, in contrast to the life and power of God: it is man, as Robinson defines him, 'in his distance and difference from God' (*op. cit.*, p. 19).

Paul builds on this Old Testament foundation. The further question has been raised whether, in addition to his Hebrew inheritance, Paul's concept of the flesh has also been influenced by trends in Greek philosophy—stemming ultimately from Plato—which, by setting matter over against mind, ended by regarding the 'flesh' or 'body', since it is composed of matter, as necessarily and inherently evil. Paul undoubtedly uses 'flesh' in what appears to be a 'theologically loaded' sense; he certainly can think of the 'flesh' (i.e. the natural life of man) as somehow the seat of evil desires (cf. 7:8). Jacob Licht (see below) contends that Paul is in the same tradition as Qumran, where 'flesh' seems to be inherently 'wicked' ('the wicked flesh'; cf. 1QS xi.9). It seems, however, that the Qumran concept represents an even more pessimistic point of view than Paul's (possibly a rationalisation of sexual disgust, not unnatural in an ascetic community). Paul's 'flesh' seems, by comparison, morally neutral, but, by virtue of its weakness, an unresisting 'host' to evil impulses. For a useful discussion, W. D. Davies and K. G. Kuhn, *The Scrolls and the New Testament*, ed. K. Stendahl (London, 1958), pp. 157ff., 94ff.; Jacob Licht, 'The Doctrine of the Thanksgiving Scroll', *IEJ*, 6, (1956), pp. 90ff.; D. Flusser, *Scripta Hierosolymitana* (Jerusalem, 1965), pp. 252ff.

The subject is one which has, naturally, aroused a vast amount of learned debate; and some may feel that the straightforward position set out above may require amplification. Essentially the view presented is the Bultmann-Schweizer theory that life 'in the flesh' is neutral, whereas life 'according to the flesh' is evil. The theory has been challenged in several studies.[1]

St Paul inherited ideas such as these from his tradition. 'Flesh' was fundamentally human nature in its weak creatureliness and mortality, in its distance and difference from God. But when St Paul thinks of the individual human being as 'flesh', just as when he thinks of him as *sōma* (or 'body'), requiring to be saved out of its weakness and mortality, he thinks in Hebraic terms, first of the whole personality responding morally to God, and so differentiated from others, and secondly of that whole personality as a social being. The individual cannot be rescued, so to speak, out of his fleshly and mortal weakness, so liable to the invasions of sin and amenable and doomed to mortality, as an isolated unit; that would be like raising oneself up by one's boot-strings. As a social personality he must be lifted out of the context of weak sinful mankind and placed into the new social context of the Body of Christ (the *sōma Christou*), the redeemed flesh, the 'second Adam'. In this sense, it is profoundly true that *extra ecclesiam nulla salus*.

In the psychology of the Old Testament, spirit (*pneuma, rûaḥ*) is the supernatural divine element which breaks into human life over against the powerless and perishable flesh. All qualities in men

---

[1]The literature on the subject is immense. Among more notable contributions are: H. W. Robinson, *The Christian Doctrine of Man* (Edinburgh, 1911); W. D. Davies, *Paul and Rabbinic Judaism* (London, 1962); O. Kuss, *Römerbrief*; E. Schweizer, in *TWNT*, s.v. *sarx, pneuma*. For some additional discussion, consult E. Brandenburger, *Fleisch und Geist: Paulus und die dualistische Weisheit* (*Wissenschaftliche Monographien zum Alten und Neuen Testament*, Neukirchen, 1968); W. G. Kümmel, *Man in the New Testament* (London, 1963); E. Käsemann, *Leib und Leib Christi: eine Untersuchung zur paulinischen Begrifflichkeit* (Tübingen, 1933).

which were deemed to be extraordinary are attributed to the workings of this divine power. Thus Samson's extraordinary physique
and his physical prowess are due to the workings of the 'Spirit' of
Yahweh; cf. Jg. 14:6f. ('And the Spirit of the Lord came mightily
upon him'); and so also it is the Spirit of Yahweh which fills the
artisans who fashion the furniture of the Tabernacle (cf. Exod. 28:3,
31:4). At Exod. 28:3 the translation: 'an able mind' is given in the
RSV, where the other versions speak of 'the spirit of wisdom', but
this is precisely what the author means by the Spirit of Yahweh in
such contexts. Similarly it is the Spirit of God which comes upon
Joseph, and gives him his wisdom and gifts of administration in
Egypt (Gen. 41:38). Above all, the prophetic spirit, the inspiration
of the prophet, is conceived of as endowing men with the gift of
understanding, wisdom and judgement; cf. Job 32:8: 'But there is
a spirit in man: and the inspiration of the Almighty giveth them
understanding' (*AV*). Here the 'spirit in man' is defined in terms
of understanding, and it is as an endowment, as it were, of the
'breath of the Almighty'.

This typically Hebraic conception of man's divinely inspired
nature and endowments is carried over into the Scriptures of the
New Testament. The early Christian Church was uniquely conscious
of the workings of this divine power in and through it; and the *fons
et origo*, the source and inspiration, as well as the medium or
channel, of this power was the Crucified, Risen and Exalted Lord.
Christian spiritual life all down the centuries has been a life inspired
by the Spirit of Jesus and drawing its spiritual resources from
worship and obedience to the Risen and Ascended Christ. As a
monk of the Greek Orthodox Church wrote in a little book called
Orthodox Spirituality (London, 1945): 'The vitalising centre of the
first Christian thought and devotion was neither a body of ethical
teaching, simply relating the individual to his Father and Maker
(Harnack, Tolstoi), nor a mere eschatological expectation
(Schweitzer). Christianity was a stream of charismatic life flowing
out with torrential might from Palestine upon the Greco-Roman
world. It was a new spring-tide of the Spirit, out of faith in, nay,
out of experience of, the Risen and Exalted Christ . . . grew the
whole efflorescence of prayer and belief, of grace and self-giving,
which we call the Holy Catholic Church' (p. 79).

St Paul speaks of the Spirit as the 'earnest' of the world to come
(2 C. 1:22 and 5:5), and the author of the Epistle to the Hebrews
(6:5) regards the Spirit as a foretaste of the powers of the age to
come. Finally, the 'spirit' confers 'eternal life' (cf. 1 C. 15:45).

These powers found expression in such extraordinary supernatural phenomena as 'speaking with tongues' (*(en) glōssē lalein*) and

in 'mighty works' (*dynameis*), but they also came to expression in what St Paul regarded as the higher *charismata* or gifts of the Spirit—that is to say, intellectual and moral endowments such as (and here there is a close parallel with the Old Testament) the words of wisdom (1 C. 12:8f.), of knowledge, and of faith, healings, the gift of administration (*kybernēsis*), powers of discernment and understanding (*diakrisis*), and so on; and, above all, what Paul regarded as the chief and indeed the sum and perfection of the gifts of the Spirit, the charisma of *agapē* ('charismatic love'). As Rudolf Otto wrote in his book, *The Kingdom of God and the Son of Man* (London, 1938), p. 342 (cf. pp. 351f. and especially p. 340): 'They are not magic powers, such as a *goētēs* (sorcerer) thought he possessed. They are mysterious heightenings of talents and capacities, which have at least their analogues in the general life of the soul'; and Dodd writes: 'by "spirit" Paul means the supernatural or divine element in human life and his test for it is the presence of a love like the love of God in Christ' (*Commentary*, p. 118). Perhaps it is Otto rather than Dodd who places the emphasis where it ought to be placed. While it is not denied that such 'endowments' are 'supernatural', it is equally important to recognise that they are familiar human faculties, including the capacity for *agapē* (which is more often toleration than passionate love). Perhaps too great emphasis has been placed on the Spirit as the (Holy) Ghost, and too little on the Spirit as *Geist*, the higher life of the spiritual being (intellectual gifts as well as qualities of character).

Sin, the Incarnation and Life in the Spirit 8:1–4[1]

1. There is consequently *now* no condemnation for those in Christ Jesus.

2. For the order of the living (and life-giving) Spirit in Christ Jesus has delivered us (set us free) from the order of sin and death.

3. For what the Law was incapable of effecting—in so far as it was weak by reason of the flesh—God sent his own Son resembling sinful flesh and as a sin-offering (or, for sin), and condemned (abolished) sin in the flesh,

4. that the just requirements of the Law might be fully realised in us who no longer conduct ourselves according to the flesh (by the order of unredeemed human nature) but according to the Spirit.

1. no condemnation for those who are in Christ Jesus: i.e. within the Body of Christ, the Church. Cf. note on 6:3 above. St Paul repeats the leitmotif; of. Chapters 1–5.

[1]On these verses, see S. Lyonnet, 'Le Nouveau Testament à la lumiére de l'Ancien, à propos de Rom. 8:2–4', *Nouvelle Revue Théologique* (Louvain), 87 (1965), pp. 561–87. Cf. also J. Tibbe, 'Geist und Leben. Eine Auslegung von Röm. 8' (*Bib. Studien*, 44) (Neukirchen, 1965).

Here and in vv. 1, 2 we again encounter the phrase 'in Christ
Jesus'. The Pauline phraseology 'into/in/with/through Christ (Jesus)'
has been extensively analysed and discussed for over a century.
That 'in Christ (Jesus)', and its related expressions, represents a
stereotyped Christological formula, for, say, 'mystical union' or 'the
body of Christ', has now been largely abandoned, in view of the
versatility of St Paul's use of these expressions in different contexts.
(This does not exclude either of these meanings in their proper
context; and Rom. 6:3 is clearly primarily intended in the second
sense. See above, p. 87). Among significant modern studies,
continuing the discussion initiated by Deissmann's famous monograph *Die neutestamentliche Formel in Christo Jesu*, Marburg, 1892
(cf. SH, p. 161), are F. Neugebauer, *In Christus*, Göttingen, 1961,
and M. Bouttier, *En Christ*, Paris, 1962, *TWNT* Bd. IX, p. 544
(Grundmann), Bd. II, p. 537, 20ff. (Oepke). Grundmann following
Neugebauer, seeks to illustrate the phrase 'in Christ', by the image
of a 'field of force' (*Kraftfeld*), the centre of which is the Risen
Christ. Such an idea of a 'magnetic field', with Christ as the divine
Magnet (cf. Jn 12:32), while possibly appealing to a modern,
popular expositor, was far beyond the intellectual horizon of St
Paul. See also now A. J. M. Wedderburn, 'Some Observations on
Paul's Use of the Phrases 'in Christ' and 'with Christ', in *Journal
for the Study of the New Testament*, 25 (1985), pp. 83–97. As Wedderburn convincingly argues, what has not been sufficiently stressed in
these studies is the central importance of considerations of subject
matter and context in each particular instance of the occurrence of
the phraseology. No less important, as Neugebauer showed, is the
recognition, not only of the spatial or causal uses of *'en'*, 'in', but
of the *associative* or *modal* use, in particular under the influence of
its semitic equivalent *be*. It is not only the equivalent of the modal
dative or the use of *dia* of attendant circumstances, but is widely
used in biblical Greek to denote any association or connection with
something or some person, and can be rendered by 'with', 'at',
'adhering to', 'depending' on' etc. (Cf. G-K §119. §(b), p. 379, and
B-D §198).

What Maximilian Zerwick has written on this subject deserves to
be quoted: '. . . we must beware of the notion that words and
grammatical usage have of themselves a definite and invariable
content of meaning. They are in reality conventional signs whose
sense is usually fairly general, the exact meaning being in each case
determined by usage *and above all by the subject matter . . . en*,
indicating of itself merely association or concomitance, may
represent, *according to the subject matter*, connections of utterly
different kinds, from that between an action and its rapidity (*en*

tachei) to that between Christ and those who are "in Christ".'
(*Biblical Greek*, Rome, 1963, §118; italics mine.)

Here at 8:1 'those who are in Christ Jesus' means simply 'baptised
Christians', members of the Body of Christ, the Church. But again,
the expression does not exclude the sense of 'mystical union', for,
in Paul's mind, whoever is 'in Christ' has 'Christ within' just as he
who is 'in the spirit' has 'the spirit within'. Cf. below vs. 8, 9, 10.
'Mystical union', however, does not exhaust the Pauline meaning:
the union or identity 'with/in Christ' includes the association with
Christ as 'the true and living way' (Jn 14:6), participating in the
'new humanity' into which the Christian is baptised. See above on
6:3 and below on 13:12, and cf. K. Berger 'Zum Hintergrund
Christologischer Titel', in *NTS*, XVII (1970–1), pp. 403f. What it is
important to exclude is that the phrase here means 'faith in Christ':
that was confessed *before baptism*, although 'being in Christ'
naturally implies a continuing faith in Christ. Cf. A. Schweitzer,
Die Mystik des Apostels Paulus (Tübingen, 1930), p. 118. In the
following verse 8:2, the nuance changes to 'the order of the life-
giving spirit in Christ Jesus (i.e. connected with, emanating from)
has liberated me . . .' (cf. 6:23. Contrast Cranfield, pp. 374ff. The
order of words is against taking the phrase as instrumental and with
the main verb.) The reading 'you' (sing) is supported by superior
textual evidence (ℵ B 1739 etc.); 'me' maintains the continuity
with Ch. 7. Whether 'me' or 'you' (or their omission) makes little
difference to the universal principle of the liberating 'order of the
life-giving Spirit in Christ Jesus'.

2. the law of the Spirit: Paul can use 'law' in a wide variety of
senses (cf. 7:23 above). But does it mean here 'authority'? (SH) Is
it not rather the 'order', 'principle' (of the living/life-giving Spirit)?
It is this new order of things, the 'spiritual order' which frees from
the old 'natural order'. T. W. Manson writes (*Peake's Commentary,
in loc.*): 'Moses' law has right but not might; Sin's law has might
but not right; the law of the Spirit has both might and right.' See
also S. Lyonnet, 'Rom. 8:2–4 á la lumière de Jer. 31 et d'Ez. 35–39',
Mélanges E. Tisserant, I (Vatican, 1964), pp. 311–23.

For the suggestion that this verse originally followed 7:25a (the
thanksgiving) see above, p. 102. Cf. Cranfield, p. 373, who connects
v. 2 with 7:6.

3. what the law . . . could not do: a pendant nominative. The
logical continuation would be: '. . . what the Law could not do (or,
what was impossible under the Law), the Holy Spirit enables us to
accomplish; because, with the help of the Spirit, we are empowered
to fulfil the demands of the Law.' What Paul, in effect, does is to
introduce the thought of *the means* by which all this was made

possible, viz. through the incarnation of the Son of God, Who imparts the enabling Spirit.

sending his own Son: cf. E. Schweizer, *ZNTW*, LVII (1966), pp. 199–210, for the 'sending' formula. Cf. also E. Schweizer, 'Dying and Rising with Christ', *NTS*, XIV (1967–8), p. 9, n. 1.

in the likeness of sinful flesh: Origen: *ostendit nos quidem habere carnem peccati: filium vero dei similitudinem habuisse carnis peccati non carnem peccati*. For the phrase 'sinful flesh', cf. 1 QS XI.9.

and for sin: *mg.* 'or **and as a sin offering**'; cf. Lev. 4. Origen understands 'an offering': *hostia pro peccato factus est Christus*. Cf., however, SH: '. . . we need not suppose the phrase *peri hamartias* here specially limited to the sense of "sin-offering". It includes every sense in which the Incarnation and Death of Christ had relation to, and had it for their object to remove, human sin' (p. 193).

4. the just requirement of the law: cf. Tyndale: 'the rightewesnes requyred of' (i.e. 'by') 'the lawe'. *NEB*: 'the commandment of the law'.

Life in the Spirit (The Spiritual Life) 8:5–11

The literary structure of these verses is similar to that at 5:12–21, and the balance of lines and clauses here is particularly noteworthy:
5. Those whose being is on the level of the natural life, concern themselves with affairs of the natural life. Those who live by the Spirit mind the things of the Spirit.

6. The natural frame of mind leads to death, The spiritual mind is (eternal) life and peace;

7. Because the natural mind is at enmity with God, it is not subject to the divine law, nor is it capable of becoming so (v. 3).

8. Those who are in the natural state of life are incapable of pleasing God.

9. But you are not in that state but in the Spirit (spiritual); since, I tell you, the Spirit of God dwells in you; and if anyone does not possess the Spirit of Christ, he does not belong to him.

10. But if Christ be in you then, as your body is dead for sin,

11. Yet your spirit is alive for righteousness, and if the Spirit of him who raised up Jesus from the dead dwells in you, he that raised up Jesus Christ from the dead will endow with life your mortal bodies through the Spirit that dwells in you.

5–7. live according to the flesh . . . live according to the Spirit . . . hostile to God: these and the following verses are of fundamental importance for Pauline Christology, no less than for his doctrine of the Spirit, with its important ideas about the inner character and inspiration of Christian life. The latter is a "pneumatic", or spiritual, life, a consciousness in which the frame of mind is one of divinely-aided obedience to the Law of God, the divine agent in obedience being the Holy Spirit. Conformity to the mind or will of God (pleasing God), so achieved or attained by the *charisma* of the Spirit, comes from the 'being in the Spirit' (cf. verses 9ff.) or having the Spirit in one.

8–11. Verse 9a defines the Spirit as the 'indwelling Spirit of God' (*pneuma theou*). Verse 9b speaks of the Spirit as 'the Spirit of Christ' (*pneuma Christou*), and 10a refers to the experience as 'Christ in you' (*Christos en hymin*). See also M. Dibelius, *Vier Worte*. (above, p. 80). All these expressions are related and, one might almost say, synonymous terms, for the same spiritual reality of the Christian character or 'spiritual' frame of mind (*phronēma*; cf. verse 6). C. H. Dodd writes (pp. 123ff.): 'This apparent equation, "Spirit of God" = "Spirit of Christ" = "Christ within you", is characteristic of Paul among New Testament writers. We may perhaps trace the lines of his thought thus: First, for Paul as for all Christian thinkers, Christ was in the fullest way the manifestation of God, and His whole life and person the expression of the divine Spirit. Further, it was the common postulate of primitive Christianity, as we have seen, that the Church was a fellowship of the Spirit, a community of those who had received the Spirit of God through faith in Christ. The one Spirit constituted the one Body. But, for Paul, with his mystical outlook, that Body was the Body of Christ, manifesting the new humanity of which He was the inclusive Representative. Hence in every member of it, possessing the Spirit of God, Christ was in some measure present and active, since the man was a member of His Body (as the whole of any organism is in some sort active in every part of it). Thus the community might be indifferently regarded as constituted by the Spirit of God, or by Christ as a "corporate personality"; and the individual as possessed by the Spirit of God, or by Christ dwelling in His member. Christ Himself, as the "second Adam" was a "life-giving Spirit" (1 C. 15:45), and Paul could speak, not only of the *Spirit of the Lord*, but, in the next breath, of the *Lord the Spirit* (2 C. 3:17–18).'

The doctrinal presuppositions of St Paul's use of this 'spiritual equation', i.e. these virtually synonymous terms, 'Spirit of God', 'Spirit of Christ', 'Christ in you', may be more simply formulated in terms of the apostolic doctrine of baptism. In baptism the believer was not only forgiven—that is, in Pauline terms, released from the order of sin and death—he also received the Spirit through his faith in Christ. It was the gift of the Pentecostal Christ; and it was Christ's Spirit yet also coming from God, the Spirit of God (cf. Ac. 2:33; 'Being therefore exalted at the right hand of God, and having

received from the Father the promise of the Holy Spirit [the promised Holy Spirit], he [Jesus] has poured out this which you see and
hear'; and Eph. 4:4ff.) The 'Spirit of God' was mediated by Christ
to his disciples.

From the point of view of Pauline 'mysticism', it may also be
described as a kind of faith union—Christ *in* you—but this was not
for St Paul an individual and purely mystical experience in the sense
of Evelyn Underhill ('The flight of the Alone to the Alone', *Mysticism* (London, 1911), p. 68); it was always an experience in Christ—
that is, within the Body of Christ, the new man, the Church. It was
to share in the upsurge of charismatic life which flowed within and
from the Christian community; it was essentially a *social*, not an
individualistic, phenomenon (cf. above, p. 105).

Dodd adds: 'Behind this rather subtle train of thought there must
have been direct experience. Paul was immediately aware that when
he was in close touch with Christ, that divine energy or power which
he recognised as the Spirit was released within him; and conversely,
the full moral effect of that power was realised only through reference to Christ as revealing the eternal Love. *In Christ, in the Spirit,
the Spirit within, Christ within* were in effect only different ways of
describing the one experience, from slightly different points of view.
This is not to say that Paul, in a strict theological sense, identified
Christ with the Spirit. But his virtual identification of the experience
of the Spirit with the experience of the indwelling Christ is of the
utmost value. It saved Christian thought from falling into a non-
moral, half-magical conception of the supernatural in human experience, and it brought all "spiritual" experience to the test of the
historical revelation of God in Jesus Christ' (p. 124).

In other terms, the 'spiritual mind' (verse 6) is the 'mind of
Christ' (cf. Phil. 2); and to possess this 'frame of mind', 'attitude',
or 'outlook' is to be concerned or involved socially—to belong, not
to the old order of humanity (the 'old Adam'), but to the new
humanity.

Christians as Sons of God 8:12–30

Verses 12 and 13 mark a transition from the section on the Spirit
to a section the main purpose of which is to present Paul's doctrine
of the status of Christians as no longer servants or slaves but as in
the category of free sons of God, and this he attributes to the
workings of the Spirit in us. Verses 12 to 17 are a Pauline paraenesis
meant to encourage Christians in their faith and hope; this exhortation follows from the previous doctrine and bridges the two parts

of the chapter—namely, first the doctrine of the Spirit, followed by
the doctrine of Christians as sons of God.

12. we are debtors: we do not owe anything to the natural life;
if we live on this level, then we are bound to die. In his choice of
verb ('we have no duty, obligation to (the flesh)'), it is as if Paul
was countering the argument that what is natural is right, and,
therefore, we owe it its 'due'.

13. you will die: if you put to death the works of the body, then
you will achieve eternal life (the latter being the force of the verb
here); by 'the works of the body' Paul is referring to the category
of the vices of the 'flesh', listed, for example, at Gal. 5:18ff.

14. All, on the other hand, who are 'led', that is to say, whose
lives are ruled by the Spirit of God—these Paul declares to be sons
of God, and in the following verse he contrasts the two spirits: one
the spirit of slavery, which is the state of the man under the Law,
and which leads to fear—fear of the consequences of the failure to
fulfil the Law—with a spirit which he describes as that of adoption,
that is to say, a status of full sonship. The thought is already
expressed at Gal. 4:5ff., and more fully developed here.

15. For you did not receive (at your baptism) **the spirit of
slavery**, here obviously referring to that state of mind, contrasted
with the new freedom of Christian sonship. It is no slavish spirit
Christians received at their baptism, a spirit which, as in the old
system under Law, relapses into fear, a fear-ridden state of mind
like that of any slave.

spirit of sonship: 'adoption' here implies the conferring of the right
to inherit, as in Babylonian and in Greek law (in Roman law it
meant the acquisition of the *patria potestas*). It is this same feature
of inheritance which is stressed in certain Egyptian documents.
Cf. L. Mitteis and U. Wilcken, *Grundzüge und Chrestomathie der
Papyruskunde*, Leipzig-Berlin, 1912, II.i, pp. 274ff.; O. Eger,
ZNTW, XVIII (1917–18), pp. 84ff.; and also F. Lyall, 'Roman Law
in the Writings of Paul—Adoption', *JBL*, LXXXVIII (1969),
pp. 458–66.

It seems probable that the Aramaic *abba* was in widespread
liturgical use, possibly as a survival from its use in the Aramaic
form of the Lord's Prayer. When Christians say: '*abba*'—that is to
say, 'my Father'—Paul declares that this is the work of the Spirit
in them, and the testimony that they have achieved the status of
sonship. Some have suggested that the strange Aramaic word *abba*
itself may have been regarded as an ejaculation of the Spirit, like
Amen, or Hosanna, or Hallelujah; cf. Dodd, p. 129, and further,
below.

spirit of slavery . . . sonship: cf. Gal. 4:7; Heb. 1:2. It was only the son, and not the slave, who had the right to inheritance.

Abba! Father!: if, as is suggested above, there is a reference here to the Christian experience of baptism, then there may be a reference to the use of the Lord's Prayer, possibly even in its Aramaic form, as one of the mysteries of admission into the Christian Church; it is well known that in the early centuries the catechumen had to profess the Lord's Prayer. It may be that, if this was said in the original baptismal ceremonies in Aramaic, it was taken to be a sign of the possession by the Spirit; cf., further, F. H. Chase, 'The Lord's Prayer in the Early Church', *Texts and Studies* I, iii (Cambridge, 1891), p. 14; and also J. Jeremias on *'Abba'* in *The Central Message of the New Testament* (London, 1965), pp. 9–30, and in *Abba: Studien zur neutestamentlichen Theologie und Zeitgeschichte* (Göttingen, 1966), pp. 15–67.

16. bearing witness with our spirit: Two witnesses, according to the *OT* injunction, establish the truth of any statement, and here the witnesses are, first, the Holy Spirit, which the Christian experiences in baptism, and then the Christian himself. They testify to the status of Christians as children of God. Cf. below on 9:1.

17. fellow heirs with Christ: Paul here goes on in an argument *a minori ad maius* to argue that, since Christians enjoy the status of full membership of the family, then they must also be heirs and joint heirs of God and fellow-heirs with Christ—that we are indeed children of God. (Note the force of the emphatic position of the 'we are' in v. 16; cf. 1 Jn 3:1.) There is no difference in Paul's use of the words 'sons' and 'children' in this passage (verses 14 and 16); cf. Jn 1:12. The usage corresponds to the Semitic usage of the word, and 'children' of course, refers generally to the *sons* of the family. It does, however, include all members of the family, and perhaps this is the reason for Paul's use of 'children' (*tekna*) as well as 'sons' here, i.e. he is using the word with the wider Greek sense to include the daughters as well as the sons of God within the family of God.

Being a full son implies the right to inherit, even if that right is acquired by adoption (verse 15).

provided we suffer with him: or lit. 'if, in very truth, we suffer with him'. Verses 18 and 36f. appear to imply that the sufferings are not by any means hypothetical but present realities; cf. Phil. 3:10, 1 Pet. 1:6, 4:13, 2 Mac. 6:30, and see E. G. Selwyn, *The First Epistle of St. Peter* (London, 1946), pp. 127ff.

The words 'if in very truth' are not a conditional sentence, and ought perhaps to be rendered 'since, as is the case'; they give the grounds for the Christian's common inheritance with Christ—

namely, their common fellowship in his sufferings. A similar use of
the conjunction occurs at 2 Th. 1:6; Rom. 3:30, 8:9.

in order that we may also be glorified with him: just as Christ is
now glorified after his passion and death, so too Christians will share
in that inheritance of glory, as they actually do now share in the
fellowship of his sufferings.

The next section, verses 18 to 25, takes up the theme of the
Christians' 'glorification' as 'sons of God' through participation in
sufferings like Christ's. The status of sonship is attained, through
the Holy Spirit's agency, in our baptism. The reality of sonship,
which is the final goal in eternal life—that is, virtually becoming
like the angels in heaven (cf. Lk. 20:36)—is a process of emancipation through suffering from corruption and death which the children of God share with the whole animate creation. According to
verse 15, we 'received' adoption as sons through the Spirit in
baptism; according to verse 23, we are still waiting in hope for this
adoption—that is to say, its realisation as sons of God, a goal which
will only be reached through our final deliverance from our bodily
life in the new reality of eternal life.

Verses 26 to 27 resume the theme of the Spirit as co-operating
with us in all things for good, and verses 28 to 30 outline the 'plan
of salvation': first the call of Christians; then their acquittal; and
finally their 'glorification'.

18. the sufferings of this present time: the simplest understanding of this verse is the rendering: 'for I do not count our
present sufferings worth considering in comparison with the glory
which is destined to be revealed'. SH are right in understanding the
words 'to us' as of the glory which is to reach and include all
Christians in its 'radiance'; but are the authors correct in understanding 'the glory' here of the heavenly brightness of Christ's
appearing? Is it not rather the glory or glorification of the individual
Christian in which he is to participate? Cf. verse 17 above. This is
the recovery of the divine image or glory originally lost at the Fall,
but restored in Christ; cf. note on 3:23 above.

19. The word translated here in the *AV* as 'the earnest expectation
(of the creation)' is highly expressive. The verb means 'to strain
forward', 'to await with outstretched head'; it appears again at Phil.
1:20, combined with the word for 'hope'. Cf. G. Bertram, in
ZNTW, XLIX (1985), pp. 264–70. See also, L. C. Allen, 'The Old
Testament in Rom. i–viii', *Vox Evangelica*, III (1964), p. 18, and
D. R. Denton, in *ZNTW*, LXXIII (1982), p. 138–40.

The usual understanding of 'creation' here is that it refers to the
whole of the created universe, and that, when Paul goes on in
verses 20ff. to speak of the emancipation of the creation from its

enslavement to corruption, he is thinking of the redemption or the renovation of nature, and in the background of his thought are such passages as Isa. 65:17ff. (See the *excursus* in SH on this understanding of the term).

An alternative interpretation is to understand the word here as the equivalent of the Hebrew word *beriyyah*, which means 'the creature' as well as '(the) creation' (see G. H. Dalman, *Words of Jesus* (Edinburgh, 1902), pp. 176ff., and cf. G. H. Box, *The Ezra Apocalypse* (London, 1912), p. 142).

This understanding of the word is preferred by E. Brunner in *Revelation and Reason* (London, 1947), p. 72, n. 16, where he argues that the term here does not refer to the cosmos, but to man as the creature of God: 'It is not the creation which is "fallen" but man; the revelation in the creation has not been destroyed but by sin man perverts into idolatry that which God has given him.' This meaning certainly fits in well with verse 21, where the creature himself, in this sense, will be emancipated from the slavery of corruption into the glorious freedom of the sons of God. On the other hand, the whole context seems to imply, especially at verses 22ff., that it is the entire created universe which St Paul has in mind.

A further possibility would be to take verse 22 as referring to 'the entire creation', but verses 19 and 20 as meaning 'the creature', man, who is part of creation.

For further discussion, see G. W. H. Lampe, 'The New Testament Doctrine of "*Ktisis*" ', *SJT*, XVII (1964), pp. 449–62. Bultmann admits that this is one place where redemption goes beyond the salvation of men (*NTS*, I (1954–5), p. 13, cf. E. Schweizer, *NTS*, VIII (1961–2), p. 3.)

20–21. for the creation was subjected to futility: what is 'futile' in the biblical sense is what is 'without result', 'ineffective', 'something that does not reach the end for which it was created'. The word is here used of the disappointing and frustrating character of present existence, and it is assumed that the whole created world had been subjected to this state of frustration, not because it wanted to, but because of its Creator who so subjected it, in the hope that creation itself would one day be freed from its mortality and decay like man himself, who would achieve an immortal destiny within the redeemed creation.

22. We know: i.e. as part of the well-known tradition of Jewish apocalyptic prophecy. Cf. W. D. Stacey, 'God's Purpose in Creation: Rom. 8:22–33', *ET*, LXIX (1957–8), pp. 178–81.

groaning in travail together until now: Moffatt: 'sighs and throbs with pain': there could be a reference to the birth-pangs of the Messiah (messianic age). The figure of speech is a familiar one in I

QH iii. 7–10, possibly with a similar reference to the birth-pangs of the Messiah or the messianic people. (Cf. M. Black, *The Scrolls and Christian Origins* (London, 1961), p. 149.)

23. first fruits of the Spirit: cf. 2 C. 5:4–5, where also 'we groan' in the 'covering' ('tent') of our physical bodies, though we have been given (verse 5) a 'first instalment' (*arrabōn*) of the life 'in the spirit'. *Aparchē* ('first-fruits') is possibly not to be pressed in its literal meaning in this context (MM., s.v.); it means simply 'foretaste', or, even more generally, 'gift'. It is probably best taken as synonymous with *arrabōn* at 2 C. 5:5—i.e. first instalment, issue, of the Spirit. It is a favourite word of St Paul; cf. Rom. 16:5; 1 C. 15:20–23, 16:15. Cf. C. C. Oke, 'A Suggestion with regard to Rom. 8:23', *Interpretation*, XII (1957), pp. 455–60.

as we wait . . . bodies: 'wait': the same word as at verse 19, indicating a 'longing expectation'. We received 'adoption' as sons at our baptism (cf. verse 15), but this apparently does not prevent us 'longing for' our 'adoption'. This can only mean our 'complete adoption', i.e. transformation into 'sons of God'; and this is further defined as the 'deliverance' of our body (for the word, cf. above, on 3:24). Cf. further, P. Benoit, 'Nous gémissons, attendant la délivrance de notre corps', *Rech. de Science Religieuse*, XXXIX (1951), pp. 267–80.

24. For in this hope we were saved: lit., 'by hope'. The meaning may be simply: 'in hope we attained our salvation', i.e. one of the integral elements of Christian 'salvation' is the Christian hope. This seems preferable to taking the dative as instrumental or as referring to the content of Christian hope as, in some sense, the means or instrument of 'salvation'. 24b stresses the essential character of Christian hope as a grasping, by faith, of the unseen.

25. with patience: again the stress is on an earnest longing for the fulfilment of the Christian hope, but one that is accompanied by patience or endurance, by holding out.

26. Likewise the Spirit helps: similarly, i.e. as we 'groan' in our longing expectation, the Spirit comes to the assistance of our weakness, with the same deep longing, also expressed 'with unutterable groanings'. Whether we are to interpret 'weakness' here of human frailty in general (elsewhere the word has an ethical connotation) or, in the light of 26b of the imperfection of the devotional life, is difficult to determine. Certainly, as an intercessor, the assistance of the Spirit is in prayer, but wider aspects of that divine help cannot thereby be excluded, since prayer itself is the inner strivings of the human spirit to transcend its weakness, strivings manifested in conduct. Probably too, as Dodd comments, prayer is here conceived as the working of the Spirit within us; our inarticulate

groans and sighings mingle with the sighs and groans that cannot be
uttered in the Spirit's joint intercession with us (cf. Dodd, p. 135).
Implied is the value of inarticulate prayer; cf. T. W. Manson (in
an unpublished meditation): 'The prayer that comes tripping from
the tongue does not always come from the depths of the heart; and
prayer that does not come from the depths is not likely to climb
very high . . . those very longings and aspirations which reach
upwards towards something that mere formal prayers can never
reach are inspired; they are themselves the work of the Spirit of
God.' See, further, E. Käsemann, 'Der gottesdienstliche Schrei nach
der Freiheit', *BZNW*, xxx (1964), pp. 142–55; and *Perspectives on
Paul*, pp. 129ff. Käsemann argues that a communal groaning is
meant—that is, the inarticulate 'sighs and groans' of the whole
congregation, similar and related to the *glossolalia* phenomena in 1
Corinthians. Cf. also K. Niederwimmer, 'Das Gebet des Geistes',
TZ, xx (1964), pp. 252–65.

27. the mind of the Spirit: St Paul seems to regard the action of
the Holy Spirit as personal and distinct from the action of God.
God knows the intention of the Spirit is to intercede for us in
accordance with the divine will; probably: 'knows *that* the Spirit
intercedes', not (as *RSV*) 'because' . . .

28. in everything God works for good with those who love him:
RSV, following *RV mg.*, adopts the reading of A B, now supported
by P[46] (cf. also Moffatt). That Paul could write: 'all things work
together for good' (*AV*, *RV*) is denied by some exegetes; Paul was
no facile or 'evolutionary' optimist. Barrett seeks to defend the
traditional rendering against this objection (*ad loc.*). Stylistically,
the repetition of 'God' as subject so soon after the phrase 'for
those who love God' is awkward. (Note how the *RSV* avoids the
repetition.) *NEB* takes 'the Spirit' as subject, unexpressed; it is the
main subject in the context: 'and in everything, as we know, he
(the Spirit) co-operates for good with those who love God'. See
further, Dodd (Fontana edn.), pp. 152ff., J. P. Wilson, *ET*, LX
(1948–9), pp. 110ff., M. Black, 'The Interpretation of Romans
8:28', in *Neotestamentica et Patristica* (Festschrift for Oscar
Cullmann, Leiden, 1962), pp. 166ff. Also H. G. Wood, in *ET*, LXIX
(1957–8), pp. 292–5; J. B. Bauer, in *ZNTW*, L (1959), pp. 106–12.

It is suggested (e.g. by Michel) that verse 28 is a *Lehrsatz* coming
out of a familiar *OT* and Jewish tradition; he compares Test. Gad
iv.7, Benj. iv.5; also Ber. 60b. Gad iv.7 reads: 'For the spirit of
hatred worketh together with Satan, through hastiness of spirit, in
all things to men's death; but the spirit of love worketh together
with the law of God in long-suffering, unto the salvation of men.'
(Charles)

called according to his purpose: this is a necessary qualification for Paul, since, without these words, the impression might have been given that divine 'co-operation' or 'furtherance' was somehow a reward for loving God. (Similarly this co-operation is 'for or with a view to good', i.e. the good life, which again defines the goal for which divine help is received.) Notice too the emphasis on the divine purpose (or plan, counsel), the divine calling, the divine pre-knowledge (i.e., choice, selection, election; cf. above, p. 19f.), divine 'pre-ordination'. Human freedom for Paul is always exercised under the gracious sovereignty of God. (Cf. Dodd, *ad loc*.)

The Hebrew tradition out of which Paul's doctrine of the sovereign grace of God in election was developed is well illustrated in 1 QS ii:22ff., iii:6, iii:15ff.: the God of knowledge created all being according to his purpose and, at the end of time, by the same purpose, there is to be a divine election of mankind. See D. Flusser, 'The Dead Sea Sect and Pre-Pauline Christianity', *Scripta Hierosolymitana* (Jerusalem, 1965), p. 220. Cf. also K. Grayston, 'The Doctrine of Election in Rom. 8:28–30', *Stud. Ev.* II (1964), pp. 574–83.

29. For those whom he foreknew . . . : four stages in the divine counsel or plan are set out: (a) the divine foreknowledge, i.e. choice and election (the divine 'fore-ordination' is virtually synonymous; cf. Ac. 4:28); (b) the divine call when the 'saints' become aware of their election; (c) 'justification', the act of salvation by faith; (d) the final 'glorification', defined as conforming to the image of the Son of God, the first-born of many brethren—the Christian's hope of final 'adoption', the 'redemption of the body'.

image of his Son: cf. above, at Rom. 3:23; and A. R. C. Leaney, 'Conformed to the Image of His Son (Rom. viii.29)', *NTS*, x (1963–4), pp. 470–9); J. Kürzinger, *BZ*, II (1958), pp. 294–9.

first-born: a term which Paul no doubt found in his *paradosis* (cf. Lk. 2:7; Col. 1:15, 18; Heb. 12:23). For a helpful note on it, see T. W. Manson, *On Paul and John* (*Studies in Biblical Theology*, 38, London, 1963), pp. 130ff.

30. predestined . . . called . . . justified . . . glorified: a climactic period (Michel, *Kettenschluss*). See also K. Grayston, *op. cit.* (pp. 577ff.).

Security from Death 8:31–39

These verses constitute something of the nature of a rhetorical climax, in which the central argument about the Christian's triumph over all the forces of evil—his groaning, travailing, persecution, even death—is summarised by a scriptural text from Ps. 44:22 (cf.

2 C. 4:11). Salvation is certain, since everything is undergirded by the love of God in Christ. It is a passage of exalted feeling.

31. What then shall we say to this? The question implies a break and summing up. Paul is still thinking out objections to his argument, and finally disposes of them all in 31b. The writer is possibly thinking in terms of a law-court; cf. verses 33 and 35, where the same kind of rhetorical questions are asked, 33 with a forensic allusion. Note again the climactic build-up of these rhetorical questions and their answers. The dialogue is reminiscent of the *OT* 'law-suit pattern' (e.g. Isa. 50); cf. Leenhardt, p. 236, and C. Müller, *Gottes Gerechtigkeit und Gottes Volk, Forschungen zur Religion und Literatur des Alten und Neuen Testaments*, LXXXVI (Göttingen, 1964), pp. 57–72 (*Rechtsstreitgedanke*). See also C. Roetzel, 'The Judgement Form in Paul's Letters', *JBL*, LXXXVIII (1969), pp. 305–12.

32. did not spare his own Son but gave him up: Paul's answer is firmly based on a Christian *paradosis* about the death of Christ, formulated in traditional kerygmatic terms, e.g. 'gave him up' (*paredōken*); cf. Rom. 4:25 and Mt. 26:2, Mk 9:31, Lk. 24:7 of the 'surrendering up' of the Son of Man; Barth points out that it is the same verb which is used at Rom. 1:24, 26, 28 for God's 'surrendering up' of man to the divine judgement; so Christ was 'given over' to judgement. Gen. 22:16, the *akedah*, or sacrifice, of Abraham's beloved son (so LXX) Isaac, probably contributed to the development of this theme (Michel, *ad loc.*). Cf., further, N. A. Dahl, 'The Atonement—An Adequate Reward for the Akedah?', *Neotestamentica et Semitica* (M. Black *Festschrift*) (Edinburgh, 1969), pp. 15–29.

all things with him: the verb 'give' here (*charizesthai*) specially emphasises the sheer goodness of this divine gift. 'All things' can hardly refer to absolute dominion over all things (*die Weltherrschaft*); more probably it embraces all the 'benefits' of salvation, eternal life, etc., which God freely bestows 'along with Christ'. The latter phrase is ambiguous: it may mean that Christ is also a freely-bestowed gift which goes with 'all things', or that God, along with Christ, is the free-bestower of all things.

33–34. may be variously punctuated (see U. B. S. Greek New Testament). *NEB* offers one of the main alternatives to *RSV*.

The style is modelled on Isa. 50:7–9, encouraging us to punctuate: 33, question: statement (exclamation) ('It is God who does the acquitting'); 34, question: statement (or exclamation), with the last relative clause resuming the subject and containing the main verb— 'Jesus Christ, he it is—the one who died, nay rather rose from the dead—who is also at the right hand of God, who does the interceding for us'. The tenses, both of the participles as well as the main verbs are probably best understood as *futures*: it is to the Last Judgement Paul is referring.

Christ's death, and its sequel in resurrection, ascension and intercessory ministry, is the demonstration of the love of God (cf. verse 39).

33. God's elect: an old name for Israel (1 Chr. 16:13, Ps. 105:6, 43), but specially used in the later apocalypses and inter-testamental writings for the 'Elect Israel', or 'Remnant', and its members (e.g. in 1 Enoch *passim* and at Qumran, e.g., 1 QHab. x.13, CD iv.3ff.). See Michel, *ad loc.*, and cf. Mk 13:20, 22, 27 *et par*; Lk. 18:7; Rom. 16:13; Col. 3:12; 2 Tim. 2:10; Tit. 1:1; 1 Pet. 1:1; Rev. 17:14.

35. Cf. 2 C. 11:23ff. Paul's experiences are typical. Seven forms of tribulation are listed, but the number is probably without significance (there are ten subjects in verses 38–39). Cf. Ps. Sol. xv. 7ff.

36. Ps. 44:22; cf. 2 C. 4:11.
For thy sake: God's or Christ's. In the context it could be either.

37. more than conquerors: a strong compound expression here only in the *NT*: 'overwhelming victory is ours' (*NEB*). The Christian's conquest of 'all these things' is not, however, through his own efforts, but through 'the One who loved us'.

38. For I am sure: the 'hymnic' rhetorical style, present throughout this passage, becomes specially noticeable in this verse. We move *a minori ad maius*, i.e. to a climax. After the seven afflictions comes a list which, beginning with 'death and life', seems mostly to be grouped in pairs, and includes ten 'powers' of evil: 'neither angels nor principalities', i.e. cosmic forces of evil (cf. G. H. C. Macgregor, 'Principalities and Powers: the Cosmic Background of Paul's Thought', *NTS*, 1 (1954–5), pp. 17ff.) It is unlikely that Paul is grouping 'death and life' among the cosmic powers of evil, but they may here be personified; and 'life' no less than death can come between us and the love of God. Cf. 1 C. 3:22.

principalities . . . powers: The words *archai* and *dynameis*, while including 'earthly powers and authorities' (the 'powers that be' in the Roman Empire, 13:1ff.), refer specifically, in this context, to the 'higher (supernatural) powers' which were regnant in this world and in human affairs no less than in their own celestial domain. For a discussion of the Jewish and hellenistic background of these and related terms, see M. Black, 'All powers will be subject to him', in *Paul and Paulinism, Essays in honour of C. K. Barrett*, edited by M. D. Hooker and S. G. Wilson, London, 1982, pp. 74–82.

things present . . . things to come: do doubt earthly calamities, present or future (Michel). Cf. 1 C. 3:22.

39. height nor depth: explained by the Fathers as heavenly and 'subterranean' powers. Modern exegetes explain as astrological terminology: the 'height' refers to the sky above the horizon, the 'depth' the sky beneath the horizon: here, however, like 'principalities and powers', the words probably refer to 'celestial powers'. For the combination, cf. Isa. 7:11.

nor anything else in all creation is rather a free translation; lit. 'nor any other created being'.

GOD'S PURPOSES FOR ISRAEL 9:1–11:36

In chapters 9–11 Paul deals with the problem of Israel's rejection—her own rejection of the Gospel and, in consequence, her rejection by God. See especially J. Munck, *Christ and Israel: an Interpretation of Rom.* 9–11 (Philadelphia, 1967), C. Müller, *Gottes Gerechtigkeit und Gottes Volk: eine Untersuchung zu Röm.* 9–11, *FRLANT*, LXXXVI (Göttingen, 1964); E. Dinkler, 'The Historical and the Eschatological Israel in Rom. 9–11', *Journal of Religion*, XXXVI (1956), pp. 109–27; L. S. Murillo, 'El "Israel de las Promesas": o Judaismo y Gentilismo en la concepción Paulina del Evangelio', *Bib.*, II (1921), pp. 303ff.; D. W. Vischer, 'Das Geheimnis Israels', *Judaica*, VI (1950), pp. 81–132; W. D. Davies, 'Paul and the People of Israel' in *NTS* XXIV (1978), pp. 4–39. See now also Cranfield, II, p. 450, n. 1.

Jeremias has argued (*op. cit.*, *Gedankenführung*, p. 148) that 9:1ff. is a reply to implied criticism of Paul. Cf. also H. J. Schoeps, *Theologie und Geschichte des Judenchristentums* (Tübingen, 1949), pp. 134ff.

The argument has two main points: (a) the Gentiles owe their salvation to the rejection of Israel; (b) in the long term, God's purposes embrace his own people.

The section is a compact and continuous whole, possibly an incorporated diatribe or missionary sermon (cf. Dodd, pp. 148ff.), distinctive in style as in content from chapters 1–8. It is, however, a natural, logical and necessary extension of the main argument. Chapter 8:38ff. gives the grounds for Israel's salvation, the unbreakable bond of divine love in Christ. Such love could not fail to embrace Israel, for whom the Gospel was first intended (1:16). The Gospel was first and foremost for the Jew (1:16; 2:9ff.; 3:9; 10:12), yet it had been rejected by contemporary Judaism. In 3:1ff. Paul included among the 'advantages' of the Jew God's loyalty, which does not give up even an apostate people. This statement alone

implies that Israel, in spite of her defection and rejection, nevertheless remains the special object of God's 'steadfast love'.

These implications of 3:1ff. are not further pursued there, but
are taken up and developed in chapters 9–11.

ISRAEL'S UNBELIEF

9:1–5

1. **I am speaking the truth in Christ:** the vehemence of St Paul's
assertion that he speaks truly about his terrible grief and unremitting
agony about Israel (verse 2) suggests that he had been accused of
indifference to the fate of his compatriots (cf. Barrett, *ad loc.*).
There is nothing specially noteworthy about the expression 'to speak
the truth' (cf. Eph. 4:25, citing Zech. 8:16, and on the lips of Jesus
in the Fourth Gospel, Jn 8:45, 46; 16:7). It seems unlikely here
that it has anything to do with the dominical locution 'Truly (Amen)
I say', but, in this context in Romans, it does have a strong asseverative force; it is as if Paul is making a declaration on oath, 'I
truthfully declare'. This full Pauline emphatic declaration (positive
statement followed by negative confirmation) 'I am speaking the
truth, I am not lying' occurs again at 1 Tim. 2:7. Paul 'truthfully
declares in Christ', i.e., either as a disciple of Christ and inseparably
united to him (cf. 8:39), or as a member of Christ's body, the
Church—the words are practically equivalent to 'I am speaking the
truth as a Christian', implying that, as such, only the highest standards of truthfulness will serve.

Paul speaks the truth *in Christ*, and his conscience supports him
in the Holy Spirit. Has he the thought here of two witnesses corrobor-
ating his statement, Christ and the Spirit (cf. Dt. 17:6, 19:15, 2 C.
13:1)? Cf. above, on 8:16. The words can hardly be interpreted to
mean: 'As one who lives in Christ (in the Holy Spirit)'.

3. **for I could wish that I myself** (were accursed and cut off from
Christ). Perhaps we should render the emphatic personal pronoun
'that I myself for my part' (see note below). 'I could almost pray to
be accursed', C. F. D. Moule, *An Idiom Book of New Testament
Greek*, p. 9, for this imperfect *ēuchomēn*: the verb carries also the
sense of a vow (*euchē*), especially in this context speaking of 'vowing
oneself' to become 'anathema', i.e. 'anathematising oneself' practically 'placing oneself under a ban' (e.g., Ac. 23:12, 14). *I myself*
(were accursed). In his remorseless sense of mission to the Gentiles,
Paul had used strong language against Judaisers as well as Jews
who had stood in his way (cf. 1 Th. 2:15), even going as far as
'anathematising' his opponents (Gal. 1:8, 9; 1 C. 16:22). Had the

word reached Rome that he was 'anathematising' all his Jewish 'natural kinsfolk' (verse 3, 'my kinsmen by race')? In that case, the words 'I myself for my part' could refer to such rumours: so far is Paul from 'anathematising' his Jewish kith and kin that he would rather wish to become himself 'anathema' and so suffer the fate of a Christless outcast. Cf. Zahn, p. 430, who recalls the later denunciations of Paul as the 'evil man' who prevented the conversion of all Israel by his false anti-Jewish Gospel, e.g., Clement, *Recognitions*, 1:70; similar voices were probably being raised against him in his life-time.

accursed and cut off from Christ: Paul says he could pray to be 'anathema', i.e. an outcast under a ban or curse. The word was originally the same as that for an 'offering' to God (*anathēma*). The Greek translation of the *OT*, however, required an expression to denote that which is offered to God *for destruction* (*herem*). Cf. Lev. 27:28, 29; Gal. 1:8, 9; 1 C. 16:22. Cf. also, however, MM, *s.v.*: in Greek thought, 'The person on whom the curse was to fall was always devoted to the vengeance of the two Infernal Goddesses, Demeter and her daughter, "May he or she never find Persephone propitious."' Paul is thinking of placing himself under the ban of total self-destruction, but in a fate worse than death, viz. in a state of severance from his Lord; cf. 8:35ff. Paul may possibly have had the 'self-offering' of Moses in mind (Exod. 32:32) in declaring himself willing to be 'devoted' to utter destruction. That we have here also a familiar type of 'ban-formula' is probable (Michel); parallels from Sanh. 2:1, Sukka 20a, Josephus, *BJ*, v.ix. 4 (419). There can be no suggestion that this was a mere 'empty wish', incapable of fulfilment (so Zahn, who compares 8:38ff.): God was, for Paul, always free to accept his self-oblation; after all, He had accepted the propitiatory sacrifice of Christ; cf. further J. Munck, *op. cit.*, pp. 29ff. Munck has drawn attention to the close parallels between this passage and Exod. 32:31–32. Certainly this part of the Moses and Israel saga was in Paul's mind; at 9:15 he cites Exod. 33:19. (The parallel with Moses is followed at 11:2 by a similar parallel with Elijah (cf. 1 Kg. 19:10, 14)).

[margin note: If possible, then why wasn't he?]

4. They are Israelites: or we may render, following closely on the preceding sentence, 'inasmuch as they are Israelites (*hoitines* = quippe qui, cf. Robertson, *Gramm.*, p. 960, giving the reason for the Apostle's unremitting agony over Israel). Paul considered himself also to be 'an Israelite' (11:1): the word is used, as at Jn 1:47 as an epithet of honour. Cf. Gen. 32:28, 2 C. 11:22.

to them belong the sonship . . .: Israel was uniquely God's 'first-born' among the nations (Exod. 4:22; Hos. 11:1 (Mt. 2:15); Jer. 31:9); individual Israelites too were 'sons of God', even though they incurred at times the divine anger (Dt. 32:19; Isa. 1:2ff.; 63:16; Ps. Sol. 17:31). 'Sons' means 'children', male or female (cf. above on 8:17)). On the concept of sonship (*huiothesia*), see above, on 8:15.

the glory: i.e. the Shekhinah, or symbol of the divine presence, or the 'restored glory' of Adam (cf. note on 3:23).

the covenants: i.e. the divine 'charters' with Israel—the old given at Sinai, the new announced by Jeremiah (31:31ff.) and now fulfilled in Christ (2 C. 3:6ff.). While Sinai was the outstanding covenant, the plural embraces earlier and later covenants (cf. Eph. 2:12), e.g., with the patriarchs (Gen. 17:2ff. recalled at Exod. 2:24, before the deliverance from Egypt, but also at all periods of Israel's history (Ps. 105:8ff., Neh. 9:8, Lk. 1:55, 72ff.)), and no doubt also the covenant with David (2 Sam. 7:8ff.; Isa. 55:3; Sir. 45:25). Cf. L. G. da Fonseca, '*Diathēkē*—Foedus an Testamentum', *Bib.*, IX (1928), p. 26; C. Roetzel, '*Diathēkai* in Romans 9:4', *Bib.*, LI (1970), pp. 377–90.

the giving of the law, the worship: *tôrāh* and *'abodāh*, originally the Temple cultus, then more widely 'worship'. According to *Pirqē Aboth*, i, 2, the world rests on three things: the *tôrāh*, worship, and the showing of kindnesses. The 'giving of the Law' follows naturally on the thought of the 'Covenants', in particular of the Covenant of Sinai.

the promises: See note on 1:2. The reference is specifically to the messianic promises of salvation. For a study of the 'Promise tradition', see D. C. Duling, 'The Promises to David and their Entrance into Christianity—Nailing Down a Likely Hypothesis' in *NTS* XX (1974), pp. 55f.

the fathers: probably refers specifically to Abraham and the patriarchs (so *NEB*); cf. 15:8, where 'the fathers' receive the promises (which Christ fulfils). But David (and other Israelite forbears) could also be known as the fathers (cf. Sir. 44:1ff and Mk 11:10, 'our father David'.)

5. and of their race, according to the flesh, is the Christ: Paul could hardly give Israel the exclusive rights of possession of the Messiah he preached, only that it was from them that Christ came, *so far as their natural lineage was concerned*. So *NEB*: '. . . and from them, in natural descent, sprang the Messiah.'

Christ. God who is over all be blessed for ever: *mg.* or, 'Christ who is God over all, blessed for ever', an interpretation widely supported in ancient as in modern exegesis. Serious doubts have been entertained, however, whether Paul would ever apply the name 'God' thus *simpliciter* to Christ. The reading of the *RSV* text, on the other hand, which suddenly introduces a doxology, is also decidedly unnatural. Dodd is inclined to favour the old Socinian conjecture

(J. J. Wettstein, *Novum Testamentum Graecum* (Amsterdam, 1751–2), *ad loc.*, reading *hōn ho* for *ho ōn*) which gives a climactic line: '*Theirs* is the God who is over all, blessed [be he] for ever'. Cf. W. L. Lorimer, *NTS*, XIII (1966–7), pp. 385f., who conjectures: 'of whom is God over all Who is blessed for ever' (cf. 2 C. 11:31). Cf. H. W. Bartsch, 'Röm. 9:5 und 1 Clem. 32:4: eine notwendige Konjektur im Römerbrief', *TZ*, XXI (1965), pp. 401–9. See especially Denney, p. 658, SH *ad loc.* (defending the tradition of *RSV mg.*), Michel, Barth, *ad loc.*, who adopts the conjecture without discussion: 'Whose is God that ruleth all things—blessed for ever, Amen'. See further, H. M. Faccio, *De Divinitate Christi iuxta S. Paulum: Rom.* 9:5 (Jerusalem, 1945).

THE DIVINE PURPOSE IN ELECTION

9:6–13

The transition seems to be: Israel has rejected the Gospel, but this does not imply the failure of God's Word to his people (cf. 3:2ff.).

The argument is a favourite one of Paul's, first set out in Gal. 4:21–31, then again at Rom. 4. There has been no failure on God's part; his scriptural promises still hold—for the Israel of the Promise, not the national Israel, since mere physical descent does not count. The argument, conducted in characteristic rabbinical form, is supported by Gen. 21:12, 18:10, 14, and 25:23. The true Israel is the 'elected' Israel.

6. But it is not as though: As we would say 'There is no question of the word of God having failed.' (*NEB* 'It is impossible that' gives the phrase *ouch hoion hoti* the force of the classical *ouch hoion te*; cf. Cranfield, p. 472 and B-D, §480(5)).

word of God: The phrase (*ho logos tou theou*) belongs to the *NT* not the *OT*, although it clearly is modelled on *ho logos tou kyriou* (cf. Isa. 1:10, 28:14 etc.). Where the phrase occurs it is used always meaning 'the word of God (about Christ)', i.e., 'the Gospel' as preached (2 C. 2:17, 4:2; 2 Tim. 2:9; Tit. 2:5; Heb. 13:7; Rev. 1:9, 6:9, 20:4, and especially in the Acts (12 times); so SH, p. 240). The phrase, since SH, however, is usually taken here in the more general sense of ' "the declared purpose of God", whether a promise or a threat or a decree looked at from the point of view of the Divine consistency' (SH, *ibid.*, Cranfield, *ad loc.*) St Paul is no doubt thinking of the whole plan and intention of God in salvation, and perhaps especially of the divine 'oracles' of Scripture, containing the (messianic) promises (cf. the use of *logia* at 3:2). But for Paul and the New Testament writers these had been fulfilled, and the divine intention realised in Christ risen and glorified; the phrase could then still mean here 'the word of God we preach', i.e., the Gospel.

had failed: The closest parallel to the meaning of *ekpiptei* here is the use of the cognate verb *diepesen* at Jos. 21:45: 'Not one of all the good promises which the Lord had made to the house of Israel had failed; all came to pass.' (*RSV*) The Greek verb renders *naphal* in its metaphorical sense of 'fall to the ground' and so of a promise or a 'word of God' 'proved empty or false' (cf. *NEB* here); for other examples of the metaphorical use of this biblical Greek verb (cf. Isa. 40:7, Sir. 34:7, 1 C. 13:8, Jas 1:11).

Paul now begins a new argument: 'It is not, however, at all true that the word of God [about Christ risen and glorified] has been proved false [because the ethnic Israel (*Israēl kata sarka*) has rejected it].'

not all who are descended from Israel belong to Israel: i.e., not all those who can trace their descent to the founding forefather constitute the true Israel, the 'Israel of God' (cf. Gal. 6:16).

7. not all are children of Abraham because they are his descendants: Similarly, *NEB*: '. . . nor, because they are Abraham's offspring, are they all his true children.' It seems preferable, however, to take the *oude hoti* clause as dependent on the *ouch hoion de* clause of verse 6 (so Zahn) and to understand 'all from Israel' (also from verse 6) as the subject: '(. . . nor is there any question) that they (i.e. all Israelites) are the (true) seed of Abraham; all are (natural) children (of Abraham), but "Through Isaac shall your descendants be named". Verse 8 goes on to explain: it is not the natural children of Abraham (*ta tekna tēs sarkos*) who are the 'children of God'. This preserves the special meaning of 'seed' as the 'true' offspring of Abraham (cf. 4:13, 16, 18). Although *sperma* 'seed' is a collective term, Gal. 3:16, 19, 29 can use it as a singular to refer to Christ as the 'true seed' of Abraham. Cf. further 2 C. 11:22, Jn 8:33ff. for the 'seed of Abraham'.

shall . . . be named: or 'divinely called' (*NEB mg.*). The argument is supported by Gen. 21:12. See G. J. Spurrell, *Notes on the Text of Genesis* (Oxford, 1896), p. 202. 'Render, '*In* (or *through*) *Isaac will a seed be called for thee*', i.e. 'in the line of Isaac will those descendants from thee come, who shall bear thy name, and as such be heirs of the divine promise, viz. the Israelites, who were the offspring of Abraham, chosen by God.' Cf. Heb. 11:18; see also Gen. 21:17, 18. The passive may have been understood by Paul (as in verse 8: 'are reckoned') as an expression of *divine* action. It is God who will name their descendants from Israel: it is God who acclaims the 'children of the promise' as the true seed. The promise was made by one of

Abraham's three angel visitants at Mamre, but it is a 'word of the Lord' he speaks (cf. Gen. 18:10, 14).

8. the children of the promise are reckoned as descendants: 'reckoned', 'counted', again *logizomai*. Cf. Barrett, p. 181: 'The word "counted" is of fundamental importance in this epistle . . . It points to the creative freedom of God, who creates "righteousness" by "counting" it, and annuls sin by not "counting" it (iv: 6, 8).' See above, pp. 65ff.; and C. Müller, *Gottes Gerechtigkeit und Gottes Volk*, (above, p. 122) p. 184.

children of the flesh . . . children of God . . . children of the promise: These are familiar Pauline terms and ideas, belonging, no doubt, to the homiletical stock-in-trade of St. Paul's Gentile preaching mission. 'Children of the flesh' recalls Ishmael. Isaac's descendants are 'children of the promise'—the promise made to Abraham after all hope had disappeared of further natural progeny—and these are likewise 'children of God'. Cf. Gal. 4:21–31.

9. The absolute priority of the promise is emphasised in this verse by a further quotation from Gen. 18:10, 14. Note the position, at the beginning of the sentence, of the emphasised word, 'promise', in the Greek order; for 'this word of the promise' is that God is miraculously at work in this election of Isaac and his descendants, as is clear from the verb 'I will come' (so, rightly, *NEB*).

10–13 seem intended to meet the possible objection of Jewish opponents that they are no Ishmaelites, but the true seed of Abraham (cf. Dodd, *ad loc.*) At the same time, Paul is clearly also reinforcing his argument of the sovereign act of God in election: Jacob was elected, his elder brother Esau rejected, and this was all revealed to Rebecca before their birth, and therefore also before they could be judged on grounds of 'works' (see note on verse 11).

10. had conceived children by one man: Ishmael and Isaac had one father, although born from different mothers: yet one, the younger, was preferred to the elder, the slave's son. Rebecca also had two sons, Jacob and Esau by one man, one father Isaac; and again one, the younger twin, was preferred to the other.

The present tense of *koitēn echousa* is to be stressed, lit., 'while she was being made pregnant': it was at this precise time, before she had given birth, that she too, like Abraham, received a divine revelation (verse 12); *koitēn echein* is a Jewish euphemism for 'to have sexual intercourse', here 'to be in the process of conceiving.' (*Koitē* here is not the bed, but the act of lying.)

Normally only exceptional circumstances would justify a father passing over an older son for inheritance. The supersession of Ishmael by Isaac was, however, justified by his being born the son of Abraham's concubine Hagar (cf. Gal. 4:21f.)—an exception which

appears to have been in accordance with social practice in Mesopo-
tamia in the middle of the second millennium B.C. (See Hastings,
Dictionary of the Bible, s.v. Ishmael.) Even so, it is here regarded
as a supersession by divine intervention. The situation was different
in the case of Jacob and Esau, both sons of Rebecca; but the passing
over of the elder in favour of the younger was justified in this case,
since it had full scriptural warrant (Gen. 25:23; Mal. 1:2, 3: see
below, note on verses 12-13.)

11. that God's purpose of election might continue: i.e. that the
purpose of God which works by the principle of *election* might stand;
the Greek verb means 'remain', 'abide'; it is the opposite of the
word used at verse 6 ('fall', or 'fail'); God's word does not collapse
or fail; so likewise his plan of selecting cannot do anything other
than 'stand', i.e. 'prevail'.

The divine purpose has been the theme of 8:28. Cf. Eph. 1:11,
3:11, 2 Tim. 1:9, 3:10.

not because of works but because of his call: the Pauline controversy, faith or works, is determinative of his thought here; it was
by a free act of gracious choice that Jacob—and so his descendants,
the spiritual Israel—was named: this choice was made by God even
before the birth of Isaac's progeny, before they had any 'works' by
which they could be judged.

12-13. The quotations are from Gen. 25:23, Mal. 1:2, 3. The
combination of a quotation from the Pentateuch with one from the
Prophets is common; together they seal the argument by scriptural
authority. The formal introduction of the Malachi quotation, 'As it
is written', shows that Paul probably thinks of this as the climax
and conclusion of his argument: 'love' here means 'prefer', 'hate'
means 'reject' (or 'love less'). (See Leenhardt, *ad loc.*).

For a valuable discussion of the *OT* background of 'election',
consult T. L. Vriezen, 'Die Erwählung Israels nach dem Alten
Testament', *Abhandlungen zur Theologie des Alten und Neuen Testaments*, XXIV (Zürich, 1953), pp. 41-50; and G. Schrenk in *TWNT*,
s.v. *eklegomai*.

GOD'S SOVEREIGN FREEDOM TO ELECT WHOMSOEVER HE CHOOSES

9:14-29, 30-33

Some Objections Rebutted and a Statement of Israel's Rejection **9:14-18**

Paul meets the obvious Jewish objection that this seemingly highly
arbitrary selection and rejection appears to imply injustice on God's
side. Paul has an answer in Scripture, Exod. 33:19 and 9:16. In

verses 19–29 the prophets are cited in support of the claim that God is absolutely sovereign in his dealings with man; cf. Isa. 29:16, 45:9; Wis. 12:12, Jer. 18:6, Wis. 15:7. Verses 30–33 conclude with a reflection on the grounds for Israel's rejection, including her own rejection of Christ, the 'rock of offence' over which she stumbled.

On the formal structure, it is noteworthy that vv. 14–18 are based on the *Tôrāh*, 19–21 on the *Prophets*, and 22–24 draw the theological consequences from this Scripture-based argumentation with references to both *Tôrāh* and Prophets (Michel, p. 236).

14. injustice on God's part: as almost always in Paul, words like *adikia* have a 'forensic' overtone: miscarriage of justice. The second phrase, 'on God's part', could have the further meaning: 'in God's assize', or 'court'.

15. Exod. 33:19. In citing scriptural authority for his doctrine of God's sovereign will in election or rejection, Paul chooses a text which first shows that sovereign election as coming from a gracious, compassionate God; and this enables him further to introduce his doctrine of pure grace. See further v. 17 for its opposite, God's rejection.

I will have mercy on whom I have mercy: for this idiom, so common in Hebrew and especially in Arabic (*idem per idem*), cf. S. R. Driver, *Notes on the Hebrew Text of the Books of Samuel* (Oxford, 1913), on 1 Sam. 23:13, pp. 185f.

16. So it depends not upon man's will: lit. 'Consequently, (the divine mercy) does not come from one who has exercised his will or run hard morally . . .' The use of 'run' for moral effort is good Stoic language; see Bauer, s.v., *trechō*.

17. I have raised you up: i.e. to bring on to the stage of history. See H. H. Rowley, *Biblical Doctrine of Election* (London, 1950), chapter 5, esp. pp. 132ff.

showing my power in you: for the phrase (and the general idea of divine sovereignty), see Wis. 12:(16,) 17, etc. I would suggest that the connection of the quotation with the preceding argument (note the connecting 'for') lies in placing the emphasis on 'showing my power in you', i.e., the purpose of God's 'raising up' Pharaoh was to exhibit his sovereign power by 'hardening Pharaoh's heart', and so rejecting him; cf. *NEB* 'I have raised you up for this very purpose, to exhibit my power *in my dealings with you*' (italics mine): God 'dealt with Pharaoh' by his act of 'hardening his heart', i.e. making him obtuse and unresponsive, and so someone to be rejected. God accepts or rejects, has mercy and withholds it, as he wills.

18 sums up. Exod. 9:16 is chosen to illustrate God's sovereign will in rejection as well as in election. God's 'hardening' of Pharaoh's heart corresponds to or typifies his rejection of the national Israel. Paul does not say this in so many words, but in this indirect way brings the argument home to Jewish readers. The question would occur at once to a Jewish reader: Is God then rejecting us (and using us) as he rejected Pharaoh?

hardens the heart: i.e. makes obtuse and unresponsive, and so disobedient (and thus by implication 'rejects').

God's Wrath and Mercy 9:19–29

If it is God himself who 'hardens' men's hearts, why then does he 'find fault'—i.e. impute blame—on the assumption that they are free creatures?

19. who can resist his will: who then is a 'free man'? (what becomes of man's free will?). This meaning seems to take the verb as a gnomic perfect. SH render: '*is* resisting God's will', explaining the tense as a perfect with a present meaning. Cf. Rom. 13:2 for a parallel. The question is then a rhetorical one, ironically put by Paul's imaginary opponent. The answer, on the argument just concluded, is: 'No one', since the man who rebels against God (Pharaoh) is only doing what God willed. The tense, however, may be simply a regular perfect tense: 'who has (ever) resisted his will?'. Cf. Wis. 12:12.

20. But who are you, a man: *NEB*; 'Who are you, sir, to answer God back?' This succeeds, as the *RSV* does not, in conveying something of the force of the vocative. It is more than 'you who are just a man': the vocative *anthrōpe* has a contemptuous ring 'You, fellow!' (Cf. Liddell and Scott, s.v.: 'You, Sirrah!') The force of the connecting particle *menounge* appears to be adversative 'But, Sirrah . . .' (cf. Moule, *Idiom Book*, p. 163).

21. The imagery of the potter and his clay is a familiar one in the prophets; cf. Isa. 20:16, Jer. 18:6; also Wis. 15:7, Sir. 36(33):12f. This verse owes more probably to Wisdom 15:7 than to the more familiar Old Testament passages, especially in this phrase: thus, '. . . out of the self-same clay he (the potter) fashions without distinction the pots that are to serve for honourable uses and the opposite; and what the purposes of each one is to be, the moulder of the clay decides.' (*NEB*).

Vv. 19–22 read like a literary adaptation by St Paul of this part of Wisdom. Cf. especially *Apocrypha and Pseudepigrapha of the Old Testament*, I, p. 526 (Holmes).

one vessel for beauty: lit., 'for honour, for dishonour', i.e., one highly esteemed (*eis timēn*), another for baser uses (*eis atimian*). Cf. 2 Tim. 2:20. The translation 'common use' (*NEB*) (or 'ordinary use', *Jerus. Bible*) for *atimia* is weak; as at Wis. 15:7, where the contest is between uses which can be called 'pure (*katharos*) and the opposite', here also the emphasis is on vessels which are highly esteemed and their opposite, utensils for menial use.

22–23. What if God . . . for glory: There is a suppressed apodosis, a not unfamiliar construction, e.g., Ac. 23:9 'What if a spirit or an angel spoke to him?', 'But what if God . . . endured with much patience the vessels of wrath made for destruction . . .?'; *RSV* then continues—with mainly the Vatican text (B) and the Vulgate in support—'in order (*hina*) to make known the riches of his glory for the vessels of mercy, which he has prepared for glory . . .'. We have then an uncomplicated sentence (which Origen also appears to have read). But the more difficult text reads *kai hina* 'and in order that . . .'. To take the *kai hina* clause closely with the preceding sentence 'endured with much patience vessels of wrath, and in order to make known the riches of his glory' gives an odd connection ('does not seem to make good sense', Barrett); to connect it elliptically with 'God, desiring to show his wrath . . . endured with much patience the vessels of wrath . . . and (did so) in order to make known the riches of his glory' is grammatically awkward, although it does give a contrasting parallel. Cf. *NEB*.

Could the text be at fault and the original here have read *hina kai* rather than *kai hina*? For examples of this type of textual error by transposition of words or letters, see Lorimer, *op. cit.*, pp. 385ff. (above, p. 126). We would then obtain the contrasting parallel without grammatical difficulties: 'But what if God, whose will it is (*thelōn*) to manifest his wrath and to make known his power, bore with much patience those vessels of wrath made for destruction, in order also to make known the riches of his glory for the vessels of mercy which he has prepared beforehand for glory . . .?' God *wills* the manifestation of his wrath:[1] the judgement is still to be reckoned with, for all God's long-suffering patience: but his postponement of it gives even his 'vessels of wrath' space for repentance (cf. 2:4); and it *also* allows him to demonstrate the wealth of his glory to his vessels of mercy. Cf. Zahn, p. 461: Zahn assumes that *kai hina* as it stands can be so construed. For *hina kai* cf. Rom. 8:17, 11:31, 14:9, and elsewhere at I C. 4:8, 7:29, 11:19, 2 C. 8:7, 14, 11:16 etc.

desiring to show his wrath: In a context where the thought of the

---

[1]The hypotactic participle *thelōn* does not require to be interpreted as either causal or concessive: it is a plain statement of the inexorable divine will to manifest his wrath in a final judgement that is still to come. Cf. Cranfield, Barrett *ad loc.*

sovereign will of God is paramount (cf. vv. 18, 19 *thelein, boulēma*)
'desire' (*RSV* and *NEB*) or 'wish' (Moffatt) do not convey the full
force of *thelein*: 'But what if God whose *will* it is (*thelōn*) to show
his wrath . . .'

with much patience: cf. 2:4 for the thought of God's forbearance;
long-suffering kindness is intended to lead to repentance. Cf. Bar.
59:6 and 2 Esd. 7:74: the idea appears to have been a familiar one
in apocalyptic circles.

vessels of wrath: The phrase *skeuē orgēs* in the LXX occurs at Jer.
27 (50) 25 for the instruments of God's wrath, (cf. also Isa. 13:5):
here it clearly means the *objects* of God's wrath. Paul is no doubt
thinking of the Jews who have rejected the Gospel, but the phrase
could also include Gentiles as well.

made for destruction: Although the verb here used, lit. 'fashioned'
(and the parallel expression in v. 23 'prepared beforehand') correspond to Hebrew terms which need mean no more than 'destined
for' (cf. S-B Bd. 1, pp. 981ff.), the Greek verbs here are selected,
especially in a context where artifacts of the potters' craft are
symbols, to convey more than 'destined', although this idea is basic.
The vessels of wrath are so fashioned (whether by God or through
their own behaviour) to be of such a worthless character as to be
'fit' or 'ripe' for final destruction, i.e. the annihilation of Abaddon
or Gehenna. For *apōleia*, 'Destruction', in the latter sense see
TWNT, Bd. 1, pp. 395ff., and M. Black, *The Book of Enoch* (Brill,
1985), p. 282.

the riches of his glory: One ms. (P) (supported by the Peshitta)
reads 'the riches of his kindness' (*chrēstotēs*) an expression from 2:4.
The scribe who introduced it, if it is more than a slip, evidently felt
that this expression was more appropriate in this context. It is a
pity the variant has such weak attestation, since a reading 'riches of
his kindness' could have become 'riches of his glory' through the
influence of the later phrase 'for glory'.

which he has prepared beforehand: Notice that God is clearly said
to have a hand in the 'preparation' of his 'vessels of mercy', and
'beforehand'—where the idea of predestination is again resumed
from vv. 11–12. For the probable background of such ideas in
contemporary, mainly Qumran, Judaism, see Käsemann, pp. 259f.
For the 'glory' which has been predetermined for the 'vessels of
mercy', cf. 2:7, 10; 5:2; 8:18.

24. even us whom he has called: V. 24 is a relative clause with
'vessels of mercy' as antecedent, identifying those predestined and
prepared by God for glory—*even us*, Paul and his fellow believers,
comprised of Jews as well as Gentiles. Paul thus introduces, in a
subordinate clause, his central concept of the seminal remnant or

Israel of God (vv. 27–28). The argument that v. 24 is a full, main clause, even though introduced by a relative, is to be rejected; cf. Cranfield *ad loc*. This use of a relative clause, giving an additional fact, is not unusual in St Paul (cf. SH *ad loc*.). We should probably render 'even us whom he has indeed called' (*kai ekalesen*, the 'ascensive *kai*', 'whom he has effectually called', Cranfield). The *kai* is certainly not otiose (E. Haenchen, *The Acts of the Apostles*, Oxford 1971, p. 140, n. 8.)

25. The argument is clinched by two quotations, the first from Hos. 2:23 (cf. 1:6, 8, 9), the second Hos. 1:10 (LXX 2:1).

As indeed he says: cf. *NEB*: 'as it says'. The subject of 'says' is probably impersonal: 'as is said' (lit., 'as one says'). Others interpret 'as he (God) says'.

in Hosea: i.e. in the Book of Hosea, cf. Mk 1:2, an apparently unique locution in the New Testament (Cranfield, p. 499, n. 1).

Those who were not my people . . . 'my beloved': At Hos. 1:6, 9, a daughter and son of Hosea are given the names 'Not pitied' (*Lo-ruhamah*) and 'Not my people' (*Lo-'ammi*) respectively, symbolising jointly the apostate northern Israel. Hos. 2:23 prophesies the restoration to favour of the rejected ten tribes of the northern kingdom (cf. 1 Kg. 11:30ff.): (a) '. . . I will have pity on Not pitied, (b) and I will say to Not my people, 'You are my people.' (*RSV*) Paul reverses the clauses (a) (b) to (b) (a), and further adapts the quotation to his argument and its context in the Epistle: (b) 'Those who were not my people I will *call* 'my people', (a) and her who was not *'beloved* (sc. *I will call beloved*)'. 'Those who were not my people, I will call my people,' comes first, since Paul has Gentiles prominently in mind, but certainly also to recall to the Jew familiar with Scripture that the original reference was to 'that other rejected Israel' (Barth), the ten lost tribes. 'I will *call* (*kalesō*) my people' instead of 'I will *say* to Not my people', has been deliberately introduced (not 'just crept in' (SH)), to link with 'call' in both the preceding and the following verses, a link which is more than formal (see next verse). St Paul then cites the second clause in a text which is close to that of Codex Vaticanus of the LXX (supported by V and several minuscules), *but not identical with it*, a clear indication that the latter has not arisen from a reminiscence of Rom. 9:25: LXX: 'And *I will love* the one who is not beloved; Rom.: 'And her who was not beloved, (sc. I will call) beloved.' (*RSV, NEB* repeat the verb 'I will call' and render 'my beloved', but the Greek text assumes 'I will call' as still the main verb and reads 'beloved' not 'my beloved'.) By adopting this translation St Paul (or the LXX translator before him) seems to be deliberately recalling the figure of the nation as the bride of Yahweh, a figure of speech not only central in

Hosea's prophecies, but perhaps even implicit in this particular oracle. The language of *agapē* of God would also particularly commend itself to the Apostle: the relation between the new Israel to God is a relationship of caring love, the love of God for his people.

26. This is a quotation from the LXX of Hos. 1:10. The reading 'will be called' (*klēthēsontai*) 'sons of the living God' from the LXX (cf. MT) continues the idea of Israel's divine call (*kalein*) at verses 24–25, here 'being called' i.e. 'designated, named'. For 'sons of God', see above, on 8.14, p. 113. Does the text refer to an actual place which was the place both of Israel's rejection and of her restoration? Most commentators nowadays prefer the alternative explanation that 'in the place of' is used, like *loco*, meaning 'instead of': so *RV mg.* to Hos. 1:10: 'Instead of that which was said to them, You are not my people, it shall be said . . .'. The use of the expression elsewhere, however, (e.g. Lev. 4:24, 33, Jer. 22:12), favours a locative sense. Jerusalem has been proposed, and Hos. 1:11 does go on to describe the ingathering from exile of the people of Judah and the people of Israel under a single head (note that Judah comes first); and the place of assembly, according to Isa. 2:2–4, Mic. 4:1–3, Zech. 8:20–23 was Jerusalem.[1] Others think of Palestine, the land of promise, itself. See H. A. W. Meyer, *Epistle to the Romans, ad loc.* (especially n. 3). The only hint of a *place* in the oracle itself is that the returning people of Judah and Israel shall 'come up from the land', a phrase from Exod. 1:10 referring to Egypt, Israel's land of bondage, but, in Hosea, presumably to Assyria, the place of their captivity. Was it when they sojourned among the nations, a captive people, that this oracle of hope was spoken; and does Paul follow this by suggesting that the place where God would call his new people would be in the Gentile world whither they had been scattered? If so, he would be following the Targumic interpretation of this verse.

27. cries out is the regular expression for inspired prophetic utterances. Cf. Jn 1:15 and R. Bultmann, *Das Evangelium des Johannes* (Göttingen, 1941), *ad loc.*

27–29 consist of two further testimonia, Isa. 10:22–23 and Isa. 1:9, for the Remnant (assumed to be the Christian Church) as the true Israel. Isa. 10:22–23 is partly assimilated to Hos. 1:10 (which links the quotation formally with Hos. 1:10 in v. 26), and is quoted in a deliberately abridged form, but one which, nevertheless, gives the gist of the Isaianic verses without loss. The verses give classic expression to the central theme of the first Isaiah (symbolised by the name he gave his son Shear-yashub) that only a remnant of

[1] J. Jeremias, *Jesus' Promise to the Nations* (London, 1958), pp. 58–62.

Israel would 'turn again' to their mighty God and so escape the judgement Yahweh had decreed. Paul reads, with the LXX, 'will be saved' (*sōthēsetai*) for the Heb. 'will turn again' (to God), and so be saved (cf. Isa. 10:20 where the remnant is defined as 'the survivors of the house of Jacob'). Paul also reads, with the LXX, '*the* remnant' (*to hypoleimma*, LXX *kataleimma*), which can hardly be construed as 'only a remnant', however legitimate a rendering this is of the Hebrew; if anything, it would mean here 'the well-known Remnant' of prophetic tradition, and now for Paul 'the remnant people of God', the Jews (and Gentiles) who had become believers. Cf. Lietzmann, *An die Römer, ad loc.*

28. The last sentence of Isa. 10:22 and the gist of verse 23 appear in this verse as an abridged and adapted version of the LXX (some mss. have the complete LXX quotation, clearly a secondary variant). The translation (and paraphrase) of SH still enjoys considerable favour among modern exegetes: 'For a word, accomplishing and abridging it, that is, a sentence conclusive and concise, will the Lord do upon the earth.' So Cranfield, 'for a sentence complete and decisive will the Lord accomplish upon the earth.' But the idea of a sentence or word of the Lord being complete but 'abridged' is without biblical parallel and seems an implausible sense, even if the words can be construed in this way.

The clue to an understanding of the LXX quotation (and Paul's use of it), is, I suggest, to be found in the biblical Greek locution, *syntelein kai syntemnein*, found usually in the passive, e.g., at LXX Dan. 5:26–28: Belshazzar's kingdom 'is destroyed (lit. cut off) and finished off' (*syntetmētae kai syntetelestai*). So also Dan. 9:24 Theod., in the different sense of the 'completion' (lit., 'cutting off' *synetmē-thēsan*) of the seventy hebdomads and the cessation (*syntelesthēnai*) of their sin. The phrase occurs again at Isa. 28:22 LXX applied to 'deeds finished and cut off', i.e., which have come to a complete and absolute end. Käsemann has suggested that we have to do with an apocalyptic formula; and certainly 'destruction by divine fiat' at Dan. 5:26 could well be so described.

The active *syntelōn kai syntemnōn* in our verse is best taken in the sense of the two verbs at Dan. 5:27, viz., 'finishing off' i.e. 'annihilating' (cf. 2 Chr. 20:23) and 'destroying', lit., 'cutting off', and both then construed together with the main verb and with subject *ho kyrios* 'the Lord' as the Agent of destruction. (The 'word' could refer to the prophetic word 'a remnant will be saved', or simply = *res*, a thing, a deed). We should then render 'for a thing/the word (of this prophecy), will the Lord accomplish on the earth, by finishing off (the reprobate Israel) and cutting (her off)', i.e. by annihilation and severance. The verb 'cutting off, severing' alludes, by implication, to the rescued rump, the remnant. Such an exegesis is close to the original MT of Isa. 10:22: lit., 'For though your people Israel be as the sand of the sea only a remnant of them will return. Destruction is decreed . . .'[1] It also leads naturally into the next quotation of Isa. 1:9: but for the seed of the remnant 'we would have fared like Sodom and been made like Gomorrah', i.e. been completely annihilated.

29. The second text from Isa. 1:9 agrees verbally with the LXX, which has interpreted the Hebrew word *sarid* '(a small) remainder' by 'seed' (*sperma*, RSV 'children'), probably influenced by the phrase 'the holy seed' used at Isa 6:13 (MT) for the new Israel. 'Sperma' 'seed' is a key word in Paul's apologetic; cf. especially Gal. 3:16ff. Here it is connected by Isaiah with the remnant, 'If the Lord of hosts had not left us (*enkatelipen*, *hypoleimma* = 'remnant'), seed (*sperma*)', thus enabling Paul to link the thought of the verse about the 'remnant seed of the new Israel' with the previous 'seed of the promise' (9:7ff.). The Remnant is to provide the 'seed', i.e., the off-spring, children, of the redeemed Israel.

ISRAEL'S FAILURE

9:30–10:13

The Stone of Stumbling 9:30–33

30. What shall we say, then? The familiar formula is usually employed to state an objection raised by an imaginary opponent. Here it summarises the foregoing argument in two paradoxical statements. Moffatt: 'What are we to conclude then?'.

did not pursue: See SH, *ad loc*. The words are correlatives ('pursue', 'overtake'), and the figure is taken from the race-course and perhaps resumed in the verbs at verses 31 and 32 (see below).

Gentiles: Paul does not say 'the Gentiles' but 'Gentiles', without the definite article, i.e. some Gentiles, and here meaning those who had, mainly by Paul's own ministry, become believers. Notice that he goes on to define the 'righteousness' which these Gentile believers have attained as 'righteousness through faith', i.e. faith-righteousness in contrast to 'righteousness of the law' of v. 31. The two verses are in antithetic parallelism.

31. the righteousness which is based on the law: The text here reads the unique Pauline expression 'a law of righteousness', so that

[1] For the relationship of the Hebrew to the LXX, see especially Zahn, p. 466, n. 44.

RSV is a somewhat free rendering, although with a respectable tradition of interpretation behind it (Cranfield, p. 507, n.4). The genitive in 'a law of righteousness' is usually explained as a genitive of quality, and as such is variously rendered ('a law which demands righteousness' (Zahn) or 'which promises righteousness' (Käsemann, Cranfield). It may also be explained as a genitive of direction or purpose (B-D §166), 'a law for righteousness' i.e. designed to ensure or enforce righteousness (the latter, for Paul, 'standing right with God.'). This is what Israel has made the chief end and goal of her life: 'Israel pursued a law to ensure righteousness . . .'

did not succeed in fulfilling that law: lit. 'did not attain to the Law' (for the verb used in this sense, cf. 2 C. 10:14, Phil. 3:16). Is the latter phrase a contraction for 'the fulfilment of the Law', or 'the justification which comes from the fulfilment of the Law?

RSV is again interpreting freely in its rendering of a difficult phrase. For an exact parallel to v. 30 we would expect 'did not attain to *righteousness*', as some Gentiles had, whereas the text reads 'did not attain to law', i.e., presumably the law of righteousness just mentioned. The TR supplies the genitive 'did not attain to the law *of righteousness*', a repetition which is stylistically ugly and un-Pauline. The idea of a text at fault has been mooted more than once; Schmiedel, in fact, proposed to emend 'law' to 'righteousness'. The difficulties the text has given rise to perhaps justify emendation. Did the original perhaps read 'did not attain to the righteousness of the Law (*eis dikaiosynēn nomou*) i.e., to the right standing with God that observance of the Mosaic Law was intended to give. Cf. the parallel expression at 10:5 'the righteousness which is based on the law' (lit., 'which is from the law'). The meaning of the verse then is that Israel, with her immense privilege of pursuing a divine Law which could have ensured her a right standing with God, nevertheless failed to attain that legal righteousness before God—and the next verse gives the reason.

32. We may paraphrase Paul's reply to the question 'Why?', 'Because (they did not pursue the *nomos dikaiosynēs*) by faith but, as if they could, by works (some inferior mss. add "of the Law")'. The last phrase reads, lit., 'but as (*hōs*) by works'. For this subtle use of *hōs* (which requires a paraphrase in English as in *RSV*), see especially L. Radermacher, *Neutestamentliche Grammatik*, pp. 22f., and SH, p. 280 (Cranfield, p. 510, seems to hesitate).

they have stumbled over the stumbling stone: Cf. 1 C. 1:23 '. . . Christ crucified, to the Jews a stumbling-block.' This sentence at 32b, introducing the testimonies from Isa. 28:16, is attached, in the best mss, asyndetically to the previous sentence 32a. Other mss. read 'For (*gar*) they have stumbled . . .', linking the sentence more

closely with its context and making it clear that here is the reason
for the failure of the Jews to realise the *dikaiosynē* of the Law; they
stumbled and fell over the Rock of Offence, namely, Christ. It is
possible that the metaphor of 'stumbling' and so 'falling' continues
that of the race at v. 30: while pursuing the *nomos dikaiosynēs*,
wrongly by 'works', they stumbled against the Rock of Christ. It is
assumed by St Paul as well known to his readers who the stumbling-
stone is. Both the texts which follow (Isa. 28:16 and 8:14 are used
elsewhere in the same connection (1 Pet. 2:6 uses the same non-
LXX type of Greek text); they were probably familiar *testimonia*,
employed by the early preachers and missionaries especially in their
controversy with Jews (see C. H. Dodd, *According to the Scriptures*,
pp. 41ff.).

33. a stone that will make men stumble . . .: at Isa. 8:14 it was
Yahweh himself who was originally the 'stone of stumbling'. At Isa.
28:16 God lays in Zion a precious foundation stone, and 'he who
trusts therein shall not be put to shame'. Already the Targum
interprets the precious foundation stone as 'a mighty King', referring, almost certainly, to the 'King Messiah'. For Paul the stone of
stumbling, which is also the foundation-stone, is Christ.
he who believes in him: cf. 1 Pet. 2:6. The Hebrew text of Isa.
28:16 has simply 'he who believes'. The LXX, however, almost
certainly read 'he who believes/trusts in him' (One codex, B, omits
ep autō, 'in him', and was assumed to be original by SH, p. 281,
who then attribute the 'addition' to Paul). The antecedent of *ep autō*
'in him' is clearly the Stone (*lithos*),[1] and the reference is to Christ
as the Stone. The passage had almost certainly already been interpreted of the Messiah in contemporary Judaism; cf. J. Jeremias,
TWNT Bd. IV, p. 276.
will not be put to shame: All versions so render, but the verb
kataischynesthai has a wider connotation. (Paul follows the LXX in
reading 'will not be put to shame'; the MT reads 'he who believes
(trusts) will not be alarmed.') In biblical Greek *kataischynesthai* can
mean 'be confounded'; and it can also mean 'be disappointed at',
e.g., Jer. 12:13, 'They are disappointed of their harvest' (*NEB*)
(rather than 'they shall be ashamed of their harvests' (*RSV*)).
Perhaps in this context, which speaks of 'trust in', 'disappointed' is
a better rendering than 'be ashamed'; cf. Isa. 20:5 LXX: 'And the
defeated Egyptians will be disappointed in the Ethiopians in whom
the Egyptians had placed their trust'. The thought of 'trust (or

---

[1]*Petra* 'Rock' is the nearer antecedent, but with such a composite subject,
'the masculine as *prior gender* includes the feminine' (G-K, §122g); 'in him'
refers to Christ as *both* Stone and Rock.

hope) in Yahweh' not being 'disappointed', 'let down', occurs at
Ps. 24(25):2 (cf. 3), 20; Sir. 2:10 (cf. 15:4) in identical phraseology,
'. . . was anyone who trusted the Lord ever disappointed?' (*NEB*).
Strictly, so far as the syntax is concerned, the 'in him' could form
the predicate of 'in him will not be disappointed', but the word
order (and certainly St Paul's intention) points to 'he who trusts in
him will not be disappointed'.

True Righteousness 10:1–13

There is no break in the argument with the beginning of the new
chapter. Paul pauses briefly to repeat his personal grief at his fellow-
countrymen's failure to accept the Gospel (the parenthetic verses
are 1–3). The rest of the chapter consists of a further exposition of
the Pauline doctrine of 'righteousness' *sola fide*, now supported from
Scripture by a fresh *catena* of texts from the Pentateuch and the
Prophets.

1. my heart's desire: the *RSV* is right in taking the word *eudokia*
here in its biblical Greek sense (Hebrew *rasōn*, 'desire'—the word
never means 'desire' *except* in biblical Greek (cf. Ps. 145:19, Sir.
18:31; so *NEB* brings out even more fully the force of the word
especially as here qualified, 'my deepest desire'. Cf., for other views,
SH, *ad loc*. It is difficult, however, to see how ideas of 'goodwill'
fit this context; cf. G. Schrenk, *TWNT*, Bd. II, p. 743.
my . . . prayer to God for them: 'Paul would not have prayed, if
they had been utterly reprobates (*si absolute reprobati essent*)' (Bengel,
Edinburgh ed., Vol. III, p. 139).
2. enlightened: lit. 'but not with discernment, percipience, recognition', as opposed to unawareness, ignorance (cf. v. 3), i.e. without
discernment or recognition of the true source of *dikaiosynē* in faith.
Cf. for the noun *epignōsis*, J. A. Robinson, *Ephesians* (London,
1903), p. 248. Cf. above, 3:20 ('recognition of sin', rather than a
'deepening awareness', knowledge of sin). The religious devotion
or enthusiasm of the Jews ('zeal' used so absolutely Ps. Sol. 4.3)
was a blind devotion and unenlightened *Schwärmerei*.
3. being ignorant of the righteousness that comes from God:
It is tempting to understand *agnoein*, *nescio* as 'to have a false notion
of'; *verkennen*, which would appropriately describe the Jewish
'misconception' of *dikaiosynē*. But there does not seem to be any
support for this meaning. The verb means 'be ignorant of' and this
is favoured by *RSV*, SH and many others. It can also mean 'fail to
understand' ('fail to comprehend', Cranfield, as at Mk 9:32) or
'fail to recognise'. In view of the previous term *epignōsis* meaning
'discernment, recognition', the latter meaning is perhaps to be

preferred: the Jews, blinded by their 'zeal', which robbed them of their powers to discern the true nature of things, failed accordingly to recognise the *dikaiosynē* of God when it appeared, i.e., the gift of 'righteousness' by faith in Christ. The translation of the *NEB* 'ignore' implies a deliberate avoidance of knowledge of the *dikaiosynē* of God; it is very doubtful if this was what Paul meant.

establish: *NEB*: 'set up'. Paul is accusing the Jews of striving to set up their own (human) system of 'righteousness' by legal works. **did not submit:** they did not commit themselves to the righteousness of God (revealed in the Gospel apart from the Law; cf. 1:17; 3:21). Since such commitment was to God, it was necessarily also a 'submitting' of oneself—hence the choice of verb. The Jew submitted himself to the righteousness of the law, 'i.e., to his own system of righteousness or right standing with God on the basis of merit acquired by performance of 'works of the law'. Cf. 2 Bar. 54:5.

4. end: Christ is the end of the law, that everyone who has faith may be justified: The exegetical debate in this Pauline apophthegm centres on the interpretation in this context of 'end' (*telos*) and 'law' (*nomos*). Both nouns are ambivalent; *telos* can mean 'end', i.e. 'termination', or 'perfection', 'fulfilment' (although this is more usually *teleiōsis*), or 'goal' (other uses can be ruled out as unsuitable here), and *nomos* (with or without the article) can be either 'law' in general (as at 2:12, 14) or the Torah. To take *telos* here, unqualified in any way, as '(Christ is) the termination of law (general or particular)' is, as Cranfield (p. 519) rightly decides, 'altogether improbable': Paul had a lofty ideal of law, in particular 'the law of faith' (*nomos pisteōs*, Rom. 3:27) or 'the law of Christ' (Gal. 6:2), but no less of 'the law (of Moses)' (7:12), and, above all, 3:31 clearly states that faith does not abrogate (*katargein*) the law, but rather puts it on a right basis (*histanein*), i.e., of faith rather than of acquired merit by the performance of ordinances and rites. The recognition of this fact has consequently led interpreters to prefer the alternative 'fulfilment' or 'goal' (not mutually exclusive), and to render 'Christ is the fulfilment/goal of the law (generally taken as the Mosaic Law)'; and Mt. 5:17 is cited in support. The concluding clause of the predicate is usually then understood as '(Christ is the fulfilment/goal of the law) so that righteousness is available for everyone who believes' (*eis dikaiosynēntō pisteuonti*, 'The *eis* is consecutive. If Christ is the goal of the law, it follows that a status of righteousness is available to everyone who believes.' Cranfield, p. 519). But is *telos* in this context unqualified? The predicate clause may be taken as a final clause qualifying *telos* 'end, termination': 'Christ is the end of law (the Jewish Torah or Gentile *nomos*) *for the* *attainment of righteousness.'* This rendering was proposed by John Murray (Vol. 2, p. 50), but is rejected by Cranfield as 'extremely unlikely in view of the order of the sentence (had Paul meant this he would surely have placed *eis dikaiosynēn* next to *nomou*.' (p. 519, n. 2). But the usual order of words has already been altered by Paul to give emphasis to the predicate 'the end of the law'; and in such a short pithy saying the other half of the predicate 'for righteousness, etc' is near enough to be construed with *telos nomou*. Perhaps Paul was deliberately making the challenging statement, 'The end of law is Christ', then adding the qualification 'for the attainment of righteousness', 'as a means to righteousness'.[1] For this final use of *eis* with an abstract noun rather than with an infinitive, cf. Rom. 3:25, B-D, §402(2). We may render: 'Christ is the end of law—as a means to righteousness'. Since the universal 'for everyone who believes' embraces Gentiles as well as Jews, SH seem right in interpreting 'law' here generally, inclusive of the Mosaic law, but recognising that 'law' was not the monopoly of Judaism. To understand *telos* here as 'end', however, by no means rules out the other main alternative, 'perfection, fulfilment, goal'. As E. G. Selwyn noted,[2] 1 Pet. 1:9 conforms more closely to classical Greek (= 'the logical end of a process or action—its issue, consummation, perfection—and thus in philosophical writings its idea of chief good'); cf. 1 Tim. 1:5: 'the end of the commandment is love'. So the 'end', the climactic development (practically 'perfection', 'perfecting') of the Law is Christ. Cf. further, E. E. Schneider, *'Finis Legis Christus'*, in *TZ*, xx (1964), pp. 410–22; R. Bultmann, 'Christus, des Gesetzes Ende', *Beitr. Ev. Theologie*, 1 (1940), pp. 3–27; F. Flückiger, *'Christus, des Gesetzes Telos'*, *TZ*, xi (1955), pp. 153–7; R. Bring, in *Stud. Theol.*, xx (1966), pp. 1–36. The two meanings supplement each other: Christ as the perfection/consummation of law (implying in this *nomen actionis* its total realisation or accomplishment) must accordingly bring an end to the 'old law' it supersedes, completes and perfects or perfectly fulfils. It is this second meaning (and both are equally important) which provides the logical link with 10:5–11 and the Pauline use of the Old Testament there.

who has faith: i.e. to every believer Christ has superseded Law as a means of attaining 'righteousness'.

5. Moses writes . . . live by it: Paul goes on to make his case

---

[1] Cf. C. F. D. Moule, *An Idiom Book of New Testament Greek* (Cambridge, 1953), p. 70. 'Christ is an end to legalism for the attainment of righteousness, as a means to righteousness.' But it is 'law' not 'legalism' *as a means to righteousness* which Christ ends.

[2] *The First Epistle of St. Peter* (London, 1946), p. 132.

for his statement at v. 4, beginning with an adapted quotation of
Lev. 18:5 which he had similarly used at Gal. 3:12. Notice the
connecting word 'For (*gar*) Moses writes': vs. 5–15 give a further
explication of the grounds for the statement at v. 4. The *RSV*
translates a text in which the adapted quotation 'the man who
practises the righteousness which is based on the law shall live by
it' is introduced directly after 'For Moses writes' (by the conjunction
'that', *hoti*). An alternative form of text is read by *NEB*, where the
quotation from Lev. 18:5 is not introduced till after 'the righteousness based . . . on the law', with the effect of making this key
expression follow immediately on 'For Moses writes', to be
construed then as an accusative of reference: 'Of legal righteousness
Moses writes, "The man who does this shall gain life by it." The
meaning, in either translation, is the same, but the second form is
preferable, as an instance of emphatic hyperbaton in which the
object of the subordinate clause is brought forward, for the sake of
emphasis into the main clause.[1]

6–8. The original purpose of the *OT* passage, Dt. 30:11–14, was
to meet the objection that the Mosaic code was impossible to keep;
it is *not* something so far removed from reality that human nature
cannot realise it. It is on the lips to utter it, and in the heart to
carry it out (the 'commandment' or 'word of God', in the sense of
the Mosaic code, the Law). Paul substitutes Christ 'the new Torah'
(see below, p. 144) for the law (law in general, but including the
'old Torah'): Christ is not so remote that he has to be brought down
from Heaven or up from Hades; the Lord, who has come down
from heaven, has also 'descended into hell' and risen from the
dead—to be present and available to Christian faith. The 'word of
faith' (corresponding to the 'word of the Law') consists of the
confession of Christ 'with the mouth' and genuine belief 'in the
heart' that God raised him from the dead. This is the saving Faith-
Righteousness. (See Selwyn, *1 Peter*, pp. 320ff. and M. Black, 'The
Christological Use of the Old Testament in the New Testament',
NTS, XVIII (1971), pp. 8ff.[2])

[1]See my *Aramaic Approach*[3], pp. 53f. I have adopted the readings of UBS[3]
and Nestle[26], for this and other reasons (cf. Metzger, *A Textual Commentary*, p. 524.) The idea that 'the man' refers to Christ and that 'righteousness' here could mean 'the merciful will of God expressed in the law' are
curiosities of Barthian eisegesis. See Cranfield, p. 521, n. 4.
[2]Cf. further, F. F. Bruce, in *Soli Deo Gloria: New Testament Studies in
Honor of William Childs Robinson*, ed. J. McD. Richards (Virginia, 1968),
pp. 35ff. See also S. Lyonnet, 'St. Paul et l'exégèse juive de son temps à
propos Rom. x. 6–8', in *Travaux de l'Institut Catholique de Paris*, IV,
pp. 494–506. Cf. also A. M. Goldberg, 'Torah aus der Unterwelt; eine

the righteousness based on faith: or Faith-Righteousness. Is Paul personifying his *dikaiosynē sola fide*, making it (her) utter a scriptural *charaz* based on Dt. 30:11–14 in a Greek version adapted to the writer's special exegetical purpose (for such personification, cf. Prov. 1:20 (Wisdom), Lk. 11:49, etc.)?

The *charaz* (see above, p. 56) which enables Paul to develop his *sola fide* doctrine, is composite and selective; it is introduced by a formula from LXX Dt. 8:17, 9:4[2], followed by two questions selected and adopted from Dt. 30:12, 13 and Isa. 14:15 (cf. LXX Ps. 106:26) respectively, the first agreeing verbally with the LXX of Dt. 30:12, the second alluding to Is. 14:15 and owing nothing to Dt. 30:13 except the question form. Paul is displaying his rabbinical expertise in weaving together this *charaz*. He is also contributing his own *pesher* or interpretation by a familiar formula *tout estin*, *id est*, 'that is' (cf. Michel, p. 257, n. 2, Käsemann, p. 272).

Paul's use or interpretation of the two main elements in this scriptural *catena* has been described as 'typological' ('a specially crass example') (Gaugler II, p. 124) or as 'allegorising' ('a drastic and unwarrantable allegorising', W. E. Kirk, *Romans* (Oxford, 1937) *ad loc*.). Superficially this is how it looks, for Paul is substituting 'Christ' for 'the law' ('the commandment' at Dt. 30:11). But, as Cranfield has argued (p. 524), Paul 'did not think of Christ and the law as two altogether unrelated entities'. 'Christ is the goal, the essential meaning, the real substance of the law' (ibid.). Or, as it may also be put, in line with our interpretation of v. 4 above, Christ is the 'perfection of law', and it is the incarnate and risen Christ, the Perfect Law or the Law of Christ, which there is no need to bring down from heaven or bring up from the abyss of hell, since in his Risen Presence he is directly accessible to faith—and as the new Torah 'his yoke is easy and his burden is light.' For Christ as the new Torah, see W. D. Davies, *Paul and Rabbinic Judaism*, pp. 147ff.; 153ff.[3]

Bemerkung zu Röm. 10:6–7', *BZ*, XVI (1970), pp. 127–31. It has been suggested that Paul has in mind the inaccessibility of Wisdom; see M. J. Suggs, ' "The Word is Near You": Rom. x.6–10 within the Purpose of the Letter', *Christian History and Interpretation: Studies presented to John Knox*, ed. by W. R. Farmer, *et al*. (Cambridge, 1967), pp. 289ff., 305.

[2]Leenhardt thinks that Paul had here the context of this introductory formula in mind (it was not by Israel's righteousness Canaan had come to be possessed) (Comm., p. 268, cf. Cranfield, p. 523).

[3]It has been noted more than once (cf. Käsemann, p. 277) that these verses from Dt. 30:11f. are applied to wisdom at I Bar. 3:29ff, but while this supplies a Jewish precedent for their wider application, the purpose of

There is another essential aspect of this 'new Torah': it is not only exemplified in the Risen Jesus, but faith in the Risen Lord (who requires obedience as well as enabling the believer to obey) offers the prospect of the fulfilment of the Law of Christ, the 'new Torah', as the 'law inscribed on the heart' (Jer. 31:31).

This creative *pesher* of St Paul (now with the authority of Scripture) shows a profounder insight than that of Moses into the reality of the human situation, viz., man's desperate need for something more than is offered by the Pelagian assumptions of the Mosaic Law.

8. But what does it say: The subject is still the personified Faith-Righteousness. The reading 'But what does Scripture (*hē graphē*) say?' is a later scribal addition.

The quotation of Dt. 30:14 is almost word for word from the LXX. Originally the 'word' referred to the 'commandments' of Dt. 5:6ff., 6:4ff. (cf. Dt. 11:22); it is said to be in their mouths and in their hearts (minds). This means at least that they knew the Ten Words by heart: after all, every pious Jew recited the Shema (Dt. 6:4ff.) twice each day. Here St Paul is thinking of the code of the law with the obligation of obedience resulting in 'works of the law'. **the word of faith which we preach** refers unequivocally to 'the Gospel', the apostolic kerygma, 'The message the subject of which is faith' (SH); cf. 1 Pet. 1:25.

9. because: The *hoti* 'because' may be taken as introducing a subordinate clause explaining 'the word of faith'. The word of faith 'that means the word of faith which we preach (namely) that if with your mouth, etc.' But the apostolic 'word of faith' needs no further definition, and the clause is best taken as in *RSV* closely with v. 8 explaining 'the word is near to you . . . because, if you confess, etc.'

. . . if you confess . . . Lord: Belief is followed by confession: the order is correctly given at v. 10, but reversed here to agree with the quotation from Dt. 30:14, where the word 'in the mouth' precedes that 'in the heart'. Clearly also the confession of Jesus as Lord depends on the belief that God raised him up from the dead (cf. Ac. 2:32, 36); 'that Jesus is Lord *as the Risen One* goes through the whole New Testament' (Foerster, in *TWNT*, Bd. III, p. 1088) (italics mine). 'Jesus is Lord' (*Kyrios Jesus*) may well have been, like *Maranatha*, an early, if not one of the earliest of Christian

---

Baruch is the very opposite of that of Paul or the Deuteronomic writer: he is seeking, by the use of this text, to emphasise the inaccessibility of wisdom not its proximity. Cf. Davies, *op. cit.*, p. 154.

confessions, possibly repeated in all acts of worship (Cranfield, p. 527). A fuller form occurs at 2 C. 4:5 and Phil. 2:11; e.g., Phil. 2:11, 'Jesus Christ is Lord.' Ps. Sol. 17:32 describes Israel's King (Messiah) as 'Anointed Lord' (*Christos Kyrios*), which could be a mistake (or a Christian 'correction') for *Christos Kyriou*, 'Anointed of the Lord'. In the fuller form of the confession 'Jesus Christ' is a proper name. Could an earlier stage in the confession, however, have read: 'Jesus is the Anointed of the Lord', becoming 'Jesus is the Anointed Lord', and eventually 'Jesus Christ (is) Lord'?

While the title 'Lord' (*mara(n)*) is applied to Jesus, the Risen Lord, in the pre-hellenistic stage of the church's development,[1] the wide use of the *kyrios* title for divine beings (not excluding the Roman Emperor) must have been influential in popularising the Christian faith in the Lord Jesus. For the full theological implications of the title 'Lord' as applied to Jesus, see below on v. 13.

shall be saved: See above on 1:16.

10. For man believes: inward faith puts a man right with God; confession of that faith brings him to salvation.

11 takes up again the closing verse of the testimony text from Isa. 28:16. St Paul alters the quotation from 'whoever believes, etc.' to 'No one who believes, etc.' thus emphasising the universality of 'righteousness' by faith.

put to shame: See above on 9:33.

12. repeats the thought of 3:22, the central plank in the Pauline 'Gospel'.

bestows his riches: lit., 'abounding wealth'.

13. Jl 2:32 (LXX 3:5). Note how St. Paul can, without comment, equate the Lord of the New Covenant with the Lord of the Old. For this important aspect of the development of New Testament Christology, consult D. E. H. Whiteley, *The Theology of St. Paul* (Oxford, 1961), pp. 106ff. The original Hebrew means, not simply 'make appeal to Yahweh', 'invoke Yahweh', but implies that the Israelite, in so doing, places himself on Yahweh's side, professes allegiance to Yahweh, and so for Paul, the words mean 'to profess oneself a Christian'. Cf. *TWNT*, Bd. III, pp. 501. 22ff. (Note also that this passage in Joel is concerned with the 'Day of the Lord'.) The verse also contains a reference to the Remnant.

---

[1] See especially J. A. Fitzmyer, *A Wandering Aramean: Collected Aramaic Essays* (Scholars Press, 1979), pp. 115–42, 87–90.

ISRAEL'S SIN INEXCUSABLE

10:14–21

These verses meet an objector's argument that Israel can hardly be
held responsible for rejecting the Gospel when she had never even
heard it or known about its meaning (God's universal salvation).
This is answered, first by a quotation from Ps. 19:4 ('their voice'
must refer to the preaching of the earliest Christian (apostolic)
missionaries), and then by two quotations from Dt. 32:21 and Isa.
65:1–2.

Verses 14–15 consist of four rhetorical questions arranged in a
'logical chain' (Cranfield, who compares 5:3–5, 8:29, 30 and v. 17
of the present chapter), where each question, after the first, repeats
a word from the previous question to produce a logical sequence of
thought. The 'chain', in fact, resembles closely the Hebrew poetic
device known as 'step-parallelism' (cf. C. F. Burney, *The Poetry of
our Lord*, p. 90), and, indeed, this Pauline rhetorical sequence of
questions could be so explained, with the final question at v. 15,
reinforced by Isa. 52:7, forming a climax to the whole. Paul is
thereby stating the preconditions of Christian confession of Jesus as
Lord—*belief*, the essential first step, depending on hearing the
gospel; hearing on the preaching of it; and the latter—the 'bottom
line'—depending on its apostolic authority ratified by Scripture:
'How lovely are the feet of the bringers of good news'—a reference
to the first Christian emissaries or missionaries sent out to the
Gentile world, including Paul's own apostolate.

how are men to call upon him: Following on vs. 12–13 ('all who
call on him', 'everyone who calls on the name of the Lord'), the
plurals are best understood as impersonal, 'men'. Others (cf. SH,
Cranfield) take them to refer to the Jews as at 9:32, 10:2, 3. (Are
the two views mutually exclusive, 'men', 'all men', includes 'all
Jews'?)

in whom they have not believed: *NEB* 'in whom they had no
faith'. If the plural verbs referred exclusively to the Jews, the aorist
could be interpreted as referring to the historic unbelief of the Jews,
their rejection of Christ as a people. More probably, however, the
aorist is ingressive (cf. Zahn, Käsemann), 'in whom they have not
come to believe', '*an den man nicht gläubig geworden ist*' (Käsemann).

of whom they have never heard: So also *NEB* 'in one they had
never heard of'. The use of *akouein* with the genitive of the person
and meaning 'to hear tell of' is by no means unknown (cf. Liddell
and Scott 54, Bauer, s.v. 3b, and contrast Cranfield, p. 534.) To
render 'how are they to believe in him whom they have never

heard', and to understand the words to refer to the hearing of Christ 'speaking in the message of the preachers' seems forced and unnatural.

15. unless they are sent: how could there be any to proclaim if they were not commissioned to go forth and preach? The 'sending' refers to the official commissioning and despatching of the mission-aries, Christians or, before them, Jews (cf. Ac. 13:3).

as it is written . . . good news!: There follows a non-LXX version and adaptation of Isa. 52:7 (cf. Nah. 1:15, LXX 2:1) describing the *apostoloi* or messengers of the gospel in the figurative language of the ancient prophets: 'feet' symbolise the bringers of glad tidings; 'beautiful' is probably best interpreted as meaning 'timely'—'how *timely* are the bringers of glad tidings' (cf. Käsemann, p. 282). The quotation is particularly apposite in this context, since the original referred to the messengers of the Return and the salvation of Israel.

16. they have not all heeded the gospel: the 'not all' stands in contrast to the statement at verse 11 about 'everyone who believes'. The 'not all', by *litotes*, really means 'only very few' (cf. 3:3 and 9:6, 27f.): 'heeded' (*hypēkousan*) gives a word-play with v.14 'hear' (*akousōsin*) and 16b 'what he has heard (*akoē*) from us', underlining the thought that the response to the 'good news' is not just hearing it, but 'heeding it', by an obedient faith. (Heb. *šama'* means both 'to hear', 'to (hear and) understand' and 'to (hear and) obey'.) The following quotation from Isa. 53:1 stresses the universality of unbelief. Such unbelief is in accordance with *OT* prophecy. A negative response is common to both prophetic and apostolic witness.

17. so faith comes from what is heard: This verse is a brief concluding summary, and not just a repetition of verse 14. Cf. J. Munck, *Christ and Israel: An Interpretation of Romans 9–11* (Fortress Press, 1967), p. 93, and p. 93, n. 131, for a survey of interpretations of this verse. The verse takes up the object in Isaiah quotation ('Who hath believed our *report?*' A D *akouē hemōn*), but with the suggestion of a Hebraic connotation for *akouē*, LXX 'report'. As Billerbeck noted (SB, Bd. III, p. 283) *akouē* here, as at 1 Th. 2:13 (cf. also Gal. 3:2, 5, Heb. 4:2) suggests Heb. *šemu'ah* a term in rabbinical usage for *doctrina*. We are to think here of the Christian 'doctrine' of salvation. Faith comes from 'indoctrination' (in the best sense of the word).

18. This verse meets the objection that some may not have heard the Gospel ('their words', i.e. 'about Christ', verse 17). This is ruled out by a quotation of Ps. 19:4 (LXX), stressing the universal proclamation of the Gospel; it has gone out, through the apostolic mission, to the ends of the earth. All Jews are acquainted with it.

Cf. Munck, *op. cit.*, pp. 96ff. (the world-wide mission to the Jews has been completed). Cf. Col. 1:6, 23.

19-21. Again, I ask, did Israel not understand? In the light of the answer to this question given in the two quotations which follow (from Dt. 32:21, Isa. 65:1), the question must mean 'Did Israel fail to understand the universal nature of the Gospel (cf. verse 12, and Dodd, *ad loc.*)? They ought to have understood in view of the words of Moses, first of all declaring that God would stir up their jealousy against a 'non-nation', and enrage them against a people with no understanding. Isaiah even went further, in his declaration that God would be found by those who did not seek him, and reveal himself to those who did not, like the Jews, enquire after him. At v. 21 Isa. 65:2 follows closely on Isa. 65:1: God's mercy had never been withheld from Israel, although she had shown herself to be an 'unruly people who went their evil way' (Isa. 65:2, *NEB*).

THE REMNANT

11:1-10

God has not rejected Israel, Paul himself is living proof of this, and there are others. Those who have not been brought into the Church are those who, for the present, at any rate, are 'hardened'. Now, however, as in the past history of Israel, although the masses are 'hardened', there is a remnant which will be saved.

1-2. rejected: a direct allusion to the language of 1 Kgd. 12:22 (LXX) and Ps. 93:14 (LXX); cf. also Jer. 31:37 (LXX 38:37). The proof that Israel has not been 'thrust away' is Paul himself, an Israelite of Israelites (cf. his boast at Phil. 3:3ff.). This personal form of appeal and apologetic—it is also a form of witnessing—continues similar personal references, e.g., at 9:3, 10:1. The Benjamites were the Israelite 'aristocracy'; cf. Finkelstein, *The Pharisees* (1938), 1, p. 39; cf. also SB, Bd. III, pp. 286ff. The variant reading 'inheritance' (*klēronomia*) for 'people', supported by P^{46}, G and some Old Latin mms., is clearly a text influenced by the parallel at Ps. 93:14 (LXX).

2. whom he foreknew: practically his chosen people. Cf. 8:29 for this familiar biblical expression, probably selected here to suggest that the divine 'election' still held good—for the new 'Israel'.

of Elijah: lit., 'in (the case of) Elijah'; a rabbinic usage. Cf. Cant. R. i.6.

how he pleads with God against Israel: The verb here (*entynchanei*) means, lit., 'bring a complaint' to God against Israel (1 Mac. 8:32, 11:25; cf. 1 Enoch 9:3).

3. An abridged quotation, practically verbatim, from LXX of 3 Kgd. 19:10, 14. Does Paul mean to compare himself with Elijah, as also being the Remnant in person? If so, he soon corrects himself.

4. What is God's reply: lit. 'What does the "oracle" (3 Kgd. 19:18) say to him?' The word for 'reply', 'oracle' (*chrēmatismos*) occurs only here in the *NT*, but also at 1 Clem. XVII. 5 (2 Mac. 2:4, 11:17). This rare and solemn word clearly is consciously selected to give prominence to the authoritative word of God that follows. Cf. further, A. T. Hanson in *NTS*, XIX (1972–3), pp. 300–2. The words of the 'oracle' are an adapted quotation from 3 Kgd. 19:18. While the LXX reads 'You (i.e. Elijah) will leave behind (as a remnant) seven thousand men', Paul agrees with the MT in reading 'I (God) have left over' (*RSV* 'kept'), adding 'for myself', thus specially emphasising the divine initiative in the survival of the 'remnant', and preparing the way for vv. 5ff, where he draws the parallel with the Christian Remnant as one 'chosen by grace', and not on grounds of their own merit. (Since the plain meaning of 3 Kgd. 19:18 is that it was by their meritorious loyalty to Yahweh and refusal to worship Baal, which was the real reason for the emergence of the seven thousand as a 'remnant', the parallel could be considered to break down on this central point. But see below on v. 6.) The 'seven thousand' who were faithful is probably best understood symbolically as a 'perfect number', a multiple of the golden number 'seven' (see Cranfield, p. 547). The reference to 'men' betrays a characteristically oriental attitude (cf. Mk 6:44).

5. A remnant chosen by grace: The fundamental common element for St Paul between the incident recorded at 3 Kgd. 19:18 and the Christian 'remnant' is that the 'sorting out' or 'election' of the 'remnant', in both cases, was solely due to the action of divine grace, and not, in any way, based on meritorious 'works' (cf. v. 4 above, 'I (God) have kept for myself . . .').

The contrary and contemporary Jewish view finds classical expression at 2 Esd. 7:17ff. (especially verses 17 and 24): the 'ungodly who shall perish' (at the Last Judgement) are those who '. . . have been unfaithful to his statutes, and have not performed his works' (*RSV*). It is 'works of the law' (Gal. 2:16, Rom. 3:20) which alone count. It is true, Qumran introduced an important modification: divine mercy (*ḥesed*, occasionally *ḥanina* 'grace') emerges as an important factor in the final reckoning, but there is never any suggestion that it could outweigh or cancel out failure in 'law-righteousness' (cf. *TWNT* Bd. IX, pp. 377f.). For Paul 'grace alone', but always conjoined with Christian faith (*TWNT*, Bd. IX, p. 385), is the sole Christian foundation of all life and morals, and takes the place of the traditional Jewish foundation, the Law and 'works of the law'. The latter were to be superseded by the righteousness that comes from faith (9:30) or 'the obedience of faith' or 'the work of faith' (1 Th. 1:3, 2 Th. 1:11).

6. grace would no longer be grace: This verse states unequivocally the Pauline doctrine: grace for Paul is not true grace unless it is totally unmerited grace. Any compromise such as the Qumran concession, i.e., of grace or mercy vouchsafed for some failure in 'law-righteousness', was still not true grace. For St Paul human nature was incapable, on its own, of fulfilling the requirements of the law of ordinances. (cf. chapter 7 above). A number of ms. authorities, supported by Syr. and some early Fathers (e.g., Chrysostom, Theophylact) expand in various ways; e.g. Chrysostom (= $\aleph$ cBΨ): 'but if it were of works, it is no longer grace, since works are no longer works (*sic*).' Most modern versions and all critical editions and commentaries since Westcott and Hort treat the addition as a gloss. (Weymouth gives it in the margin.) This is not surprising, since the last clause 'otherwise work is no more work' (*AV*) is virtually unintelligible as it stands. Could the clause be a corruption of 'since (i.e., where there *is* grace) there is no need of work(s)' (reading *tou ergou* or *tōn ergōn* for *to ergon*, and for this use of '*ergon esti*', Liddell and Scott, s.v. *ergon*, p. 683, IV 1b)? The whole sentence, beginning 'But if it be of works . . .', is parallel in structure and content to the previous sentence 'And if by grace, etc.': both together have an effective rhetorical repetition of 'no longer' (*ouketi*). Bengel argued (p. 148) for the originality of this 'addition'. If we accept the above conjecture, was the original order perhaps as follows (transposing the last clause of the 'gloss' with 6b):

But if it (the Remnant) is chosen by grace, it is no longer (chosen) on the grounds of works, *since there is no longer any need for works*;

If it (is chosen) through works, then it is no longer grace, *since grace is (then) no longer effective as grace.*

7. Israel failed to obtain . . . the elect obtained: Cf. 9:31: *hē eklogē* is abstract for concrete, 'the selected few' (*NEB*).

hardened: cf. above. It is incorrect to stress the passive, as if Paul was avoiding any suggestion that God did the 'hardening'; indeed, the opposite is true, and the passive here could be an idiomatic Hebraic locution to avoid the use of the divine name; but it is God who is the real subject. See above, p. 27; and cf. Mk 6:52; Jn 12:40; 2 C. 3:14. 'Paul does not shrink from the conclusion that it was God's will (determined ultimately by his mercy) that this should be so, and confirms the conclusion by Old Testament quotations' (Barrett, *ad loc.*). See, further, A. Škrinjar, in *Bib.*, XI (1930), p. 295, n. 2.

8–10. Paul clinches his argument and conclusion by his customary *OT* authorities—a mixed quotation from the Pentateuch (MT + LXX) (Dt. 29:4), supported by the Prophets (Isa. 29:10) and the Writings (Ps. 69:22ff., 35:8). The quotations are woven together, *charaz-fashion* (see above, p. 56) from Torah, Prophets and Writings, thus providing a solemnly authoritative climax and scriptural coping-stone to the argument. The first word from Dt. 29:4 is a condemnation of Israel, the second ('And David says') is virtually an invocation of David, pronouncing a curse on Israel. The imagery in the quotation should not be pressed.

9. their feast: lit. 'their Table (*trapeza*). The Psalm quotation (69:22–24) which follows, and in which this key word is the subject, 'their Table', is again adapted from the LXX. The previous verse of the Psalm (v. 21) reads 'They (the psalmist's enemies) put poison in my food . . . May their table be a snare to them' (*NEB*). The psalmist's petition—it is really an imprecation—is that, in retribution (so LXX) for his foes' attempts to poison his food, their feasts should likewise spring such a 'trap' a 'snare' upon them, perhaps also by poisoned food. (The use of poisoned snares for trapping wild animals was no doubt well known.) Cf. also Ps. 35:7–8. The quotation in Paul is also an imprecation on the unbelieving mass of the Jewish people: but how are we to understand 'Table' in the context of this part of Romans? A literal meaning 'their food', but referring in general terms to 'the good things they enjoy' (Cranfield), seems jejune; 'table-fellowship' (Barrett), or 'Table' in a cultic sense (Käsemann), have also been suggested, but in any of these senses it is difficult to see the connection of the subject 'Table' with its predicate (cf. Käsemann, p. 289). It does less than justice to Paul's use of the Old Testament to suggest that he simply understood these verses 'in a general way suggestive of the divine hardening', and that verses 22–23 are quoted only for the sake of v. 24a (Heb. 23a). (Cranfield). Paul expands the quotation beyond the LXX or MT to read 'May their Table become a trap and a snare (net)' or 'and for prey' (*eis thēran*), and, in doing so, I suggest, is thinking of some way in which the Jews might be trapped and caught in the toils of their 'Table'. Was he thinking of their festivals or their food restrictions? At Mal. 1:7, Ezek. 41:22, 44:16 the 'Table of the Lord' refers to the Temple cultus in Jerusalem, the 'altar' or sacrificial system of the Second Temple still operative in A.D. 57 when Romans was written, and which was, in fact, along with the Torah, the very heart and soul of Judaism. Cf. also SB, Bd. III, p. 289, for 'Table' in the sense of 'Altar'. SH note (p. 316) that Lipsius (who is not otherwise given to theories of interpretation) suggests that verses 9–10 are a marginal gloss *after the fall of Jerusalem*; Zahn also

believed that there was such a reference here but to the *future*
judgement on the Temple and Jerusalem. Munck (*Christ and Israel*,
p. 116) thinks it can be assumed that others within the period of
early Christianity also interpreted these verses of the fall of the
Temple. May not Paul actually himself here, like his Master, be
making a prediction of the fate of the Temple and its cultus? The
words are then not a *vaticinium post eventum*, but an actual imprecation on the Jerusalem Temple and its worship as the place where
ethnic Judaism would be finally trapped and become a prey (*eis
thēran*), meeting their downfall and their nemesis—as actually did
happen in A.D. 70, when the survivors of the siege were literally
trapped in the Temple precincts and became a 'prey' to the Roman
legions.

10. bend their backs for ever: The figure of speech may be
variously interpreted in this context, perhaps of an oppressed people
suffering under foreign yoke. We should probably render 'bend
their backs *continually*', i.e. without respite, rather than 'for ever';
the *RSV* of Ps. 69:23 rendering the MT, reads 'make their loins
tremble continually.' An imprecation by Paul for God to enslave or
oppress with grievous burdens his ancient people *for ever*, would
exclude the possibility of the eventual redemption of Israel which
Paul cherished (11:26ff.).

THE REJECTION OF ISRAEL IS NOT FINAL

11:11–24

11. stumbled so as to fall: the first figure was possibly suggested
by *skandalon* (verse 9; 'pitfall', lit. 'stumbling block'). 'Fall' in this
context suggests final destruction ('irreversible ruin', Cranfield) in
contrast to 'stumbling', from which it is possible to recover.
Certainly *piptein* = *naphal* can be used of a fatal fall, to 'fall in
battle', and hence figuratively 'to go to ruin', 'to perish'. But the
verb can also mean 'to remain prostrate' (*liegen bleiben*, Käsemann),
or 'to fall away' 'to defect', and this latter sense would accord well
with the following *paraptōma* (cognate with *piptein*), a word which,
etymologically means, lit., 'falling from the right way', 'a false step'
(cf. Liddell and Scott, s.v., p. 1322). The noun comes to have the
more general meaning of 'transgression', 'sin' (cf. especially the
plural *paraptōmata*, Mt. 6:15, Rom. 4:25, Eph. 2:1, etc.), but the
noun is especially appropriate in its context here in this verse.
By no means: stronger, 'Heaven forbid!' (cf. above, p. 54).
to make Israel jealous: recalling 10:19 and Dt. 32:21. Cf. Ac.
13:45ff.

12ff. For the style of these verses (parallelism, balance of clauses, etc.), cf. note on 5:16.

12. riches for the world: i.e. an enrichment of (for) the world; cf. 10:12.

their failure: *Hēttēma* is a rare word in biblical Greek (Isa. 31:8 and 1 C. 6:7 only, and otherwise unattested in profane Greek). At Isa. 31:8 LXX it mistranslates Heb. *mas* 'forced labour' ('. . . his young warriors shall be put to forced labour', *NEB*) as if it were Heb. *mas* (Job 6:14) or *massah* lit. 'melting, failing' and so 'despairing'. Since SH it has been taken to mean 'defeat', but, as has been frequently observed, it seems related by contrast to *plēroma*, 'fullness, full inclusion' (cf. Käsemann, p. 292), so that the sense of 'a falling short', e.g., of prescribed norms or requirements, and hence (with no doubt a religious or ethical connotation) 'failure', the meaning of the noun at 1 C. 6:7 (cf. *NEB*). The Vulgate *diminutio*, in the sense of the 'falling-off' (*NEB*) of Israel, is possible, if not actually with reference to numbers, and cannot be excluded from the intention of the text. Cf. 1 En. 103:9, 15.

how much more: for this argument *a minori ad maius*, cf. 5:9.

full inclusion: cf. Rom. 11:25 where the same word (*plēroma*), applied to the Gentiles, supports the interpretation: 'until the full number of the Gentiles comes in'. The meaning, then, presumably is that, if the deficiencies (failures) of Israel enriched the Gentile world, their full inclusion—i.e. full enrolment in the Church, the Kingdom of God—will bring an even vaster increase of wealth to the world.

However, the word has also eschatological overtones (cf. the parallels at verse 15); some take it as synonymous with *teleiōsis* ('consummation'). There may also be hellenistic philosophical parallels; see J. B. Lightfoot, *St. Paul's Epistles to the Colossians and to Philemon* (London, ⁸1886), pp. 255ff. For the eschatological-apocalyptic use of the word, perhaps in a sense like 'their Final Inclusion' (in the People of God), see J. Jeremias, *Parables of Jesus*, trans. S. H. Hooke (London, 1962), p. 152, n. 92; D. W. Vischer, *Das Geheimnis Israels* (1950), (above, p. 122), p. 120, assumes that Paul is using the terminology of the money market. Israel's debt or loss was the enrichment of the world. When the whole debt is paid up, and Israel makes its full contribution to mankind's spiritual resources, then what an enrichment that will be! Such an interpretation, however, seems forced and artificial. On the whole, 'full' (or 'final') inclusion, or even 'final total' or 'total number' (see, further, note on 11:25 below), is preferable.

13. to you Gentiles: i.e. to the Gentile component of the Roman Church, and, no doubt, through them to the whole Gentile world.

V. 13 is an aside to the Gentile members of the Roman church, in which the Apostle, while reminding them of his peculiar apostolate to the Gentiles, declares that he magnifies this office only to make his own flesh and blood jealous, in the hope that he might save some of them: lit., 'To you Gentiles, however, I say: in so far as I am, indeed, Apostle of Gentiles, I magnify my ministry, if perchance I might make my own flesh and blood jealous and save some of them.'

magnify: I bring my office (as Gentile apostle) to honour (see Bauer). 'I make much of my office (to see if I may provoke to envy my own flesh and blood . . .)' (Barrett).

14. my fellow Jews: (see *NEB*: 'men of my own race'); better, and more literally, with Barrett, 'my own flesh and blood'.

save some: Paul confidently expected the eventual salvation of 'all Israel' (v. 26), but, at this stage in his ministry, his expectation is limited to saving 'some'. Cf. 1 C. 9:22 for the lengths to which Paul was prepared to go 'to save some'. One such individual was Crispus, the leader of the synagogue in Corinth (Ac. 18:8): Zahn and others would include Sosthenes (either Crispus's colleague or successor) (cf. Ac. 18:17, 1 C. 1:1). While 'save' here means, in effect, 'to bring to the Christian faith' (Barrett), the term has also a wider connotation, and probably refers here to the eschatological 'salvation' of Israel (cf. above on 1:16).

15. rejection . . . acceptance: i.e. by God. V. 15 develops v. 12 and cf. the corresponding contrast: 'failure', 'full inclusion', which helps us to define the parallel terms. God 'accepts' (Rom. 14:3), Christ 'accepts' (Rom. 15:7) by an act of 'grace' what is 'unacceptable', in this case the apostate Israel (and likewise Christians each other (Rom. 15:7)). Cf. the gloss at Sir. 10:21: 'The fear of the Lord is the beginning of acceptance (*proslēpsis*); obduracy and pride are the beginning of rejection (*ekbolē*).'

reconciliation of the world: The abstract noun *reconciliation* (*katallagē*) occurs again only once in *Romans* (5:11), but the concept, like 'justification', is central in Pauline teaching (see especially Barrett on Rom. 5:10). SH think of it here as 'the immediate result of St Paul's ministry, which he describes elsewhere (2 C. 5:18, 19) as a ministry of reconciliation': it could also mean reconciliation of Jew and Gentile (cf. Eph. 2:16). In the present context, however, it seems more likely to refer to the reconciliation of the Gentiles ('the world') to God through Christ (cf. 5:10–12, 2 C. 5:18, 19). It is doubtful if Paul would include Jews with Gentiles in 'the world'.

life from the dead: i.e., the climax of the eschatological drama of salvation, the 'general resurrection', conceived, not as any special renewal of Israel such as that envisaged by Ezekiel (37:1–10) or

Hosea 6:2–4, but the kind of resurrection from the dead which the Targumist envisages in interpreting Hos. 6:2–4—one which, on Paul's understanding of it, was a resurrection of the faithful and elect, both Jew and Gentile. See further my article on 'The "Son of Man" Passion Sayings in the Gospel Tradition', in *ZNTW*, Bd. LX, 1969, pp. 4ff.

16. dough offered as first fruits: the reference is to the custom of the harvest offerings of the 'first fruits' of the dough, i.e. probably the first loaf baked (cf. Num. 15:17ff.). Were these 'first-fruits' popularly supposed to consecrate the rest of the dough which was thereby released for general consumption or was the idea Paul's own? The parallel at Lev. 19:23–25, where the fruits of the trees are to be regarded as 'forbidden' until an offering has been made, would tend to support the first explanation. Cf. Cranfield *ad loc*. The identity of the 'first-fruits' which 'sanctify' the whole of Israel is disputed: many take the reference to be to the Patriarchs, others the Jewish Christian community (cf. 1 C. 16:15) and others still identify with Christ himself (cf. 1 C. 15:20). The first alternative seems to be supported by the rest of the verse referring to 'the holy root' and by v. 28. But the 'root' could also be Christ or the Jewish-Christian Church. Is the Pauline figure of speech a blank cheque, as it were, which leaves interpretation free, but within the limits of these three possible alternatives? The Fathers explain the 'first-fruits' (*aparchē*) as 'Christ' on the basis of 1 C. 15:20: the figure is a not uncommon one in the *NT*, and is variously applied (e.g., Rom. 8:23, 16:5; 1 C. 16:15; 2 Th. 2:13; Jas 1:18; Rev. 14:4).

The Allegory of the Engrafted Wild Olive 11:17–24

The process here described is said to be entirely unnatural (cf. Dodd, *ad loc*.), and that this is admitted by Paul himself (verse 24). The opposite process is said to be usual: the wild olive (*agrielaios*) becomes the cultivated olive (*kallielaios*) by the engrafting on it of a cutting from a cultivated olive.

On the other hand, the engrafting of a fresh cutting from a wild olive into an old olive-tree does not seem to have been unknown, or possibly even uncommon, in the ancient world (cf. Michel, pp. 275ff., who also cites parallels from Philo for a similar figure of speech applied to Israelites and proselytes (*de Exsecr.* 6)). (See also SB, III, pp. 291ff.) Paul is building on earlier traditional figures of speech about Israel and its Gentile converts. According to Yeb. 63a (SB, *loc. cit.*) Israel had twice had a fresh cutting engrafted into it, viz. Ruth and Naomi.

Neither of these cases, however, is exactly parallel to the Pauline allegory (cf. SB *loc. cit.*) which assumes the engrafting of a wild-olive shoot into the severed branches of the old, cultivated olive, and later (verses 23–24) the grafting in again of the severed branches into the new vine-stock. The Apostle is more concerned with his allegory than with horticultural details: '. . . the verisimilitude of the metaphorical details is not important; the important thing is that the author's meaning should be quite clear' (Cranfield, p. 566).

The analogy, however artificial, is a vivid and telling one. More-over, if the Jewish-Christian congregation which formed the nucleus of the Roman Church, had its beginnings as an 'off-shoot' of the synagogue of the Olive Tree in Rome (Intro., p. 7, n. 3: *synagōgē elaias*), the allegory would be even more appropriate; cf. further, M. M. Bourke, *A Study of the Metaphor of the Olive Tree in Romans XI* (Washington, 1947).

Cf. Jer. 11:16, Hos. 14:6 where the olive tree is similarly used as a symbol of Israel and which may have inspired the Pauline allegory.

17. to share the richness of the olive tree: *mg.* 'rich root'. The word 'root' has, according to the *RSV* (possibly correctly) been scribally inserted or interpolated into the text. Textual support for *RSV* is good, and includes P[46] D* G it.[d, f, g], though the alternative, with 'root' in the text, has slightly better support. If we read 'root' in the text, the genitive must be qualitative: 'a root of fatness' = 'a fat root'; but we may also construe: 'the fat proceeding from the root'.

18. do not boast over the branches: *NEB*: 'make yourself superior to the branches'; the verb is stronger than 'give yourself airs', and more like 'bragging about your superiority'—so 'be contemptuous of'. ('become proud' (verse 20) is practically a synonymous and equally strong expression.) 'If you do find yourself "glorying" in your position' (the verb 'boast' is not necessarily used in a pejorative sense) 'then [remember—this verb has to be supplied] it is not you that supports the root, but the root that supports you.'

Were these Gentile Christians 'spiritual enthusiasts' (*pneumatikoi*), as the Corinthians at 1 C. 2:6ff.? Cf. Michel. It is very doubtful if the evidence exists to support this attractive possibility, any more than the assumption that the Gentile Christians at Rome were anti-Semitic.

19. In this question and answer style of the diatribe, the Gentile Christian 'comes back' with: 'You will then say (*ereis*), So the branches were broken off for the sake of *my* engrafting.'

20. That is true: true, indeed (*kalōs*)—Paul's reply is ironical. But Israel was cut off on account of her unbelief, while your present security ('you stand fast') is entirely due to your faith. (In that case, it is implied, you have no reason for self-glorifying.)

stand fast: the word here used (lit. 'to stand') is employed in this connection especially in a sense the opposite of that of the verb 'to fall' (i.e. 'to fail'). 'To stand (fast)' is to enjoy a state of inward stability (or security) as a Christian; passages with such a meaning are Rom. 5:2; I C. 7:37; 10:12; 2 C. 1:24; Jn 8:44. The Hebrew '*āmad* is also used in a similar figurative sense, but the Pauline term has taken on a meaning of its own in relation to the 'firmness' of the Christian in his faith and calling.

become proud: cf. 12:3, 16; cf. I Tim. 6:17. These words are quoted frequently as a *sententia* by the Fathers; they read like a sentence from the Wisdom literature.

21. neither will he spare you: We should perhaps prefer the reading of P[46] D G etc. and render (20) '. . . but stand in awe (lit. be fearful). (21) For if God did not spare the natural branches, (repeat "be fearful") lest perchance you too he will not spare'. Cf. Bengel, p. 152. 'Paul employs *mēpōs* 'lest perchance' some nine times (once only elsewhere in the New Testament).[1] As Cranfield remarks (p. 569, n. 6), 'the addition of *mēpōs* is . . . a considerable softening of Paul's categorical statement.'

22. severity: the word in Greek (*apotomia*, lit. 'severing off') carries on the figures of speech of the branches being 'lopped off': but the word, of course, is regular in the meaning 'severity', 'hardness' (the opposite of 'mildness, gentleness, kindness' as a trait of character).

22–24 prepare the way for the Pauline *mystērion*, his eschatological 'secret', now disclosed at verses 25–26. It is God's ultimate purpose, when the 'fullness of the Gentiles' is reached, that he will reverse his judgement—the rejection of Israel has been, in any case, only a partial rejection (verse 25)—and all Israel will be saved. Paul introduces this final 'mystery' by the argument that, if the wild olive could be engrafted against nature, then the cultivated plant can, by the power of God, be engrafted back into the new Israel, its own natural 'olive plant'. In customary fashion, Paul concludes and clinches his argument from Scripture (verses 26, 27, a contraction of Isa. 59:20–21 (cf. Ps. 14:7), Isa. 27:9, and Jer. 31:33–34).

24. from what is by nature a wild olive-tree: More precisely, 'from what is a natural (*NEB*, native) wild olive tree', i.e., the wild olive to which you naturally belong, in contrast to the unnatural grafting of a wild olive on a cultivated tree.

---

[1]Cf. B. M. Metzger, *A Textual Commentary on the Greek New Testament*, London, 1971, p. 526f.

COMPLETION OF GOD'S PLAN

II:25–32

25. **wise in your own conceits:** See below on 12:16 for the source
of the phrase. At verses 18 and 20 the Apostle warns his readers
against 'boasting' (18) and 'highmindedness' (20), and again at 12:16
he exhorts them 'never be conceited'. Such phrases have led
commentators to suggest that there were problems in Rome similar
to those at Corinth: *cognoscenti*, claiming special *gnōsis*, 'spiritual
enthusiasts' (*pneumatikoi*), were laying claim to special 'wisdom'.
The force of the phrase here would seem to be 'lest you have
ideas of your own about the destiny of Israel': Paul confronts their
speculations, possibly their uncharitable condemnation of the unbelieving and hostile Jews, with a divine revelation of their ultimate
destiny: everything might seem to reason to be against their
salvation—nevertheless, they would all be saved.

I want you to understand this mystery, brethren: For the
'disclosure formula' see on 1:13: Paul is seeking to emphasise what
he is about to say. *Mystērion* (*mystēria*), a word borrowed from the
religious terminology of the hellenistic mystery religions, and one
which came to enjoy a wide application in Greek philosophy, in
Jewish apocalyptic and rabbinical sources, as well as in the New
Testament and in later (or possibly contemporary) Gnostic writings.
Basic to all is the thought of a transcendental reality (*ens divinum*
or *res divina*) into which the neophyte or philosopher can somehow
be conducted or initiated. In the 'mystery' cults the central idea
seems to have been that of participation, by the initiated, in a ritual
drama, symbolising the triumph of life over death in the Nature
cycle (mythologised as the dying and rising of the 'earth deities',
Demeter, Adonis, Isis etc.), and so guaranteeing his own 'salvation'
and 'eternal life.' (See especially *TWNT* Bd. IV, pp. 813f.
Bornkamm). Unlike the closely guarded *arcana* of the mystery cults
(or of the Essenes), the 'mysteries' in Jewish apocalyptic are 'open'
or 'revealed' mysteries, and concerned, not with the 'metaphysical'
or the 'ontological', but with *historical revelations* of the divine in
the affairs of creation and of mankind. They are focussed upon a
transcendental eschatology, the coming Judgement and its sequel in a
'new heaven and a new earth' (cf. especially Dan. 2:18, 19, 27 etc.,
I En. 91:15–17, 93:2ff. etc.) In the Pauline Epistles (where the
word occurs more than twenty times) the *mystērion* is 'Christ' (cf.
Eph. 3:4), i.e., the revelation of God in Christ in the drama of
'salvation-history'; and in this 'mystery' is included (cf. verse 26

and Rom. 16:26) the reconciliation and restoration of 'the whole Israel'.

a hardening has come upon part of Israel: lit., 'has partially come to Israel'. Virtually 'a partial hardening' (*NEB*: 'this partial blindness has come upon Israel . . .'). Israel's unbelief is not a total 'obduration', but partial, only affecting some—no doubt many—'Israelites'; Paul has to allow for the many 'Israelites' who had become Christians. Cf. further, O. Glombitza, 'Apostolische Sorge. Welche Sorge treibt den Apostel Paulus zu den Sätzen Röm. 11:25ff.?', *Nov. Test.*, VII (1965), pp. 312–18.

until the full number of the Gentiles: According to the rabbis, after the Fall the precise number of mankind was decreed until the Last Judgement, and the latter could not take place till this number was complete. At 2 Esd. 4:36, Rev. 6:11, 7:4, 14:1 it is the number of the saints that has to be 'fulfilled', or 'filled up'. Here it is the number of the Gentiles (cf. 2 Bar. xxiii. 4, 5,). The term begins to be used as a semi-technical apocalyptic term in Paul (see above, p. 154).

come in: some understand 'into the Kingdom of God', and it is argued that the term 'enter' is beginning to be used thus absolutely at Mt. 7:13, 23:13, Lk. 11:52. It may be, however, that the word here is used (as so frequently in the LXX for *bō'*) in the simple sense 'has come', i.e. 'has arrived', and so 'been realised'.

26. And so all Israel will be saved: lit., 'and in this way (*houtōs*)', i.e., through the partial 'blinding' (or 'obduration') of some Israelites until the full complement of Gentiles in the Kingdom is reached. (cf. *NEB*, 'when that has happened'.) 'All Israel' here seems to imply the whole national or ethnic Israel: the statement at 9:27 about a remnant only being saved would then refer simply to a stage in Israel's salvation-history on this earth: the final salvation of all Israel will be, not on this earth by their inclusion in the Church of Christ (so SH), but at the *eschata*, the Last Judgement (cf. Cranfield *ad loc.*) Cf., however, Zahn, p. 523, n. 67a, who understands 'all Israel' to mean 'Israel as a whole', no matter whether it is represented by many individuals, or how many individual Israelites are excluded.

The Deliverer will come from Zion: In his usual style Paul sums up with a concluding scriptural quotation (or combined quotation, Isa. 59:20–21 (Ps. 14:7), 27:9 (Jer. 31:33–34)) which recalls the prophecy of the coming out of Zion of *the* Deliverer, to remove—turn away back—his impieties from Jacob; it recalls also the ancient covenant promise of forgiveness.

The first part of the prophecy ('out of Zion will come the Deliverer') seems to refer to the saving of Israel at the Parousia, Zion

being understood to mean the 'heavenly Jerusalem' (cf. Gal, 4:26,
1 Th. 1:10). The prophecy may be understood, however, from the
point of view of the prophet, to refer to the coming 'out of Israel'
of the Christ and to the redemptive 'work' of Christ on behalf of
Israel—achieving her forgiveness and inclusion in the 'New
Covenant'.

The LXX reads: 'on account of Zion', the Hebrew: 'and a
Redeemer shall come *to* Zion'. The Pauline 'variant' may come from
Ps. 13:7, 52:7 (LXX): 'O that deliverance (salvation) for Israel would
come out of Zion'. Paul may have changed the preposition in the
interests of his soteriology; Isaiah had promised that the Messiah
would come *out of* Zion and bring salvation to Israel. 'Zion' would
then most probably signify the 'City of David'. See also, L. G. da
Fonseca, in *Bib.*, IX (1928), p. 28.

Verse **27** is a combination of LXX Isa. 59:21a 'and this will be my
covenant with them', with a clause from Isa. 27:9 'when I take away
their sins' (the previous reference at 27:9 to the removal of Jacob's
sin also links the verse with Isa. 59:20–21). This *charaz* may be
Pauline, or come from a collection of messianic testimonia (cf.
Barrett). There is also an implicit allusion to the New Covenant of
Jer. 31:31–33: by the removal of Jacob's sin, Jacob who is Israel
will, finally, at the Parousia, be brought within the New Covenant
community of the Christian Church.

28. As regards the gospel . . . as regards election: i.e. from the
point of view of the gospel, from the point of view of *their* election,
'beloved for the sake of their forefathers'.

for your sake: The rejection of the Jews is for the sake of the
Gentiles. SH interpret freely 'for your sake, in order that you by
their exclusion may be brought into the Messianic Kingdom.' The
idea is more fully expressed by Paul himself earlier at verse 11:
'Through their (the Jews') trespass salvation has come to the
Gentiles.'

The sentence has a characteristic rhetorical structure of clauses:
a b c, a b c; the balanced structure is continued to verse 32. To the
rhetorical style of the Greek schools Paul has added the parallelisms
of Hebrew tradition. Cf. Barrett, *ad loc*. In vv. 28–29, 30–32 respectively, we have two sentences, vv. 28–29 in antithetic parallelism,
vv. 30–32 in synonymous parallelism, each set of verses completed
by a climactic sentence:

(28) a As regards the gospel . . . *enemies* of God, for your sake;
    b but as regards election . . . *beloved* for the sake of their
      forefathers.
(29) c For the gifts and call of God are irrevocable.

(30) a . . . *you* were once *disobedient* to God but *now have received mercy* because of their disobedience,

(31) b so *they* have now been *disobedient*, in order that . . . *they also may receive mercy*.

(32) c For God has consigned all men to disobedience, that he may have mercy upon all.

enemies of God: simply 'with reference to the Gospel, enemies'. The interpretation of the versions 'enemies of God' (cf. *NEB*) is justified, but the Pauline shorter form does not exclude the further sense of 'enemies of the Church'. So also, 'beloved' can refer to Jews who are 'beloved' even to Christians as the elect of God.

for the sake of their forefathers: cf. B. Reicke, 'Um der Väter willen (Röm. 11:28)', *Judaica*, XIV (1958), pp. 106–14.

29. the gifts and the call of God are irrevocable: While 'irrevocable' 'irreversible' are legitimate interpretations, the strict meaning of *ametamelētos* is 'not to be repented or regretted', and all instances of this relatively rare adjective (here in the New Testament and at 2 C. 7:10 only) are of an act or state of mind etc. of a personal subject about something of which he does not repent or which he does not regret. Clearly it is the latter meaning 'not to be regretted' which seems intended here, with the implication that God's gifts and call are 'not things ever to be regretted by God', or, put in the active, are 'not things God will ever regret'. The adjective retains the biblical anthropomorphism that God can 'regret' or 'rue', i.e., feel deep or bitter sorrow for an action which he could wish otherwise or even, by his divine power, reverse (cf. the use of the verb at LXX Ps. 110:4 = Heb. 7:21). The modern renderings 'irrevocable' 'irreversible' are too impersonal to convey the personal nuance of the original. The *charismata* or 'gracious gifts' (*NEB*) are Israel's special divine endowments listed at 9:4–5. Calvin took the phrase as a hendiadys, i.e. God's gracious endowments by virtue of which Israel was called. (cf. Cranfield, p. 581). That there is anything 'legalistic' (Käsemann, *juridisch*) in the phrase seems unlikely. Cf. C. Spicq, '*Ametamelētos* dans Röm. 11:29, *RB* LXVII (1960), pp. 210–19.

30–31: Paul makes effective use of the correlative clauses 'Just as (*hōsper*) . . . so (*houtōs*), especially in Romans (5:12, 19, 21; 6:4, 19; 11:30; but cf. 1 C. 11:12, 15:22, 16:1, Gal. 4:29). Cf. above on 5:12. In verses 30–31 note the balanced parallelism of clauses between the protasis and the apodosis (cf. Cranfield, p. 582).

were once disobedient to God: The Vulgate renders '(you once) did not believe in God' (*non credidistis deo*) with a parallel in verse 31, 'so they have not believed in thy mercy' (*non crediderunt in vestram misericordiam*). This seems more suitable for Gentiles rather than that, as Gentiles, they had 'disobeyed' a God they did not know; the reference in v. 31 would then be to the parallel 'disbelief' of the Jews in the Gospel. But *apeithein* in the sense 'to disbelieve' is not attested in Paul's time (See Cranfield, p. 583, n. 1.)

because of their disobedience: Moffatt, '. . . (and now you enjoy his mercy), thanks to their disobedience'. *NEB* takes the dative, *tē apeitheia*, as temporal not causal, 'in the time of their disobedience', parallel to 'when you receive mercy' (*tō hymeterō eleei*) in verse 31.

by the mercy shown to you: (*tō hymeterō eleei*) This clause is taken by the *RSV* (and many authorities) along with the following verb ('. . . by the mercy shown to you they also may receive mercy'). The word order is unusual, but may be explained as a hyperbaton construction to underline the clause: 'by the same divine mercy you Gentiles were vouchsafed, Israel will also be received'. It is possible also, however, to construe the clause with the previous verb 'they have now been disobedient', as the Vulgate does (above 162), or *NEB*, 'so now, when you receive mercy (temporal dative), they have proved disobedient', or, 'so now they have become disobedient, all for the sake of the mercy shown to you' (dative of advantage) (so Dibelius, *op. cit.*, Käsemann, p. 303). The clause then corresponds to the earlier clause 'because of their disobedience'.

31. they also may receive mercy: *mg.*: add 'now'. At verse 25 Paul seems to speak of the final salvation of Israel as still lying in the future; and this makes the reading of 'now' here difficult; this was felt by a number of scribes who omitted the adverb, P[46] A D G, etc. We would expect the adverb *pote*, 'some future day', to correspond to this adverb in the parallel clauses, in verse 30, and some mss. read *hysteron*, 'later' for 'now'.

The 'now' is, however, the more difficult reading. Paul could be contrasting the former disobedience of the Gentiles, who have, through Jewish apostasy, come to enjoy a present mercy, with the present apostate Jewry, to whom, however, the door of mercy is always open, even now: '. . . in order that God might show mercy, to them too—now!'

32. consigned: the figure is a military one; cf. Ps. 77:62 (LXX): 'He gave his people over unto the sword'. 'Used (in this verse in Romans) with the pregnant sense of giving over so that there can be no escape' (SH). For a similar figurative use, cf. Gal. 3:22. The literal meaning of the verb is 'to imprison' (1 Mac. 5:5), then in general of the 'delivering up', synonymous with *paradidōmi*. The figurative sense, of 'being delivered up captive to', is clearly intended by St Paul in both passages where he uses the term. The sense here is: 'All men without exception were, as it were, "locked up in unbelief" that God might show his mercy to all.'

all men: should we interpret in terms of 'universalism', i.e. every single individual without exception, or as 'all', looked at collectively, like the phrase 'fullness of the Gentiles', or 'all Israel'? SH is quite definite: 'The reference is not here any more than elsewhere to the final salvation of every individual' (p. 339). So too is Dodd, but from the opposite point of view: 'Whether or not . . . Paul himself drew the "universalist" conclusion, it seems that we must draw it from his premises.' (p. 184) The point has been exhaustively debated (cf. Käsemann, p. 303, whose own view is not immediately obvious to the reader). Cranfield (p. 588) seeks to maintain both positions, but a compromise between 'universalism', the salvation by God's mercy, of every man, and 'the final exclusion of some from the embrace of God's mercy' (Cranfield, *ibid.*) is impossible: this must be an either/or decision. Dodd's argumentation, on the basis of a survey of related Pauline passages, seems convincing: Paul meant the salvation of every human being from the universal slavery of sin and death.

DOXOLOGY

11:33–36

Verses 33–36 are described as a *Hymnus* ('hymn') by Michel. They are, in fact, more of the nature of a concluding doxology (familiarly Pauline, cf. Rom. 16:25) cast in *OT* language (verses 34–35 combine elements from Isa. 40:13; Job 15:8; Jer. 23:18; Job 41:11), and continue the 'poetic' style of the section. The outburst is prompted by St Paul's having just fully revealed the 'mystery' of verse 25, the divine purpose for Israel, salvation through an apostasy serving God's purpose for the Gentiles. 'God works in a mysterious way his wonders to perform'.

33. the depth of: cf. H. M. Dion, 'La Notion paulinienne de "Richesse de Dieu" ', *Sciences Ecclésiastiques*, XVIII (1966), pp. 139–48.

riches and wisdom: some prefer to make 'wisdom' and knowledge depend on 'wealth': '. . . the depth of God's wealth both of wisdom and knowledge'. Most modern interpreters tend to take 'wealth' independently, meaning all the infinite resources of God, in goodness (cf. for this figure of speech, Rom. 2:4; 9:23; 10:12.)

34. For who has known . . . counsellor: agrees exactly with LXX. Isa. 40:13 except for the Pauline *gar* (for). Cf. Sir. 42:21 '. . . he needs no one to give him advice.' Cf. also 1 En. 14:22.

35. given a gift to him . . . repaid: This Pauline quotation appears to be a rendering, quite independent of the LXX, of Job 41:11a (MT

41:3a). (The addition of this sentence at Isa. 40:14 is clearly an interpolation from Romans.) The verb *prodidonai* is regularly used meaning 'to give beforehand, pay in advance', but are the EVV right to give the verb the meaning here 'to give a gift'? Could the sense not be 'Who has ever advanced him a loan (*proedōken*) to be repaid?' Cf. the somewhat free rendering of the *Jerusalem Bible*: 'Who could ever give him anything or lend him anything?' 'The purpose of the quotation is to underline the impossibility of man's putting God in his debt.' (Cranfield). Such 'bankers' language might be especially familiar in Rome. The answer to this rhetorical question is obviously 'No-one', and v. 36 then explains why: 'For from him and through him and to him are all things.' Cf. Job 41:11b, LXX, AV [in 'Stoic' phraseology (cf. Cranfield)].

36. The formula 'from-through-to' is said to be a Pauline adaptation of a hellenistic prayer (cf. Michel, *ad loc*.) Michel claims that Paul avoids the mystical 'in him'. God is the Creator, Redeemer, and the eschatological God of Creation and Redemption; cf. 1 C. 8:6. The threefold form ('from-through-to') is reflected in the 'riches-wisdom-knowledge', and in the threefold question in verses 34–35—an illuminating example of St Paul's rhetorical composition in a 'hymnic' passage.

PRACTICAL EXHORTATIONS 12:1–15:13

There follows Paul's concluding *paraenesis*—practical exhortations based, for the most part, on the doctrine of the Epistle; they are applications of the fundamental tenets of the doctrine of justification *sola fide* and the 'life in Christ'. The central idea is that of the peace and concord of the Church in the world. The same type of *paraenesis*, characteristically Pauline, is found in 1 Th. 4, 2 Th. 3:6ff., Gal. 5, Col. 3 and Eph. 4.

CHURCH MEMBERSHIP

12:1–8

1. I appeal . . . by the mercies of God: It is doubtful if 'appeal' or 'implore' (*NEB*) or 'beseech' (*RV*) convey the exact nuance of *parakalein* in this context: this is the beginning of the Pauline *paraenesis*, the apostolic homily that flows from the apostolic doctrine, the appeal to awakened Christian consciences, encouraging them towards Christian behaviour, comforting, admonishing, rebuking them. In this context 'I exhort' is no doubt closest to the original meaning (so Cranfield) but it lacks the urgency of the Greek verb: perhaps 'I call upon and enjoin you . . .'. In the injunctions that follow Paul is not issuing moral advice or admonition, but speaking 'in the power of the Spirit' (cf. Rom. 15.19, Ac. 11.23–24, and see *TWNT* Bd. v, pp. 794ff.). The accompanying formula, 'by the mercies of God', may mean little more than: 'I enjoin you, for the love of God, to present yourselves' . . .; but cf. Barrett, pp. 230ff. The 'exhortation' to obedience is consequential on the Christian experience of the 'mercies of God'. Alternatively, we may explain that here and at verse 3 ('. . . by the grace given to me I bid everyone') it is Paul, the Apostle to the Gentiles, who is speaking, but in both cases he declares that it is by the mercy and grace of God alone, which so exceptionally has been shown to him, that he can so charge his hearers.

your bodies: cf. 6:13. Paul means their *whole selves*, but his choice of term perhaps reminds his readers that they are still 'in the body'.

living sacrifice: this may imply a contrast with the 'dead' sacrifices of 'irrational' worship, i.e. the dead bodies of sacrificial animals (cf. SH). Cf. Rom. 6:13 (cf. Michel, *ad loc.*); and further, P. Seidensticker, *Lebendiges Opfer (Röm. 12:1). Ein Beitrag zur Theologie des Apostels Paulus (Neutest. Abhand.*, xx, Münster, 1954).

For the Pauline use of the language of the altar, see above on 3:25 (pp. 59f., 63f.) SH note the metaphorical use St Paul makes of sacrificial language at Phil. 2:17, 4:18 (cf. Lev. 1:9, 2 C. 2:14, 16, Rom. 15:16, and cf. 1 Pet. 2:2–5. Such language was not unfamiliar in contemporary hellenistic writers: thus Philo, *De spec. leg.* 1.209: '. . . the soul which honours the (Supreme) Being (*to on*) ought to honour him not irrationally (*alogōs*), but with knowledge and reason'. The *Corpus Hermeticum* 1.31 contains the petition to God to receive 'holy, rational sacrifices from a soul and heart stretching out to thee' (cf. Käsemann, p. 313). Cf. also 13:31 (cited by Dodd, *The Interpretation of the Fourth Gospel*, p. 437). The expression 'rational sacrifice' (*logikē thysia*) corresponds to 'living sacrifice' . . . (lit.) 'your rational worship' (*logikēn latreian*). A close parallel to this verse and to Phil. 4:18 also occurs in the Test. Levi 3, where the angels are said to 'offer to the Lord a sweet-smelling savour, a reasonable and bloodless offering' (*logikēn kai anaimakton prosphoran*, trans. Charles). The idea of such 'spiritual worship' is prominent in the Qumran *Hodayoth*[1] and *Manual of Discipline*[2]

---

[1] Cf. J. Becker, *Das Heil Gottes: Heils- und Sündenbegriffe in den Qumrantexten und im Neuen Testament* (1964), pp. 129ff.

[2] See my *Scrolls and Christian Origins*, pp. 42f., Millar Burrows, *The Dead Sea Scrolls*, New York, 1955, p. 383.

'offerings of the lips like a true sweet-smelling savour and a perfect way of life as a free-will offering pleasing (to God)'

holy and acceptable: That 'holy' means no more than 'open to God' and is without an ethical connotation is maintained by Käsemann (against Cranfield). The ethical dimension, however, of such Christian 'sacrificial' offerings of themselves is central, and *Corpus Hermeticum* 12. 23 expresses this negatively in its simple statement: 'the service of God is one thing, to refrain from evil'. The ethical character of Christian 'spiritual worship' is brought out beautifully in the *Odes of Solomon* (No. 20, ed. J. H. Charlesworth, Oxford, 1973):

The offering of the Lord is righteousness,
Anc purity of heart and lips.
Offer thy inward being faultlessly . . .

spiritual worship: cf. *NEB*: 'the worship offered by mind and heart'; and *mg.*: '. . . for such is the worship which you, as rational creatures, should offer.' 'Spiritual worship' (*logikē latreia*) is said to refer in hellenistic literature to the act of spiritual thanksgiving which replaced the offering or sacrifice in early forms of worship (so Michel). 'Spiritual' seems the best rendering, provided we include the worship of all that is highest in man—mind, spirit, will. It is possible too that the word had associations, among Roman 'spiritual' enthusiasts (the *pneumatikoi*), with a 'higher life' above the physical; and this could account for Paul's choice of the term 'bodies' to emphasise that it is the whole man, in his bodily life, that is the holy and acceptable offering.

This 'spiritualising' of Christian 'worship' and the metaphorical use of 'liturgical' language, in particular the language of sacrifice, does not, in any respect, render Christian worship proper, including sacramental worship, redundant. It might do so for a Stoic philosopher, but never for anyone brought up, like Paul, within a Jewish religious tradition. But it does bring the whole of the secular world, in which the Christian lives, within the sphere of the sacral: he has now no 'secular' life, i.e., a life apart from the 'spiritual worship' of God. This becomes a new, transformed life, as the next verse states.

2. conformed . . . transformed: note the Greek distinction between *schēma* (outer (passing) fashion) and *morphē* (inner transformation, and in Platonic thought the 'real'). Cf. SH and J. B. Lightfoot, *Epistle to the Philippians* (London, [12]1898), pp. 130ff. This distinction has recently been questioned (Cranfield, pp. 606ff.), and perhaps too much emphasis has been placed on *schēma* and its cognates as implying outward and transient change: certainly *metaschēmatizein* can also be used of inward change (Phil.

3:21). But *schēma* and *morphē* (and their cognate verbs) cannot be regarded as 'simply synonymous'. There is a fundamental difference between the two words: thus Trench (*Synonyms of the New Testament*, [8]1906 p. 246) explained, '. . . if I were to change a Dutch garden into an Italian this would be *metaschēmatismos*: but if I were to transform a garden into something wholly different, as into a city, this would be *metamorphōsis*.' So in our verse Christians are not 'to fall in with' i.e. to be conformed to this present world, e.g., by 'falling in with its lusts' (1 Pet. 1:14), but to be 'transmuted, transmogrified, metamorphosed', totally changed into a different mode of being, that of the 'newness of mind' of the new *aiōn*, under the reign of the Risen Christ. This 'transubstantiation' of the Christian's whole being has very probably baptismal associations (cf. Käsemann, p. 314).

world: *mg.*, '*age*', i.e. this present evil age under the dominion of Satan and the powers of evil.

renewal of your mind, that you may prove: the second clause may be consequential or purposive, more probably the latter. The object of such spiritual dedication and transformation is to enable the Christian to discover, by a process of trial and error ('testing'), the good, well-pleasing, perfect will of God.

It is *the mind* in which this inner 'transformation' takes place; and this is in keeping with the rational or 'spiritual' nature of our service. Cf. Heb. 5:14 ('. . . *perceptions* . . . trained by long use to discriminate between good and evil') and Phil. 1:9–10: 'love' which grows richer 'in *knowledge* and *insight* of every kind' bringing 'the gift of true discrimination' (*NEB*). True dedication of spirit is to engage powers of mind, in the quest for perfection, or rather for the perfect will of God for us. Cf. Mk 12:30. See also H. E. Stoessel, 'Notes on Rom. 12:1–2: The Renewal of the Mind and Internalising the Truth', *Interpretation*, XVII (1963), pp. 161–75.

3. For by the grace given to me: cf. the opening of verse 1. The two phrases are parallel.

every one among you: there are no exceptions.

to think of himself . . . judgement: no English translation can bring out the word-play in the original *phronein* ('to think'), *hyperphronein* ('to think overmuch of oneself'), *sōphronein* ('to be sober-minded', not only in one's self-esteem, but in the sense also of leading a righteous, godly and sober life). Cf. Phil. 2:2–3.

each according to the measure of faith: The meaning of these words has been endlessly debated, and a consensus of interpretation is no more likely nowadays than it was in patristic or Reformation exegesis, a situation which could point to a 'primitive error' in the transmitted text, although there are no significant variants. Objections can be made to all the traditional options (see Cranfield, pp. 613ff., for a detailed survey). The two most widely adopted are (a) the measure (amount) of 'faith', *pistis* in the familiar Pauline sense of 'justifying faith', *fides qua creditur*; (b) the degree of the divine gift of 'faith', the latter in the sense of *pistis* at 1 C. 12:9, 13:2, as a charisma, a 'power given by God to do certain things (for example, to remove mountains)' (Barrett, p. 235), i.e., a 'miracle-working faith' (Cranfield).

The main objection to both views is convincingly stated by Cranfield: '. . . then the implication would be that a Christian is to think of himself more highly than he thinks of his fellow-Christian who has a smaller quantity of faith . . . It is surely extremely unlikely that Paul intended to imply this; for such an intention would scarcely be consistent with . . . vv. 4ff.' (p. 614). Cranfield then argues for the meaning 'a standard' (by which to estimate oneself), namely, his 'faith' i.e. *fides qua creditur*, which 'is really to recognise that Christ Himself . . . is the One by whom alone one must measure oneself and also one's fellow-men' (p. 616). But 'standard of faith (in Christ)' cannot simply be equated with 'standard of Christ Himself'. Pallis, *ad loc.*, takes the phrase in a passive sense: 'the measure of that which has been entrusted to us by God', i.e. to the limit of the capacities we have been entrusted with (by God), Lat. *fideicommissum*; cf. Polybius v. xli. 2: 'This Hermeias was a Carian who had been set over the affairs of Seleucus, Antiochus's brother, who had committed this trust *(pistis)* into his hands.' Could *pistis*, which has a wide range of meaning (cf. Cranfield, p. 697), come to mean, from 'that which has been entrusted to us', 'our responsibility'? Certainly 'according to our measure of responsibility' within the Church, the Body of Christ, would give an appropriate meaning. It would be less appropriate, however, in the context of the parallel phrase at v. 6, 'according to the proportion *(analogia)* of faith' *(RSV)*. Confronted with such an *aporia*, the exegete is perhaps justified in considering the possibility of a 'primitive error', in this case a scribal error (or alteration) of an original *pneumatos* changed to *pisteōs*.[1] The meaning in both verses would then be 'each according to the measure of the Spirit which God has assigned to him', 'if prophecy, in proportion to the spirit (assigned to him)'. This accords with 1 C. 12:7ff.; cf. Eph. 4:7 'the measure of the gift of Christ . . .'. Michel, *ad loc.*, draws attention to the Hebrew idea of the Spirit being apportioned by God 'according to measure (weight)', i.e. capacity (cf. SB, Bd. II, p. 431: 'one prophet

---

[1] Could it have arisen by mistaking a contraction πς for *pneumatos* as *pisteōs*? Or was *pisteōs* in both verses 3 and 6 an anti-Montanist 'correction'?

prophesied *one* book, another (like Jeremiah) *two*.' In this context 'spirit' means '*Geist*', i.e. spiritual endowment (see above, pp. 105f.).

Is Paul perhaps using this familiar idea of 'measure' (with its associations with 'fitting measure') to curb the excesses of Roman 'spirituality'? See, further, J. N. Birdsall, '*Emetrēsen* in Rom. 12:3', *JTS*, XIV (1963), pp. 103f.; C. E. B. Cranfield, '*Metron pisteōs* in Rom. 12:3', *NTS*, VIII (1961–2), pp. 345–51.

4–5. The comparison of a community with a living body is a commonplace of ancient literature (e.g. Livy, ii.32; Senate and people are said to belong together as much as stomach and limbs; and for other classical parallels, Käsemann, pp. 321ff.; Cranfield, p. 617, n. 1.; cf. the use Paul makes of the figure at 1 C. 12:12ff.; Eph. 4:15ff.; Col. 1:18ff.).

The connection with v. 3 ('For', *gar*) seems to me to be best accounted for in the light of 1 C. 12:22ff. which develops a fuller version of the simile of the Body of Christ. Some of the 'members' of the Church in Rome as in Corinth (the *pneumatikoi*?) no doubt considered themselves the 'spiritual' superiors of the more humble and less 'gifted' members, probably the 'silent majority'. These are now reminded that all are members of the Christian Body ('one body in Christ', see above on 6:3, 11 and Cranfield, pp. 833ff.), where even the 'weakest' members are 'necessary' for the body to function harmoniously—even the 'less honorable' members (*RSV*), (perhaps referring to the 'outcast' or the slave members of the early Church) who are even to be more highly esteemed—to receive 'positive discrimination'—*vis-à-vis* the more highly honoured members.

5. so we, though many: Could this be the Semitic use of 'many' inclusively when we prefer 'all', i.e. 'so we all . . .' See above, p. 83.

7. in our serving: the *diakonia* here is usually interpreted of general service in the Christian community or including the 'service of tables' (Ac. 6:2), the care of the sick or the poor (cf. 2 C. 8:4); the order—after 'prophesying' and before 'teaching' (the latter follows 'prophecy' at 1 C. 12:28)—may be without any significance.

It is perhaps worth noting, however, that the 'ecstatic charismata' (Käsemann) (e.g. 'miracles' (*dynameis*), 'speaking with tongues' (*glossolalia*)) are omitted here in Romans: no doubt the situation in Rome was different from that which prevailed in Corinth. But 'prophecy' and 'teaching' are central in both lists as also at Eph. 4:11. The 'service' (*diakonia*) of the congregation is also mentioned at Eph. 4:12. In all these lists the 'organisation' of the Christian community implied is evidently still at an embryonic stage of development, that of the era of the unifying, guiding and inspiring power of the 'Spirit' (cf. Käsemann, p. 325), where 'prophecy' (*prophēteia*) and 'teaching' (*didaskalia*) comprised the 'ministry of the Word', consisting of the preaching of the Gospel, but also the prophetic or 'inspired utterance' of the Spirit, declaring the mind and will of God relative to the situation of the believers in Rome or wherever the word was proclaimed (which, following Hebrew tradition, could be conducted on the basis of scriptural texts and their interpretation). Cf. M. A. Chevallier (*Esprit de Dieu paroles d'hommes* (Neuchatel, 1966), p. 198): 'Prophecy has as its function the illumination by the revelation of God of the life of Christians, whether as a community or as individuals'. 'Teaching' no doubt included catechetical instruction in the Old Testament, the *didachē* of Jesus and the apostles, baptism, the Lord's Supper etc. See especially David Hill, *New Testament Prophecy* (London, 1979), Chapter Five, 'Paul and the Phenomenon of Prophecy in the Early Church', pp. 110ff.

teaching . . . exhortation: both go together, and no doubt include 'counselling' (*nouthesia*, 1 Th. 5:12ff.). Notice the use of the participles, tending to emphasise function rather than status.

8. liberality: *NEB*: '. . . give with all your heart'. It is doubtful if either is correct, though the sense of 'liberality' is also claimed for 2 C. 9:11, 13. The *Testament of Issachar* (cited by SH) gives the clearest meaning: *haplotēs* means 'purity, or simplicity of heart', i.e., a self-forgetful attitude, entirely innocent of any ulterior motive. Cf. R. H. Charles, *Testaments of the Twelve Patriarchs* (London, 1908), Issachar III, pp. 102f., Cranfield, p. 625.

he who gives aid: *NEB*: 'if you are a leader'. The verb is ambiguous. In the second sense it is used by Justin Martyr of the *proestōs*, or president, who officiates at the celebration of the Eucharist (1 Apol. lxv. 5). Cf. also for such Church 'leaders', 1 Th. 5:12.

he who does acts of mercy with cheerfulness: The reference could be to a special 'diaconate' concerned with *eleēmosynē*, i.e. the distribution of alms, rather than as referring to 'the person whose special function is, on behalf of the congregation, to tend the sick, relieve the poor, or care for the aged and infirm' (Cranfield, p. 627). Cf. 2 C. 9:7 (Prov. 22.8 LXX); Sir. 35.9a, (*RSV*) 'With every gift show a cheerful face' is not quite parallel, since the reference is to 'gifts' or offerings made to God (9b reads 'and dedicate your tithe with gladness'.)

PARAENETICAL MAXIMS

12:9–21

These verses represent a more or less self-contained unit of Christian *sententiae*, very much in the style of the Hebrew Wisdom literature. The main theme is *agapē*. Barrett thinks that there may even have been a Semitic source at Paul's disposal. The use of participles with the force of imperatives is a feature of Hebrew style, especially when these are used to express, not direct commands, but rules and codes; cf. Selwyn, *I Peter*, Appended Note on 'Participle and Imperative in 1 Peter', by D. Daube. They are by no means all logically connected; occasionally the only connection appears to be that of a *Stichwort* (a catchword), where word-association, not logic or meaning, is the link (e.g. between verses 13 and 14, the use of the term *diōkein* in two different senses, in verse 13 'practising (hospitality)', in verse 14 'persecuting'). There is no formal *schēma* in the verses (so Lagrange: 9–16 love to Christians, 17–21 love to all men; but verse 14 belongs to 'love to all men'); the *agapē* theme is renewed at 13:8–10. The form of the *sententia* is sometimes a negative formulation followed by a positive exhortation (e.g., verses 17, 19). On 12:9–13:10, see A. Viard, 'La Charité accomplit la Loi', *Vie Spirituelle*, LXXIV (1946), pp. 27–34.

9. The transition from verse 8 reminds us of the transition to 1 C. 13:1ff. at 1 C. 12:31; here too reflections on *agapē* follow a similar passage on the exercise of 'spiritual gifts'. *Agapē* is the precondition in the Christian community for the exercise of all *charismata*.

genuine: lit. 'without hypocrisy'. It is perhaps better to render by a negative equivalent; hypocrisy is just what Christian *agapē* can become. This description of *agapē* (or *philadelphia*) appears to have been in the paraenetical tradition; cf. 2 C. 6:6, 1 Pet. 1:22. The idea supplements 1 C. 13:4.

hate . . . hold fast: *NEB*: 'loathing . . . clinging to'; *AV*: 'abhor . . . cleave to', perhaps bring out better the force of the original. They are both strong expressions, conveying a passionate hatred of evil and zeal for good, the latter here to be defined as at verse 1, i.e. the pursuit of the will of God.

10–13 yield a number of pairs of parallel *sententiae*, beginning with 'brotherly love' (verse 10), and concluding with 'hospitality' (verse 13); the rhetorical structure is in the style of such writing. Cf. Cranfield, p. 636, n. 2.

10. with brotherly affection: lit. 'be warmly affectionate' (*philo-storgoi*). The Christian shows the same love to his fellow-Christian as he does within his own family; it is a caring concern. The word

here used—verb, adjective, and noun—has special associations with
the intimate, tender love of a family; see Liddell and Scott, s.v.
outdo one another in showing honor: If *proēgeisthai* is given this
meaning we would expect '*allēlōn* (gen.), but, in fact, the verb
(which means 'to lead') is not attested meaning 'to outdo'. The
meaning 'to anticipate (one another)' has patristic support. See Cranfield, p. 632, and cf. Pesh., Vg. and Bengel (p. 165): 'The Talmu-
dists say: 'whosoever knows that his neighbour has been in the habit
of saluting him, should anticipate him by saluting him first.' Cf. SB
III, p. 296, II, pp. 553ff.

The usual rendering of the verb here with a following accusative,
(as in *AV, RV*) is 'in honour preferring one another'. The translation
'prefer', however, does not fully convey the meaning of *hēgeisthai*,
especially as biblical Greek, viz., 'to consider, give thought to,
count, reckon, esteem' (cf. Heb. *hašab* and Vincent, *Philippians*
(I.C.C.) p. 56). The compound *proēgeisthai* would then mean that
we are 'to give thought to', 'to consider' others before ourselves.
This does not mean that we are not to consider ourselves—that
would be asking the humanly impossible—but that our priorities
must be consideration *first* for our neighbour before we think of
ourselves. *NEB* 'esteem' is preferable to 'honour': 'Give pride of
place to one another in esteem' (*NEB*). Phil. 2:3 puts this thought
even more strongly: '. . . you must humbly reckon others better
than yourselves' (*NEB*). (English 'better' suggests morally or spiri-
tually better, but the Greek verb *hyperechein*, while capable of being
so interpreted, is used especially with reference to persons of consequence, e.g. rulers, social 'betters' etc. so that we should perhaps
render '. . . you must humbly reckon others more important than
yourselves'.)

This goes far beyond the ethic of Lev. 19:18, the command to
love one's neighbour as oneself. To suggest that the theological
reason for such an attitude is that one encounters in a brother
Christian the Lord who calls and accepts us is to read too much
into the expression. (Käsemann, p. 330, Cranfield, p. 633, cf.
Barth, *Shorter Commentary*, p. 154: 'to prefer the other man as a
representative of the Lord'). It seems more likely that this radical
Christian ethic has been inspired by the teaching and example of
Christ himself (cf. Lk. 14:7f.).

11. zeal: mentioned here only and at 2 C. 7:7 as a Christian
characteristic and a genuine sign of the spirit's working.
aglow with the Spirit: *NEB* 'in ardour of spirit'; the same
expression is employed to describe the ardent spiritual zeal of
Apollos at Ac. 18:25 ('fire' is a familiar biblical figure for the Spirit's

consuming power: Isa. 4:4; Mt. 3:11 and par.; Ac. 2:3), and, for similar figures of speech, 1 Th. 5:19; Rev. 3:15.

serve the Lord: a variant 'serve the opportunity' is attested by the 'Western' ms. group D* F G etc. (a contraction KR (*Kyriō*, 'Lord') may have been misread as *kairo* (opportunity), or vice versa), *NEB mg.*: 'meeting the demands of the hour'. 'To serve the time' in Greek means 'to be an opportunist'.

'Lord' is better attested textually, and gives a less difficult meaning; some, however, prefer the harder reading on the grounds that it is more in keeping with the context; besides, St Paul was not opposed to opportunism.

In favour of the more difficult 'serve the time (opportunity)' is the occurrence elsewhere of the phrase, e.g., *douleuein tō kairō*, (Liddell and Scott s.v. *douleuō*); *kairos* too is a rich concept in profane as well as in biblical Greek. Its biblical meaning 'the eschatological 'Time', 'the Last Time' is quite unsuitable here, but its use generally in hellenistic Greek virtually as a synonym of *Tyche*, '*dia Glückstunde*', could be relevant, especially in its religious connotation, e.g., in the magical papyri where *ho kairos*, 'Opportunity' is a deity bringing good fortune, or an 'angel', and mankind its 'slave' (*doulos*). Cf. *TWNT*, s.v. *kairos*, Bd.III, p. 458 (Delling). St Paul is not then thinking of 'time-serving' (cf. Cranfield, pp. 634ff.) but of opportune or 'timely service'.[1] On the whole, however, the better attested 'serve the Lord' seems preferable.

12. hope: i.e. of the final revelation at the Parousia, when the Christian would exult in the (restored) glory of Adam. Cf. note on 5:2, 3:23.

patient in tribulation: patience (endurance, long-suffering) is inspired by 'hope'; cf. Rom. 5:2ff., where we find the same order: hope—patience (endurance). The 'tribulation' was not necessarily identical with persecution; but, as verse 14 implies, it must have included it.

constant in prayer: the phrase is an old one—no doubt well-established in Christian paraenesis; see Ac. 1:14, 2:42; cf. Col. 4:2, 1 Th. 5:17, Eph. 6:18. Paul practised what he preached; cf. Rom. 1:9–10. In the practice of prayer, the synagogue was the school of

---

[1] The expression is not connected with the phrase 'redeeming' (lit. 'buying') the time at Eph. 5:16 (cf. Col. 4:5) any more than the latter expression has to do with Dan. 2:8, 'to gain time'. In Eph. the phrase, I suggest, means 'as redeemed from (lit. purchased out of) the (evil) *kairos* (i.e. the Last Time).' Cf. Rom. 13:11 and *Martyrdom of Polycarp* 2.3 'at the cost of one moment (martyrdom) being redeemed from (purchased out of) everlasting punishment' (*tēn aiōnion kolasin exagorazomenoi*).

the Church; Judaism in Paul's day not only produced in Pharisaism a system of legalism covering all possible behaviour; it also produced prayers covering every moment of the entire day. Such prayer was naturally especially evident in time of persecution. Cf. *TWNT* Bd. II, pp. 801, 35f. (Greeven).

13. Contribute to the needs of the saints: *koinōneō*, to share out one's property. For the verb and the noun *koinōnia*, cf. Phil. 4:15; Rom. 15:26; 2 C. 9:13; Heb. 13:16. A variant, obviously late and secondary, reads: 'sharing in the commemoration(s) of the saints' (*mneiais* for *chreiais*, with D* G it vg, etc.).

While *hagioi* has become a proper name for Christians (see above, 24), it can also refer specifically to the 'poor among the saints' in Jerusalem (cf. 15:25–26) and St Paul has no doubt these specially, though not exclusively, in mind in this verse.

14. This *logion* (cf. Mt. 5:44 par. Lk. 6:28) stands alone in its context, but is further developed in verses 17ff. Michel describes the sayings as a Pauline Targum-like version of the original dominical *logion*, which no doubt by Paul's time had become firmly embedded in catechetical tradition; cf. 1 C. 4:12, 1 Pet. 2:23. 'Blessing' and 'cursing' (the latter of 'enemies') was a regular feature of synagogue practice; 'cursing' recalls the synagogue custom of formally 'cursing' its opponents; Jesus' word abolishes it (cf. Jas. 3:9ff.). The unity of theme between this verse and verses 17 to 21 gives the impression of a dislocation in the text; verse 16 certainly follows more logically on verses 9–10. The variant 'you' after 'persecute' is strongly attested, but appears to come from a reminiscence of Mt. 5:44.

15. The Christian *sententia* here is a commonplace of Jewish and hellenistic moralists. Parallels are cited from Sir. 7:34: 'Do not fail those who weep, but mourn with those who mourn.' The Christian injunction is a positive one; cf. 1 C. 12:26, Phil. 2:17–18.

16. live in harmony with one another: recalls verse 3. The injunction is frequent in Paul; cf. Rom. 15:5, 2 C. 13:11, Phil. 2:2, 4:2. Was it a necessary exhortation in these early congregations?

do not be haughty, but associate with the lowly: lit., 'do not be high-minded, but go along with the humble.' We may then interpret with special reference to the ideas and claims of the Christian enthusiasts, whose minds were to such an extent on higher things— the *charismata* of prophecy and tongues—that they despised the humbler aspects of Christian service. Cf. further, A. Fridrichsen, 'Humilibus consentientes', *Horae Soederblomianae* I. i (1942), p. 32. The verb *synapagein*(*esthai*) in the sense of 'associate with' (*NEB* 'go about with') appears to be unattested in any Greek source (cf. Liddell and Scott s.v.). In the only other two places where the verb occurs in the *NT* it is used metaphorically meaning 'to be carried away' by, e.g., by error (2 Pet. 3:17) or by falsehood (Gal. 2:13), and the verb can be so interpreted in this verse, '. . . do not be high-minded, but be carried away—not like the gnostic enthusiasts by tongues or ecstatic prophesies—with the humbler tasks (*tapeinois*, neut.) of Christian service' (cf., e.g., Grundmann in *TWNT*, Bd. VIII, p. 20, especially n. 56.). This, however, seems a less satisfactory meaning than 'associate with', which would be fully conveyed by *synagomenoi* (cf. *synagōgē*, an 'assembly'). Has there been a textual error *synapagomenoi*, in which *ag* has been repeated as *ap*? It seems best to take the predicate *tapeinois* as masculine, as elsewhere in the New Testament: 'come together/assemble with the lowest' would be apostolic advice to admit, not the 'lowly', but the socially depressed, the poor, the outcast and the slave into Christian fellowship. (Cf. Michel, p. 307, n. 3). Cf. also Käsemann (p. 332): 'the congregation of Jesus is able to take its stand on the side of the socially deprived (*die Niedrigen*) and socially to break down the ghetto of the classes.' The Church is a classless society.

never be conceited: a Pauline adaptation of Prov. 3:7 (LXX), 'Be not wise in thine own eyes . . . (*AV*)'). Cf. Rom. 11:25. This is not the only echo in tradition of this verse. See SB, III, p. 299.

17. Repay no one evil for evil: cf. 1 Th. 5:15, 1 Pet. 3:9. Again, evidently a well-known Christian injunction, firmly embedded in the paraenetical tradition. The *OT* deprecates the returning of evil for good (Gen. 44:4; Jer. 18:20; Prov. 17:13). There is frequent discussion in late Judaism of the question of retribution (cf. Prov. 20:22); but this never appears to have gone further than negative injunctions such as: 'Do not rejoice over the misfortune of thine enemy', or 'Return not evil for evil' (SB, I, p. 368; III, p. 299. Michel, p. 308, n. 1.). In this Christian injunction, the negative injunction is always followed by a positive—here presented by verses 17b and 18ff.

take thought for: *NEB*: 'Let your aims be such as all men count honourable.' Paul is supporting his paraenesis (as he does his arguments) by an adaptation of Prov. 3:4 (LXX) (cf. 2 C. 8:21). The words can also be translated 'harbouring the best intentions towards all men', and this is more nearly parallel to the thought of verse 18. Prov. 3:3–4 reads in the *RSV* version 'Let not loyalty and faithfulness forsake you; . . . So will you find favour and good repute (*NEB* success) in the sight of God and man.' LXX renders after 'So will you find favour', lit., 'and give thought to things that are right (*pronooun ta kala*) in the sight of the Lord and of men.' In Paul's adaptation the clause may be taken as continuing the thought of 17a, or as a new participial imperative: '(Repay no one evil for evil,) giving thought to (doing) right in the sight of all men' or '(Repay no one evil for evil.) Give thought to (doing) right in the sight of all men.' Cf. 2 C. 8:21, *Jerusalem Bible*: '. . . for we are trying to do right (*pronooumen . . . kala*) not only in the sight of God, but also in the sight of men.' Is the Pauline emphasis on 'all'? There are no exceptions; taking careful thought for what is right is required in all circumstances, even when we are dealing with someone who has wronged us.[1]

18. so far as it depends upon you: Others may not be prepared to live at peace with you; then your attitude must be that defined in verses 19ff. The *AV*, 'so far as lieth in you', suggests that we may not always be ourselves capable of peaceable relations with others, a thought which is not in the text. This thought of peacemaking no doubt ultimately stems from the teaching of Jesus (Mt. 5:9, Mk 9:50). Paul repeats the exhortation at 1 Th. 5:13, 2 C. 13:11, etc.; but he is thinking here of the Christian virtue as exercised beyond the Christian congregation (as at Heb. 12:14); cf. Epict. IV. v. 24. The Hebrew foundations of the thought of these two verses 17 and 18 are found at Prov. 3:4 and Ps. 33:15 (LXX); cf. Dodd's comment (pp. 199ff.).

19. For the literary form, see above, p. 172f.; on the theme, cf. K. Stendahl, 'Hate, Non-Retaliation and Love: 1QS x. 17–20 and Rom. 12:19–21', *HThR*, LX (1962), pp. 343–55.

Beloved, never avenge yourselves: The form of address ('Beloved') is an indirect reminder of the Christian's obligation to *agapē* (including love of enemies).

leave it to the wrath of God: (*mg.* Greek: 'give place'); *NEB* 'leave a place for divine retribution'; *RSV* is an idiomatic and exact rendering of the meaning of the (originally Hebrew) idiom: 'give place to': The Hebrew expression is *nathan maqom le* (cf. SB, Bd. II, p. 204, III, p. 300) and is used in a variety of ways, e.g., cf. Sir. 13:22, Lk. 14:9, Eph. 4:27, 'give the devil a wide berth.'[2]

---

[1] A text closer to the *OT* quotation is found in several mss. ('not only before God but also before all men' (F G etc.) or 'before God and all men' (A). This 'addition' is usually explained as an accommodation to LXX Prov. 3:4 and 2 C. 8:21. But LXX Prov. 3:4 reads 'Lord' not 'God', and at 2 C. 8:21, the Pauline quotation may have read 'God' not 'Lord' (P⁴⁶ reads 'God'). The 'addition' has claims to be considered as a possible original. Why should Paul omit 'before God (the Lord)' in this verse and not at 2 C. 8:21?

[2] Its opposite is '*amadh kenegedh, antistēnai*, 'to resist' (S-B., l. c.). Should Mt. 5:39, 'do not stand up to the Evil One', be understood as parallel in meaning to Eph. 4:27, 'give the devil a wide berth', and meaning, not 'do not resist', implying taking measures to oppose and defeat, but 'do not confront', 'face up to', meaning simply 'avoid'?

it is written: as usual the Christian *didachē* is authoritatively summed up by a scriptural text or interwoven texts (see note on p. 56). The first, Dt. 32:35, is the Pentateuchal prohibition of vengeance, on the grounds that it is a divine prerogative.

20. The second text, Prov. 25:21f., comes short of the Christian attitude of love to one's enemies, since the motivation is still revenge. For the figure 'coals of fire', see W. Klassen, 'Coals of Fire: Sign of Repentance or Revenge?', *NTS*, IX (1962–3), pp. 337ff. The repetition of Dt. 32:35 at Heb. 10:30 suggests that this verse had a firm place in Christian catechesis. Cf. also M. J. Dahood, *CBQ*, XVII (1955), pp. 19–24; S. Morenz, 'Feurige Kohlen auf dem Haupt', *Theol. Ltzg.*, LXXVIII (1953), pp. 187–92.

21. sums up (both verse 20 and verses 17–21) negatively and in a succinct and pregnant *sententia*, the basis of all Christian behaviour towards others. Within its context, following verse 20, evil here not only means evil in general within ourselves, but also the ill (*kakon*) that an enemy can do to one; cf. Bengel's note (p. 168) 'by the evil of your enemy, and of your own nature.'

OBEDIENCE TO RULERS

13:1–7

The group of maxims ending at 12:21 resumes and is completed at 13:9–10; 13:1–7 consists of Christian teaching on the attitude of Christians to the civil powers. For literature and views, consult O. Cullmann, 'Zur neuesten Diskussion über die *Exousia* in Röm. 13:1', *TZ*, X (1954), pp. 321ff.; cf. also O. Cullmann, *The State in the New Testament* (New York, 1956), and C. D. Morrison, *The Powers that Be* (*Studies in Biblical Theology*, 29, London, 1960). E. Wolf, 'Politischer Gottesdienst', *Festschrift K. O. Schmidt* (Göttingen, 1961), pp. 51–63; V. Zsifkovits, *Der Staatsgedanke nach Paulus in Röm. 13* (Vienna, 1964); H. v. Campenhausen, 'Zur Auslegung von Röm. 13:1–7, Die dämonistische Deutung des Exousia-Begriffs', *Aus der Frühzeit des Christentums* (Memorial volume for A. Bertholet, Tübingen, 1950); E. Käsemann, 'Grundsätzliches zur Interpretation von Röm. 13', *Beitr. Ev. Theol.*, XXXII (1961), pp. 37–55; C. E. B. Cranfield, 'Some Observations on Rom. 13:1–7', *NTS*, VI (1959–60), pp. 241–9; A. Strobel, 'Zum Verständnis von Röm. 13', *ZNTW*, XLVII (1956), pp. 57–93; O. Michel, 'Das Problem des Staates in neutest. Sicht', *Theol. Ltzg.*, LXXXIII (1958), pp. 161–6; E. Bammel, 'Ein Beitrag zur paulinischen Staatsanschauung', *Theol. Ltzg.*, LXXV (1960), pp. 837–40; G. Delling, *Röm. 13:1–7 innerhalb der Briefe des Neuen Testaments*

(Berlin, 1962). For an extended bibliography (with related discussion) see Käsemann, pp. 334f. and Cranfield, pp. 651ff. Especially important is the study by the late W. C. van Unnik, 'Lob und Strafe durch die Obrigkeit: Hellenistisches zu Röm. 13:3–4' in *Jesus und Paulus: Festschrift für Werner Georg Kümmel*, ed. by E. E. Ellis and E. Grässer, Göttingen, 1975, pp. 334–43.

Verse 1a lays down the general thesis of Christian submission to the supreme authorities, i.e. clearly the Roman governing or civil authorities, in Rome itself or wherever the Christian congregation or Christian believer is located; the repetition of this injunction at verse 5 shows that it is the central thought of the whole passage, which is argued out in the style of the Wisdom literature as a rational appeal to the individual conscience. Verse 1b gives the theological grounds for such 'submission', that such authorities are in existence as ordained by God. Verses 2 to 4 draw the consequences of verse 1b.

The passage leaves the clear impression that St Paul is addressing his remarks to a definite situation or situations which had arisen in relations between some early Christian communities and the state or local authorities. Christians may even have been refusing to pay taxes. The situation is quite different from that at 1 C. 6:1ff. where Paul advises Christians to avoid litigation outside the Christian congregation, no doubt to prevent scandal. Here in Rome he accommodates his paraenesis to a different situation: the danger here was to avoid disturbing the *pax Romana* which specially favoured the new religion. (It was not many years before that trouble had broken out in the city through disturbances *impulsore Chresto*. (See above, p. 6).

The connection of 13:1–7 with its context—12:19–21 and 13:8ff.—is not immediately obvious; it is sometimes explained as an 'interpolated' section of teaching. Cf. Käsemann, who regards it as 'an independent block' which can be called an 'alien body' (*Fremdkörper*) in the Pauline paraenesis. It is doubtful, however, if there is anything 'alien' in the passage, except perhaps Paul's indebtedness to 'the terminology of hellenistic administration' (Käsemann). Even more important for the understanding of the Christian attitudes to the state inculcated here and at 1 Pet. 2:13ff. is the recognition that St Paul is employing identical ideas and expressions as hellenistic writers from the 5th century B.C. to the 4th century A.D. (See W. C. van Unnik, *op. cit.*) More probably, the passage represents a traditional Jewish (or Jewish-Christian) body of doctrine on relations with the civil power, which had already been formulated and in circulation, in the light of current hellenistic attitudes, and which Paul is here adapting from such a source of catechetical or paraenetic material utilised by early Christian *dida-skaloi* (cf. especially, E. G. Selwyn, *The First Epistle of Peter* (London, 1946), Essay II, pp. 426ff.) There is no question of this piece of paraenesis being an 'interpolation'. (So J. Kallas, in *NTS* XI (1964–5), pp. 365–74.)

The logical link is with 12:19–21, where the fundamental Christian ethic, to leave all retribution to God, is unambiguously stated: '. . . do not avenge yourselves, beloved, but leave a place for divine retribution. "Retribution belongs to me", says the Lord, "I will repay."' The Christian ethic is clear: good is to be returned for evil. But this does not mean that there is no redress of wrongs or retributive justice in this life. God deals out this retribution, and he does so *in this world* through his divinely constituted authorities, the civil magistrates. Paul, at this point, fills in a gap in the Sermon on the Mount which leaves open the question: 'If we suffer wrong and do not seek revenge, but return good for evil, does the offender get off scot-free? Is the injustice to be righted only at the Last Judgement?' 'No', Paul replies. 'It is for this end civil law exists, to mete out divine justice on this earth. And this kind of law no man can take into his own hands.' St Paul's argument is reinforced if the 'authorities' (*exousiai*) are for him, like the 'principalities and powers', divine agencies. Cf. SH, p. 366: 'The idea of the civil power may have been suggested by verse 19 of the preceding chapter, as being one of the ministers of the Divine wrath and retribution (ver. 4); at any rate the juxtaposition of the two passages would serve to remind St Paul's readers that the condemnation of individual vengeance and retaliation does not apply to the action of the state in enforcing law; for the state is God's minister, and it is the just wrath of God which is acting through it.'

1. **every person:** lit. 'every soul', a Hebraism.

governing authorities: i.e. of the state, the state 'authorities', abstract for concrete, and equivalent to 'rulers' at verse 3. The rendering 'supreme authorities' (*NEB*) seems, on the whole, preferable (contrast Cranfield, p. 659). Moreover, while the term could refer to the Roman establishment anywhere in the Empire, the reference to *supreme* authorities does strongly suggest the imperial civil service (from the Emperor down) in Rome itself. Cf. 1 Pet. 2:13, 'Be subject . . . to the emperor as supreme' ('supreme' renders *hyperechein* in both verses). Some interpret in terms of the 'authorities'; cf. 1 C. 15:24, Col. 1:16, 2:10, 15, i.e. *exousiai* = 'demonic agencies'; and it has been persuasively argued that the Romans conceived of the state as 'divinely appointed in relation to a cosmic system of spiritual powers' (Morrison, *op. cit.*, p. 99 and cf. Cullmann, *op. cit.*, pp. 95ff.). Käsemann, however, (and cf. now

Cranfield, p. 659) rejects any such metaphysical ideas—indeed any kind of political philosophy—in these verses, noting that the terminology throughout was that of Roman hellenistic administration. The use of the plural 'authorities' (*exousiai*), however, by Paul in the specially Jewish sense of 'demonic agencies'[1] makes it not improbable that the Apostle is deliberately introducing this special extra nuance of meaning into the word in his reference to the Roman establishment (cf. Tit. 3:1); for contemporary Jews (as for Christians; cf. 2 Th. 2:8ff., Rev. 13:18) Rome was a demonic power. (A variant text—supported by P[46] D* G etc. has: 'To *all* the higher powers subject yourselves'.)

be subject to: a strong word expressly used in this connection; cf. Tit. 3:1.

there is no authority except from God: *RSV* appears to be reading the 'Western' text, 'from (*apo*) God', whereas the better reading would normally be rendered as 'No authority exists except by (*hypo*) God.' Translations generally render 'from God' or freely paraphrase '(There is no authority but) by act of God' (*NEB*); 'for no one is a ruler except by God's permission' (Weymouth); 'For no authority exists as such except by God's appointment' (Cranfield). The preposition here could perhaps be given the sense of 'under', i.e., 'subject to God': everyone is to be subject to the authorities, as they are subject to the Almighty.[2] 'This is a sentence, about which, in the ancient synagogue, differences of opinion hardly existed' (SB, III, p. 303). Cf. Dan. 2:21, 37ff., Wis. 6:3, En. 46:5, Josephus, *BJ*, II.viii (140), Jn 19:11. It was also accepted Graeco-Roman doctrine (by which the ancient synagogue was not uninfluenced): cf. Morrison, *op. cit.*, p. 93: 'His (the Emperor's) authority was not merely the highest among men, but specifically established by God for the benefit of men.' The idea persists in rabbinical Judaism; even though Rome destroys the Temple, and slays the pious Israelite, she is nevertheless the heaven-appointed ruler (SB, III, pp. 303ff.).

those that exist: lit. 'the powers that be' (*ousai*), clearly referring to the imperial establishment (cf. Cranfield, p. 663).

have been instituted by God: lit. 'are ordered (*tetagmenai*) by (under) God.' Verse 2 speaks of resistance to the divine order (*diatagē*).

2. he who resists the authorities resists what God has

---

[1]See my 'All powers will be subject to him', in *Paul and Paulism*, Essays in honour of C. K. Barrett (above, p. 121).

[2]We would expect *hypo theō* (or *theon*), but the genitive is attested with this meaning, Od. 19:114, *hyp' autou*, 'under his rule,' and, but also rarely, in biblical Greek, LXX Job 9:13, Num. 5:20, 29.

appointed: lit., 'he who sets himself up against authority'. Moffatt: 'anyone who resists authority is opposing the divine order'. The second verb is even stronger than the first: it is used especially of the 'resistance' of rebellion or revolt. Cf. Josephus, *Antiq.*, XIV. xv, 5 (424).

Does this mean unqualified obedience, in all circumstances, to the 'powers that be'? If the latter are divinely appointed, can civil disobedience ever be justified? Cranfield argues that, since Paul had here in mind an authoritarian state, Christian submission to the authorities 'is limited to respecting them, obeying them so far as such obedience does not conflict with God's laws, *and seriously and responsibly disobeying them when it does.*' (p. 662, italics mine).

The idea that divinely appointed state authorities, whose function it is to punish evil-doers and praise the good, will themselves be 'doers of good' is virtually assumed in Graeco-Roman political philosophy (*euergētai*, 'benefactors' is a title attributed at Lk. 22:25 to rulers), and it is made explicit in Hebrew tradition.[1] But what happens if the authorities are unjust or tyrants? In these circumstances guide-lines to Christian conduct are contained at 1 Pet. 2:20ff.: '. . . if, when you do right and suffer for it you take it patiently, you have God's approval. For to this you have been called, because Christ also suffered for you, leaving you an example, that you should follow in his steps.' The Christian's duty is to do right, as his conscience directs. If this brings him into conflict 'with the authorities', and he suffers punishment, he is to 'follow in his (Christ's) steps', i.e. endure suffering by submitting to the punishment meted out to him by the 'powers that be'. But this is not the same as what we mean by 'civil disobedience'.

will incur judgement: lit., 'will receive (bring) condemnation (*krima*) for (upon) themselves'. *AV*, 'shall receive to themselves damnation' is clearly thinking of the Last Judgment. It is certainly a *divine* condemnation that is meant, although a sentence pronounced and carried out by human authorities. The phrase 'to receive condemnation' occurs in the *NT* at Mk 12:40 (Mt. 23:14 TR), Lk. 20:47, Jas 3:1, but is not attested in the LXX or elsewhere in *Koinē* Greek; Michel suspected a Semitism (p. 318). Could the expression (which had evidently established itself in New Testament usage) have been a Jewish Greek equivalent of the Heb./Aramaic *nasa hēt'*/*'awōn*, 'to receive punishment', e.g. Ezek. 4:5 'you shall receive the punishment for Israel's iniquity.' The Aramaic equivalent at Ezek. 4:5 is *qabbēl ḥobh*, LXX *lambanein adikian*. Aramaic *ḥobh* covers both *adikia* and

---

[1] Cf. Philo, *De vita Moses*, I § 134, van Unnik, *op. cit.*, p. 337: Moses, the model ruler, distributes praise and blame by the standards of the Law.

krima, and the *Koinē* locution *lambanein* (*lambanesthai*) *krima* could be the kind of translation Greek we find at Mk 12:40, where 'punishment' rather than 'condemnation' seems required. See my *Aramaic Approach*³, p. 140, n. 3. The Greek *krima* elsewhere in the New Testament seems best rendered by 'punishment', e.g., 2 Pet. 2:3, Jude 4. Cf. Bauer, s.v. *krima*, 3b, and *TWNT*, s.v. *krima*, Bd. III, pp. 943, 31, n. 5.

3. good conduct: abstract for concrete, i.e. those who behave themselves.

. . . do what is good: Käsemann interprets, not of moral qualities, but as referring to 'political goodwill' (p. 338). In contrast to 'wrong-doing' (cf. v. 4), 'good social behaviour' at least is meant: but 'good acts', 'doing what is good', in the best sense of that phrase, i.e., actions which benefit others, and so society, and not just 'that which is morally good' or 'political goodwill' is surely intended. For Jewish or Jewish Christian readers *gemiluth ḥasadim* is meant, i.e. 'the imparting of kindnesses', 'the active kindness, comfort and support, given by members of the Covenant-people to one another . . .' (T. W. Manson, *Ethics and the Gospel*, S.C.M. 1960, pp. 37ff.)

4. he is God's servant: a consequence of the principle of verse 1 that temporal authority is instituted by God. 'Rulers are ministers of God for the care and safety of mankind, that they may distribute or hold in safe keeping the blessings and benefits which God gives to man . . .'. Plutarch, *Princip. Inerud* v. 13.22–14.2, cited by Morrison, *op. cit.*, p. 79). The words here are in a prominent position opening the sentence (with the emphasis on the genitive: '*God's* servant he is') and are repeated, stressing this fundamental thought, later in the verse. Cf. also note on verse 6.

to execute his wrath: lit. 'bringing retribution to the evil-doer', a retribution which effectively constitutes the out-workings of the wrath of God.

5. conscience: as in Stoic thought, 'conscience' is the individual's sense of right and wrong, his moral judgement, his recognition of the inherent claims of the good, and the grounds for rejecting what is wrong. It also includes the recognition of the divinely given authority of the state in executing justice which may include the *ius gladii*. See above, p. 18.

6. ministers of God: the word used for 'ministers' has liturgical associations. Is Paul seeking to convey that the state authorities have a sacred task to perform?

taxes . . . revenue: i.e. direct and indirect taxation, the first probably the poll-tax, the second duties and taxes on goods (see Michel, *ad loc.*).

attending to this very thing: the verb 'to attend to' (*proskartereō*) has also special associations with liturgy, cf. of constant occupation with prayer, e.g. above, Rom. 12:12; Ac. 1:14; cf. also Ac. 2:46.

7. **Pay** (*apodidonai*) . . . **their dues:** The words recall the word of Jesus at Mk 12:17. These closing paraenetic chapters of Romans contain several versions of words of Jesus interpreted and adapted by Paul for his own special purposes, e.g., Rom. 12:14, 17, 21; 13:9.

respect . . . honour: to this outward conformity in payment of taxes, etc., Paul adds the inward attitude of 'fear and honour'. (So *Jerusalem Bible*.) Greek *phobos* includes 'respect' but is closer to 'fear', 'awe'. In this we can detect the influence of tradition (cf. SB, III, p. 305), as well as of a Christian attitude to the State recommended by the early Church (1 Pet. 2:17). Cf. further, A. Strobel, 'Furcht, wem Furcht gebührt: zum profangriechischen Hintergrund von Röm. 13:7', *ZNTW*, LV (1964), pp. 58–62.

BROTHERLY LOVE AS CONSUMMATION OF THE LAW

13:8–10

There is no division in thought between verses 7 and 8; indeed, on the contrary, verse 7 leads logically into verse 8 and prepares the way for this striking Pauline aphorism. (*NEB* begins a new paragraph at verse 7. Bengel, however, notes at verse 9 *nova pars adhortationis*.) The train of thought of 12:14ff. is resumed after the intervening section on the Christian's attitude to the State.

8. **owe no one anything:** The Greek word 'to owe' (*opheilein*) evidently here shares the ambiguity of its Aramaic equivalent *hobh*, Michel, *ad loc.* (cf. A. Fridrichsen, *Theol. Studien u. Kritiken* (1930), pp. 294ff.): it means, literally, 'to be in debt to', but also 'to be under an obligation to', and so 'to have a duty towards (cf. 15:27 and the note on 1:14 above). What Paul is arguing is that no debt to anyone must be left outstanding, with the exception of the love which Christians are in duty bound to show to one another. The reference is to the scriptural commandment at Lev. 19:18, which, since its use by Jesus, had come to feature so prominently in Christian teaching. (The article in the phrase 'except the well-known injunction—to love one another' is anaphoric.) There must surely have been in the mind of the Apostle not only a negative 'owe no one anything', but also the positive meaning of the verb 'to be under obligation to', especially in view of the prominence in Jewish tradition of the idea of man's 'debt' or 'obligation' to fulfil the commands of the Torah. (Cf. *TWNT* Bd. v, pp. 561, 563, 29ff.) Furthermore, it seems hardly coincidental that the same consonants

give the word in Aramaic 'to love', *ahebh* or *hebbebh*. (See M. Black, *Aramaic Approach*[3], pp. 180ff.) The paronomasia is reproduced in the Peshitta Syriac: *wal 'enash medem la tehubun 'ella had lehad lemahabu*. As Meyer points out (*Jesu Muttersprache* (Leipzig, 1896), pp. 125ff.; see also E. Nestlé, *Philologica Sacra* (Berlin, 1896), pp. 49ff.), this proverbial-like saying was just the kind to lend itself to a 'punning' word-play. Paul is probably reproducing in Greek an Aramaic *sententia*, possibly a Christian one, conceivably even a dominical pun.[1] Lietzmann would confine 'one another' to fellow Christians, but this seems an illogical narrowing of the scope of this universal Christian obligation, especially following verse 7: 'Pay *all* . . .' We should be in debt to no one (including the tax authorities): our obligation to everyone, however, is *agapē*. For the influence on Paul's language and style, see especially W. C. van Unnik, 'Reisepläne und Amen-Sagen, Zusammenhang und Gedankenfolge in 2 Korinther 1:15–24', in *Studia Paulina*, de Zwaan *Festschrift*, Haarlem, 1953, pp. 215–34 (especially pp. 232ff.), and below, p. 213. On 8b, see D. G. Hughes, in *Estudios Biblicos*, II (1943), pp. 307ff.

for he who loves his neighbour has fulfilled the law: the perfect is that of a general truth; 'fulfilling the Law' is the same as 'doing the Law' (2:13): *agapē* produces the results aimed at by the Law. Cf. W. Marxsen, 'Der *heteros nomos* Röm. 13:8', *TZ*, XI (1955), pp. 230–7. This proposal to take *heteros nomos* together meaning 'another law' is to be rejected. Cf. Cranfield, p. 675. For *heteros* in the sense of 'neighbour', see above note on 2:1.

9. Here we have a brief summary of the 'second' Decalogue (i.e. Dt. 5:16ff.), the addition 'and any other commandment' serving the purpose of 'etc.'. These summaries were well known. The order of the commandments here follows the same tradition as at (LXX B) Dt. 5:17; Lk. 18:20; Jas 2:11; Philo, *de Decal.* xxiv; Clem. Alex., *Strom.* vi. 16. Such summaries were no doubt useful for catechetical purposes as well as for reference. Whether any significance attaches to the use of a summary placing of the seventh Commandment first in a paraenesis on *agapē* is not certain.

Philo divides the Decalogue into two sets of five commandments, the first set being concerned with 'the divine', the second with 'the

---

[1]In an original Aramaic the *ei mē* would probably correspond to the adversative *'ella* (= *alla*; cf. Michel, p. 324, n. 4) and the infinitive alone, independently of the previous infinitive, implies obligation. Cf. *limehabbeba* (Dt. 33:3, Frag. Targ.): *le'enash mande'am la tehubun 'ella had lehad limehabbeba/lemahabu*: Owe no man anything/But to love one another.

human' (*loc. cit.*, xxiv). It is the second set Paul is summarizing. Was this division already known to him?

in this sentence: i.e. Lev. 19:18. What is meant is that every injunction, exhortation, and whatever in the Law concerns human relationships, are all comprised in this comprehensive 'portmanteau' rule. In every human situation *vis-à-vis* others the obligation to *agapé* is paramount. Although 'neighbour' at Lev. 19:18 is 'fellow-Israelite', the term here, as at Lk. 10:25ff., 'has a universal range' (Cranfield).

10. fulfilling of the law: the sentence in the original is arranged in a chiastic order: subject/predicate/predicate/subject, the sentence beginning and ending with 'love'. So *NEB*: 'Love cannot wrong a neighbour; therefore the whole law is summed up in love' (*mg.*: 'or the whole law is fulfilled by love'.) 'Fulfilled' (*RSV, NEB mg.*) is better, since the word refers to the active carrying out of this commandment *usque ad finem*, while the love which is the fruit of such obedience is the whole, rich fullness of the Law.

The noun 'fulfilling' (*plērōma*) has a wide variety of associations; see above, pp. 154, 160; a close parallel to its meaning here is its use of a 'complete', 'finished' performance. Cf. Theophrastus (*Char.* xxvii. 7) of the full performance of a conjurer's entertainment.

A REMINDER OF THE IMMINENT PAROUSIA

13:11–14

These verses echo 1 Th. 5:1–11, but there is a change of tone. In 1 Thessalonians the tone is one of intense, almost excited, urgency; here the tone is more that of an earnest preacher, but not that of the herald of an imminent catastrophe; cf. C. H. Dodd, in *Bulletin of the John Rylands Library*, XVIII (1934); 'The Mind of Paul: Change and Development', pp. 69ff.; 'Gospel and Law', pp. 28f.; also Selwyn, 1 *Peter*, pp. 396ff.

11. Besides this you know what hour it is: *NEB*, 'in all this'; for the idiomatic use of *kai touto*, Cranfield *ad loc.* = 'and that', '*und zwar*', drawing special attention to an additional reason for the conduct enjoined: 'And all the more so, as you know' . . . that 'salvation is nearer', i.e., the 'End-Time', the imminence of the Parousia.

RSV, 'what hour it is' is a free rendering: the Greek *kairos* has the special eschatological meaning of 'the End-Time', the reference in this context being probably to the Parousia which signalled the End, the Last Judgement and the consummation of the Reign of God. *NEB* renders '(In all this, remember) how critical the moment is.'

The word *ho kairos* '*the* Time' has become a technical term for the
Last Judgement or for other related phenomena of the End-Time.
(*TWNT* Bd. III, pp. 462f.) In this usage the *NT* has not only been
influenced by the *OT* and the LXX, but, probably even more directly,
by Qumran: cf. 1QS IV. 25(20), 'the decreed End-Time' (*qeṣ*,
Season) (*mo'ēd*) (cf. Dan. 9:26), 1 QM 1.5, 11–12.

how it is full time now: lit. '(knowing that) it is by now high time
(to wake from sleep)'. While *hōra* (*estin*), 'it is high time' is a
common Greek idiom (Cranfield), the noun *hōra*, like *kairos*, carries
in itself eschatological overtones: it fits perfectly here into its eschatological context. (Cf. Barrett, *ad loc.*)

wake from sleep: 'sleeping', 'waking', 'day', 'night', 'light', 'darkness' are familiar images in the apocalyptic eschatology, Jewish and
Christian, of the period, for the passing of the 'period of wickedness'
and the 'dawn' of the messianic era (Kingdom of God). Cf., e.g.,
Eph. 5:14, (8), 1 Th. 5:4, etc., and in Qumran (sectarian) Judaism
(e.g., 1QS I. 9, II. 16, III. 13, 1QM 1.1, Test. Lev. xix. 1, Joseph
xx. 2, etc.).

salvation is nearer to us: here clearly means the final 'deliverance'
from evil, sin, and death, to be realised at the Parousia. Cf. 8:23–24.
On *sotēria*, 'salvation', see above, pp. 29ff. It is possible to construe
the text as 'Now is our salvation nearer' (so the Vulgate), but the
context requires 'nearer to us.'

first believed: So also *NEB*, but lit., 'when we came to believe'
(ingressive aorist). So Cranfield, p. 681, n. 6.

12. **the day is at hand:** cf. Mk 1:15. Very early morning, as dawn
breaks, and at sunset, are the periods of maximum activity in the
East, because of the heat of the day. Thus we learn that King
Agrippa I was already, along with the populace, in the theatre at
dawn (Josephus, *Ant.* XIX. viii. 2 (344)). It was the busiest period
of the day in the Temple, as preparations were made for the daily
offering; it was then the *Shema'* was recited; it was then the Essenes
made their devotions, turned towards the rising sun (Josephus, *BJ*,
II, viii. 5 (128). Then was also the time for Christians to be awake
and about their Lord's business. The suggestion that the words 'in
the day' (v. 13) are intended also to convey the idea that Christians
are now to behave as if the Last Day had come is somewhat far-
fetched.

I cannot see any defensible alternative to the literal understanding
of these words, *viz.*, that they refer to the imminence of the
Parousia, to come within at least decades, not centuries, of
subsequent Christian history. Paul certainly here appears to share
the belief implicit at 1 Th. 4:15, and made explicit at Jn 21:23 that
the End was anticipated by some believers in the proximate, if

not the immediate, future. 2 Pet. 3:3ff., however, provides a later reflective, but also a canonical scriptural modification of this primitive belief, and one which commends itself more widely to present Christian expectations. Christian faith cannot surrender the essential feature in the kerygma, which is expressed in the doctrine of the Second Advent—the final consummation of all things, when the Kingdom of God, inaugurated in Christ, will be finally and fully realised, not on this earth in the present Age, but in a 'renewed heaven and earth' (2 Pet. 3:13).

cast off . . . put on: the metaphor is that of putting off garments. The expression in the connection and context belongs to a set of formulae evidently connected with baptism and possibly deriving from a primitive baptismal liturgy; cf. Selwyn, pp. 396ff. The figure is used less frequently of the putting on of the 'armor of light', cf. 6:13, 'arms of righteousness', than of the 'donning of Christ' (or the 'new man'), e.g., Gal. 3:27; Eph. 4:24; Col. 3:9, 12. It seems unlikely that the imagery was first suggested by the undressing of the catechumen at baptism, and by the donning, after the ceremony, of a (white?) baptismal garment, symbolic of new life.

13. as in the day: cf. 1 Th. 5:5: Christians are 'children of the light' and 'children of the day', not 'of the night' or 'of darkness'. Lagrange detects a suggestion of the Roman idea that 'in the night everything is permissible'. Some interpret like Bengel: 'See that you bear yourself so now, as you would desire to be seen to be at the last day.' But while 'Day' does have this eschatological nuance at v. 12, it seems here also to be used metaphorically—as at 1 Th. 5:5ff. along with 'light'—to describe the life that had 'put on' Christ—one pure and clear as daylight, in contrast to the 'dark deeds' of self-indulgence in drunkenness, sexual excesses, strife and envy.

reveling and drunkenness . . .: cf. 1 Th. 5:7.

debauchery . . . jealousy: The nouns in Greek are all in the plural; cf. *Jerusalem Bible*, 'no drunken orgies.' The plurals may be explained as stressing repeated acts (abstract plur.?) or perhaps as having the force of the 'intensive plur.' in Hebrew (cf. Jn 1:13, Ps. 5:10 (LXX 11), 'impiety' (LXX *asebeiōn*), Ps. 37:13 'deceit' (LXX *doliotētas*)); cf. G-K, § 124, d (abstract plur.) e (intensive plur.). The 'pairings', 'reveling and drunkenness', 'debauchery and licentiousness', 'quarrelling and jealousy' may be explained as examples of hendiadys, 'drunken revelries', 'sensual debauchery', 'jealous strife' (cf. Cranfield *ad loc.*) The English noun 'debauchery', however, has a wider connotation than Greek *koitē(ai)*, lit. (a) 'sleeping together', which, along with its paired *aselgeia(ai)* refers here unambiguously to illicit sexual intercourse or related sexual aberrations. The noun *koitē* is especially used of the 'marriage-bed'

in Greek, but can also be used generally of sexual intercourse in
both Greek and Hebrew: in the Old Testament it corresponds to
Hebrew *mishkabh* (vb. *shakabh*), where both verb and noun are
employed especially of illicit sexual acts, both heterosexual and
homosexual (e.g., Num. 5:20, Jg. 21:11, 12, Lev. 18:22 etc.). It
was a common vice in the hellenistic world, and is listed and
condemned at 2 C. 12:21, Gal. 5:19, 1 Th. 4:3; Eph. 4:19; 1 Pet.
4:3, 2 Pet. 2:18.

14. put on the Lord Jesus: Cf. above on v. 12.

make no provision . . . desires: The second half of this verse
defines, negatively, what, in this context, being 'clothed' with the
Lord Jesus Christ means, viz., to cease 'intending', and so 'making
provision for' 'carnal acts' (Gal. 5:19). Here the meaning of 'desires',
'lusts' (*epithymiai*) has clearly a sexual connotation. Cf. above, on
Rom. 1:24, 6:12, 7:7, 13:9.

The suggested interpretation that these words imply 'a qualified
approval of care for the natural life of the body' (Cranfield) as
Luther and Bengel understood them, is rightly rejected by Cranfield
and by commentators; we would then have expected *sōma* not *sarx*
(although *sarx* = *basar* can be neutral in Paul as in the Old
Testament).

ATTITUDE TO CHRISTIANS, WEAKER IN THE FAITH

14:1–15:13

The fellow-Christian here is the Jewish Christian still harbouring
legalistic scruples about feast-days or food, and still, no doubt,
finding it difficult to accept Gentile participation in the Gospel (cf.
A. George, 'Les Écritures, Source de l'Esperance (Romains
15:1–6)', *Bible et Vie Chrétienne*, XXII (1958), pp. 54ff.). These are
the 'weaker brethren'; Paul identifies himself with the 'strong',
those able to exercise their Christian freedom, but he pleads for a
charitable exercise of it. The argument is that it is the same Lord
with whom we all have to do, and it is to him each must give
account. We are not, then, to sit in judgement on our brother, but
rather to make up our minds not to place a stumbling-block in his
path; and this we do if we give offence to a 'weaker' brother for
whom 'clean' and 'unclean' are still questions of conscience.

1. weak in faith: for this kind of debility or impotence, cf. 4:20,
where it is also contrasted with strength and vigour (cf. below 15:1).
Cf. also 2 C. 12:10, 13:9.

welcome: *NEB*: 'accept'. The word is used in the papyri of
'receiving' into a household (once of 'accepting' for the army). See

MM, s.v. Here it is not only receiving fellow-Christians with a 'weak' faith into the household of faith, but taking them as full partners. Cf. verse 3 of God's acceptance of all such; 15:7, Christ's acceptance. Cf. also Phm. 17.

for disputes over opinions: *NEB*: 'attempting to settle doubtful points' (*diakriseis*, 'resolvings (by judgement)'; *dialogismoi*, 'controversies'). Perhaps 'quarrels' is better than 'disputes' for *diakriseis* (cf. Liddell and Scott, s.v.), and the following *dialogismōn* a genitive of definition, 'without quarrels over disputed matters' (e.g. whether Jewish ritual requirements were binding on the Christian). Paul is here recommending unconditional acceptance of the 'weaker' brethren into the 'fellowship' (including 'table fellowship'); even arguments about Christian freedom are not to be allowed to jeopardise the brotherly relationship of *agapē*.

2. vegetables: cf. verse 21. The controversy evidently had to do with eating meat, with which also went the drinking of wine (cf. 14:21). Cranfield lists no fewer than six different theories about the nature of the 'weakness' of the 'weaker' brethren, of which two are probably nearest to the original intention of the author: (1) a suggestion which sees the twofold abstinence (from meat and wine) 'as a manifestation within primitive Christianity of ideas and practices which were characteristic of various religious-philosophical movements in antiquity and which persisted with remarkable vitality down the centuries.' (pp. 693ff.) Among practices listed (p. 693, n. 5), is the vegetarianism of the Jewish Therapeutai of Egypt (Philo, *Vit. Contempl.* ix.37), who actually abstained from *both* meat and wine (Philo, ed. Loeb, ix. 73–74). (2) The second possibility is that 'the weakness' of the weak consisted in a continuing concern with literal obedience to the ceremonial part of the *OT* law, though this was not necessarily the same kind of 'judaising' as that referred to in 1 Corinthians and Galatians. The conclusion is reached that, while it is not possible to decide with absolute certainty between (1) and (2), the latter seems the more probable explanation.

So far as (2) is concerned, such legalistic scruples would not be surprising considering the Jewish character of Roman Christianity (above, p. 7), but (2) still does not account for the combination of food and wine. According to one interpretation of v. 5, the arguments were also about 'feast-days'. Does all this not perhaps point at least to the presence in Rome of 'sectarian' Jews, similar to the Therapeutai, the Egyptian Essenes, who had embraced Christianity, but wanted to retain their 'asceticism', with regard to meat and wine, and perhaps their own views of the festival calendar (See especially Schürer, *History*, Vol. II, p. 592 and below, pp. 192ff.). As Jews they would also share the scruples of the more orthodox

Jerusalem Jews about what was ritually 'clean' and 'unclean'. (cf. verse 14). See further, below, on verse 21. Were these people the ancestors of the later Encratite heretics? Cf. also 1 Tim. 4:3ff., where these *abstinentes*, like their Marcionite descendants, abstained from marriage as well; see, further, note at verse 21.

3. despise: *NEB*: 'hold in contempt'.

welcomed: cf. above, verse 1. 'God has taken him into his household (*familia dei*)' (Michel). The same argument is repeated with reference to Christ at 15:7. The figure of speech is confirmed by the use of 'household servant' at verse 4.

4. the servant of another: The word 'servant' (lit. 'household servant', *oiketēs*) is synonymous with *doulos*, 'slave'; the only difference is that *oiketēs* defines more accurately the status of probably most *douloi* in Graeco-Roman society. Just as at v. 10 Paul refers to the non-abstainer as the Christian 'brother' of the abstainer, here he describes him as also 'household servant', i.e. his fellow-slave in the family of God, both servants of the same God and Lord Jesus Christ.[1]

It is the 'weak' Christian who abstains from 'meat and drink' who is here addressed (for the style, cf. 2:1): he has no right to pass judgement on his 'brother' who does not abstain. Cf. the parallel v. 10: 'Why do you (who abstain) pass judgement on your brother (the non-abstainer)? Or you (the non-abstainer), why do you despise your brother?' Here, at v. 4 Paul asks 'Who are you to pass judgement (*in malam partem* = condemn) the servant of another (*allotrion oiketēn*)?' The adjective *allotrios* is usually rendered and interpreted 'the servant of another, i.e. Christ or God.' Cf. Cranfield, p. 703: 'The point made by *allotrion* is not, of course, that the strong Christian belongs to a master other than the one to whom the weak Christian belongs, but that he belongs to a master other than the weak Christian—he is not the weak Christian's slave, but Another's, i.e. Christ's (or God's), and therefore not answerable to the weak Christian'. This view that by passing judgement on his 'brother', the 'weak' Christian is usurping the place of their common Lord, goes back at least to Zahn, *ad loc*.[2] There is, however, an alternative interpretation: Käsemann renders: 'Wer bist du denn, der du den fremden Knecht zu richten wagst.' If this means 'the foreign/alien

---

[1]While *doulos*, 'slave', is well attested as a description of the Christian in his relationship to God (or Christ), (cf. Rom. 6:16, *TWNT*, Bd., II, pp. 276f.), *oiketēs* is rarer in this connection (but cf. Lk. 16:13). It is chosen here to serve the argument about the relationship of these two 'servants' of the Lord. They are equals before their Master.

[2]Cf. the Syriac Peshitta version, 'a servant who is not yours.'

(i.e. the Gentile) servant (of God)', it would correspond to the use of *allotrios* in biblical Greek = Heb. *nochri*, i.e. the non-Israelite, the Gentile.[1]

In this context in Romans the reference would then be to the Gentile 'liberal Christian', in contradistinction to the Jewish Christian, anxious to observe the ritual law. Is there, in the background of Paul's thought, Lev. 25:55 '. . . to me the people of Israel are servants (LXX *oiketai*), they are my servants whom I brought forth out of the land of Egypt: I am the Lord your God.'? These Roman Jewish-Christian *abstinentes* were no doubt making exclusive claims to be the true 'servants' of the Lord. Paul is stating that both Jews and Gentiles alike are all 'servants' in the *familia Christi*, responsible to the same Lord and Master.

stands or falls: For the phraseology cf. Ps. 37:24, 145:14, Prov. 24:16. The household slave is responsible only to the *pater familias*, his master. For the total subservience of slave to master in Graeco-Roman society, see *TWNT*, Bd. II, pp. 273ff.: the slave had no will other than that of his master. The dative is one of advantage or disadvantage: 'it is with regard to (not "before", *RSV*) his own master he stands (succeeds/survives) or falls, is dismissed, fails.)'[2]

is able: better, *NEB*: 'has power to enable', used also of God at 2 C. 9:8 and of Christ at 2 C. 13:3.

5. **esteems one day as better than another:** lit. 'prefers (*krinei*) one day over another'. Ancient interpreters understand the reference to be to the observance of particular days as days of abstinence, and this view is also shared by modern exegetes (cf. Leenhardt, pp. 348ff. and Cranfield, p. 705). Others think of festival days, Old Testament celebrations, in the Roman Jewish, but also in the Jewish-Christian Calendar. Much less probable is the suggestion that Paul is thinking of 'lucky' or 'unlucky' days, or of differences relating to the transition from the observance of the Sabbath to the Lord's Day.

esteems all days alike: This is the usual rendering ('regards all days alike', *NEB*), 'makes no difference between days' (Cranfield). If the reference, however, is taken to be to the *OT* festival days, then the impression is given of Pauline indifference or even carelessness about such 'special days' (cf. Zahn, p. 572)—unless we interpret (with Zahn) '(one man) treats every day as a Sabbath'; cf. also

---

[1]Cf. 2 Chr. 6:32 'the stranger (*nochri*) who is not of thy people, Israel.' Cf. Josephus, *Ant.* XVIII, iv (47), 3 Kgd. 11:1.

[2]The variant 'God' for 'Lord' of the TR is usually explained as a scribal adaptation to verse 3. If original, it would then be an intended parallel to verse 3.

Bengel, 'He judges that he should equally do good at all times'. Both interpretations are unconvincing; and it seems very unlikely that Paul would ever have deliberately offended the 'weaker brethren' by implying carelessness on the part of the 'stronger' towards the Jewish festive seasons.

On the traditional view that the reference is to days of 'abstinence', Leenhardt writes '. . . we shall not regard this as an allusion to the Sabbath but to practices of abstinence and fasting on regular fixed dates. What such practices were we do not know, and it is a great pity, since great interest attaches to the apostle's estimate of them.' (p. 349) On this view, the meaning of the second clause would then be that, whereas 'one man prefers one day rather than another to abstain from meats' etc., i.e. to fast, another approves of any date, (lit. regards every day as suitable (for fasting)). Although we have no information about such practices in the Roman Church in Paul's day, the position as set out in the Order of Hippolytus would confirm this interpretation; for then there were two fixed days only for fasting, viz. Good Friday and Holy Saturday— 'special fasts for all might be directed on *any* special occasion' (B. S. Easton, *The Apostolic Tradition of Hippolytus* (London, 1934), p. 96 (italics mine); cf. H. Lietzmann, *Geschichte der alten Kirche*, Berlin and Leipzig, 1936, Vol. 2, p. 129: '. . . the Roman congregation of Hippolytus fasted generally still *completely as desired* (nach Belieben) and knows of one binding rule for fasting, only on Good Friday and Holy Saturday' (italics mine).

It may be objected that 'abstention' from meat etc. at this period and 'fasting' were two different things, but the difference may be academic only. It is not surprising to find one *NT* ms. (von Soden, cursive 367) reading 'fasts' (*nēsteuei*), twice in this verse for 'esteems' (*krinei*), a reading supported by the Ethiopic version.

The meaning would then be that, while one man considered fasting appropriate only on certain *Festtage*, another regarded any day as suitable for fasting, if some occasion warranted or justified one. Was Paul referring to the observation by Jewish Christians in Rome of the two weekly Fast-days, Wednesday and Friday (or Thursday and Monday)? Cf. *Didache* XVIII.

be fully convinced . . . mind: i.e., everyone must not only make up his own mind on these controversial issues, but come to a firm conviction by himself. The words were probably directed at the 'waverers' who were 'tossed to and fro . . . with every wind of doctrine' (Eph. 4:14). See further, below on verse 23.

6. in honour of the Lord: the dative (*tō Kyriō*) may have the force given by the *NEB*: 'has the Lord in mind'; both senses are possible. Such 'days' were days of special thanksgiving; even he

who fails to keep such a day, if he does it with a good conscience,
in the name of Christian liberty, is giving thanks to God.

give thanks to God: Is there an implied allusion to grace before
meat?

Equality Before God 14:7–12

Like other similar passages in Paul, this gem of Christian teaching,
where an argument is built up to a doctrinal climax by literary
features such as balance of clauses (negative, then positive) and by
polar opposites—life, death, embracing all attitudes in life—the
whole clinched from Scripture, arises in the course of the discussion
of a long-forgotten controversy in the Roman Church on clean and
unclean foods, the observance of Sabbaths, feast-days, etc. For the
'hymnic' style, cf. 2 Tim. 2:11–13.

7–8. None of us lives to himself . . .: Cf. D. M. Baillie, *God
Was in Christ* (London, ²1956), pp. 204ff.: '. . . the very essence of
sin is self-centredness.' Behind St Paul's proverbial and Hebraic
sententia lies the hellenistic as well as, no doubt, Jewish reflection.
Terence presents a different view of self-sufficiency (*Adelphoe*, v.
iv. 9) but Plutarch (*Vita Cleom.*, 31) declares that it is 'a disgraceful
thing to live and to die for ourselves alone'. The problem is to find
an alternative to self-centred living.

8. to the Lord . . . so then . . . we are the Lord's: we only live
and die, Paul declares, 'for the Lord' (dat. of advantage), or 'before
the Lord', and therefore responsible alone 'to the Lord', the reason
being that we belong to the Lord; we are his servants (verse 4: cf.
1 C. 6:19ff.).

9. lived again: *NEB*: 'came to life again' (the oldest reading).
Christ's death and resurrection alone establish his right to be Lord
of the living and the dead.

10. Judgement belongs to the Lord. Christians have enough to
do minding their proper business.

judgment seat of God: the variant 'Christ' is explained as due to
the influence of 2 C. 5:10. Origen noted that Paul wrote 'God' to
the Romans, but 'Christ' to the Corinthians. SH rightly reject the
line of interpretation taking 'God' of Christ in his divine nature, on
the grounds that it is contrary to Pauline usage (cf. however, Heb.
1:8). It is, however, very important to see how easily St Paul passes
from Christ to God; cf. SH, p. 389. Sanday argues that God is here
mentioned as Judge because he judges the world through Christ.

11. As I live, says the Lord: there are two salient features in the
Pauline 'quotation' of Isa. 45:23 which owe nothing to the LXX or
MT: (a) the asseverative formula prefacing the quotation, 'As I live',

probably derived from Isa. 49:18, which is introduced by St Paul, not just as a formula of asseveration (an 'honest to God!'), but with the clear intention of identifying 'the Lord' in the quotation with the Lord Christ who 'lived again' (verse 9; lit. 'came alive', i.e. rose from the dead), and is the Lord both of the dead and the living (verse 9). It is to the Risen and Living Lord that every knee shall bow; cf., however, Cranfield, p. 710, '. . . it is by no means clear that this was St Paul's intention'; it is the Lord God (Cranfield argues), before whose tribunal we shall all stand (verse 10), who is the subject of the quotation. The prominence of the theme from verses 7–9 of the Christian living and dying, and as belonging to the Lord who died and lived again to be our Lord (*kyrieusē*), does suggest, however, a deliberate alteration of the formula from 'by myself I swear' (LXX Isa. 45:23) to 'As I *live*, says the Lord' (LXX Isa. 49:18), in order to identify the Lord in the quotation with Christ the Lord. Phil. 2:10ff. does show that the quotation was given a christological application. (b) The second part of the quotation should be rendered: 'and every tongue shall praise God'— universal worship of the Risen Lord is to be accompanied by universal thanksgiving to God. (On the basis of the Pauline exegesis of Isa. 45:23, see the present writer's article 'The Christological Use of the Old Testament in the New Testament', in *NTS*, XVIII (1971–2), p. 8.)

give praise to God: *mg.* 'confess', i.e. to acknowledge God (so *NEB*); this is certainly the meaning required at Phil. 2:10, '. . . and every tongue confess that Jesus Christ is Lord'. The more common meaning of *exomologeisthai*, however, in biblical Greek is 'to give praise to', as *RSV* renders here.

12. to God: The omission of these words by mss. like B, 1739, G, and the early Fathers might possibly be explained as necessitated by reading 'Christ' at verse 10; it could also, however, be an addition dictated by the change from 'Christ' to 'God' there; cf. J. Hugh Michael, in *JTS*, XXIX (1938), p. 154.

The Rule of Love 14:13–23

13. decide: the same Greek word as for 'pass judgement' (*krinein*). Cf. Mt. 7:1.

stumbling-block or hindrance: both words are biblical, and when combined give a characteristically biblical locution. The messianic use of the expression is quite independent of the usage here or in parallel passages, e.g., at 1 C. 8:9. Cf. Hermas, *Mand.* ii 4, where 'religiosity' (*semnotēs*) of a kind different from that discussed here is the stumbling-block.

14. I know and am persuaded in the Lord Jesus: Paul gives the fullest possible apostolic emphasis to his conviction. Is he thinking of the dominical teaching at Mt. 15:11, Mk 7:15? First, the general principle of Christian 'freedom' is thus categorically laid down; then follows the qualification: it is better to tolerate another's prejudice than to advocate one's beliefs at the expense of a breach of *agapē*. Cf. 1 C. 8:7–13.[1]

15. is being injured: *NEB*: 'is outraged'; the literal rendering, 'is pained', is as adequate as any. It is the grief and pain caused by outraged feelings Paul is stressing as a breach of charity.

walking in love: better, *NEB*: 'guided by love' (lit. '(is no longer) walking *according* to love'). Cf. Eph. 5:2. *Agapē* provides the standard of Christian conduct; it is also the inner disposition of the Christian believer.

for whom Christ died: that Christ died for mankind is the core of Paul's Gospel (cf. 5:6, 8). The repetition of this 'advice' here in the same terms as at 1 C. 8:11 may indicate that Paul used this stereotyped expression regularly in this connection. The solemn form the injunction takes shows how seriously the Apostle regarded any breach of charity of this kind. By giving such offence, or in leading a 'weaker' brother astray, when his conscience was still troubled by such things (cf. 1 C. 8:10), the 'strong' Christian believer was undoing the work of Christ—destroying one whom Christ had saved.

16. spoken of as evil: a strong verb in Greek. The meaning is well brought out by *NEB*: 'What for you is a good thing must not become an occasion for slanderous talk.'

17. For the kingdom of God: Paul has several 'Kingdom of God' sayings, mostly bearing the character of general truths, e.g., 1 C. 4:20; 15:50; Gal. 5:21 (in the later two cases it is conceived as a kind of inheritance). 'Kingdom of God' is virtually here *regula dei* (like *regula fidei*), as in the rabbinical idea of taking on oneself the 'yoke' of the *malkuth* of God. In other words, it is here a spiritual absolute, though naturally also eschatologically conceived; the righteousness, peace, and joy are the righteousness, peace, and joy of faith.

righteousness and peace . . . Holy Spirit: Cf. above at 5:1–2. 'Righteousness' for Paul is always 'faith-righteousness', and no doubt he also has in mind here, as clearly at 5:1–2, the 'peace of mind' which comes from reconciliation to God. That the third item of the triad at 5:1–2, viz. 'hope', corresponds to 'joy' is unconvinc-

---

[1] For a useful discussion of the problems of this verse (and section), cf. O. E. Evans, 'What God requires of man', *ET*, LXIX (1957–8), pp. 199–202.

ing. Cf. Michel, p. 346, n. 3 and Cranfield, p. 719, n. 4. Both terms here, however, as also *chara* 'joy', are used of Christian *charismata* (the fruit of the spirit), so that 'righteousness' has the rich meaning of Heb. *ṣedhaqah* (cf. above, p. 32) and 'peace' (*eirēnē*) that of *shalom*, not only a state of peace with God but the 'wholeness' and 'integrity' of the life of faith. Clearly, however, Paul also is thinking here, as at verse 19, of 'peace' within the Christian community.

joy in the Holy Spirit: it is best to take the last phrase as defining 'joy'. Joy is the outward manifestation of the Spirit; cf. 1 Th. 1:6, Gal. 5:22, Ac. 13:52.

18. he who thus serves Christ: or, 'he who in this (Holy Spirit) serves Christ'. Probably to be understood, as *RSV*, more generally: he who serves Christ also by 'righteousness, peace and joy in the Holy Spirit', rather than by insisting that God's rule refers to kosher distinctions, or by uncharitably claiming that it does not—he is well-pleasing to God, and approved by men. 'This principle cuts both ways, for it hits Jewish-Christian kosher-complexes as hard as the freedom of the enlightened' (T. W. Manson).

19. peace: the phrase and ideal is a characteristically Hebrew one (see SB, I, pp. 215ff.) which passed into Christianity (in a similar sense, Heb. 12:14, 1 Pet. 3:11, Rom. 12:18).

mutual upbuilding: peace is the foundation of any community's strength. The ideal of community, 'compactly built together' by the Gospel and its exponents (through word and life), is a central Pauline thought, especially in the Corinthians correspondence (1 C. 14:3, 5, 12, 26; 2 C. 12:19, 13:10). That *oikodomē* ('upbuilding') here means, correctly, the *ecclesia Christi* is argued by E. Peterson, in *Bib.*, XXII (1941), p. 441.

20. work of God: 20a corresponds to 15b; cf. 1 C. 8:11. The 'work of God' could conceivably refer to the individual man as 'the noblest work of God', or refer to the 'community' which has been built up. Other commentators, e.g. Michel, *ad loc.*, tend to interpret it, in line with verse 15b, of the 'work of Christ', in his death, resurrection, etc. 'God's work in the weak brother, the new man he has begun to create.' (Cranfield)

it is wrong: the general sense is that 'all things are pure'; cf. Mt. 15:11. Nevertheless, it is no good thing—indeed the very opposite, a wicked thing (*kakon*)—for anyone to give offence by his 'freedom' in eating anything set before him.

21. it is right not to eat meat or drink wine: abstention from meat and/or wine was a not unfamiliar feature of ancient ascetic practices; cf. the Rechabites in the *OT*; cf. above on 14:2 and Dan. 10:3. The latter passage reminds us of the practices of the Egyptian *Therapeutai* (Philo, *Vita Contempl.* ix. 37) and possibly also of the

Essenes. Judaism was probably not uninfluenced in this connection
by Pythagorean (Orphic) practices (cf. Philostratus, *Life of Apol-
lonius*, ed. Loeb, Bk. I, Ch. VIII, where wine is not in the category
of things ceremonially impure, but condemned because it impairs
the mind and disturbs the mystical union with the gods).

Was there an ascetic Jewish-Christian group in Rome, or was
wine objected to as having been 'dedicated' by a libation to a pagan
deity (Michel), like the 'meat offered to idols' (1 C. 8)? The probability is that there was a stricter group of *abstinentes* in the Roman
church, abstaining from meat and wine, if only as a protest against
pagan excesses.

your brother stumble states the principle of Paul's own conduct,
enunciated at 1 C. 8:13.

Mg. adds 'or be upset' or 'or be weakened'. This longer text is
not badly attested (B D G), but finds only a few supporters. For
the conjecture: '. . . or do *not even one thing* by which your brother
stumbles' (*mēde hen hō* (Hofmann), *mēde hen, en hō* (Mangey), see
Michel, p. 349, n. 2. *RSV* translates 'or *do* anything (that makes
your brother stumble)' (italics mine). The verb 'do' does not appear
in the text, but requires to be supplied to complete the sense. (So
also *NEB*). (The *AV* is closer to the original, 'nor *anything* (whereby
thy brother stumbleth)'). Did the original read 'or *to do a single
thing* by which (*mēde poiein hen en hō*) your brother stumbles,' where
poiein, 'to do', has fallen out of the text by 'haplography', caused
by the earlier *piein* 'to drink (wine)'?

22–23 state certain conclusions; cf. 14:2. An alternative text would
read: 'Do you have (this) faith? Then keep it to yourself and God.'
The 'faith' in question is the liberal doctrine that 'all things are
pure'.

happy is he . . .: The translation is very obscure. Paul is stating,
sententiously, as *NEB mg*. rightly renders: 'Happy is the man who
does not bring judgement upon himself by what he approves!' The
liberal-minded Christian approves of non-discrimination in food and
drink; but if this attitude leads a brother into trouble, then such a
Christian does bring judgement on himself.

23. But he who has doubts: Greek *diakrinomenos*, giving a word-
play with *krinō, katakrinō* ('judge', 'condemn' (verses 22, 23) (cf.
the conjectured *piein, poiein*, verse 21.) T. W. Manson: 'He who
wavers in his opinion is self-condemned, if he eats (regardless of
tabu).' 'Faith' here is (Christian) conviction. The doing of anything,
such as eating non-kosher food, is sinful if it does not proceed from
the conviction that 'all things are clean', since such a man is doing
what he is still inwardly convinced is wrong. See, further, R. Aroud,

'Quidquid non est ex fide peccatum est (Rom. 14:23)', *Mélanges H. de Lubac* (Editions Montaigne, Paris, 1963–4, 3 vols.)

On the position after verse 23 of the Doxology at 16:25–7, see Introduction, pp. 12ff.

The Action of Love 15:1–13

There is no sense division between 14:23 and 15:1; the chapter division has been determined by a rule of thumb without taking account of the contents.[1]

Verses 1–13 represent the third section of St Paul's exhortation on Christian 'freedom', or the relation of the 'strong' to the 'weak' about ritual matters. Verses 1–6 and 7–13 are to a certain extent parallel in thought, both concluding with a prayer (verses 5–7, 13): common to both is the reference to the lowly service of Christ in the interest of the 'upbuilding' (*oikodomē*) of the Christian community. The liturgical character of the second section is more marked; teaching, exhortation, and doxology are all present.

1. bear with the failings of the weak: the reference is probably more general now, namely, to Jewish Christians whose 'weaknesses' the emancipated Christian must 'bear'. Earlier the 'strong' have been exhorted not to lead the 'weak' astray; now, more positively, Paul enjoins them to adopt the attitude of the Isaianic servant which was also Christ's, to 'bear' (i.e. tolerate in charity) these immature Christians. There seems to be an unmistakable allusion in these words, 'bear', 'weaknesses', to the Christian's duty as a 'servant of the Lord' outlined at Isa. 53:4 (cited at Mt. 8:17). Cf. Lev. 25:55 (above on 14:4).

2. please his neighbour: contrasted with self-pleasing; cf. verse 3. Christ did not 'please himself'; the phrase is virtually synonymous with 'living for oneself' (cf. 14:7). Its opposite is stated at 1 Th. 2:4, 'pleasing God'. Cf. 1 C. 10:33 for St Paul's own attitude: 'I try to please all men in everything I do'—the context is a similar one. There is an indirect allusion to the obligation of Lev. 19:18. Cf. earlier at 14:19; all is for the good of the congregation.

3–6. Verse 3 recalls, not only the attitude of the Servant-Christ, but his long-suffering, forbearance and fortitude; the same qualities are enjoined on the Christian (verse 4)—and they are also the attri-

---

[1] On the last two chapters, consult especially R. Schumacher, 'Die beiden letzten Kapitel des Römerbriefes', *Neutest. Abhandlungen*, XIV. iv, Münster, 1929; C. H. Turner, in *JTS*, x (1909), pp. 365ff. Cf. also J. B. Lightfoot, *Biblical Essays* (London, 1893), pp. 285–374.

butes of God himself (verse 5). Paul frequently uses the same or similar expressions of God and Christ.

3. reproaches: Ps. 69 was evidently widely used as a Christological *testimonium* in the early Church (cf. Rom. 11:9–10, Ac. 1:20, Jn 2:17, 15:25, Lk. 23:36, Mk 15:36). The insults directed at God, the Psalmist believed had fallen upon himself; likewise Jesus bore men's reproaching of God.

4. for our instruction: cf. Rom. 4:24, 1 C. 9:10, and especially 1 C. 10:11. This is the purpose of Scripture. The formulae here used belong to an *OT* and rabbinical type; cf. Bruce Metzger, 'The Formulas Introducing Quotations of Scripture in the New Testament and the Mishnah', *JBL*, LXX (1951), pp. 297ff.

steadfastness: *NEB*: 'fortitude', i.e. following the example of the patience and long-suffering of Christ himself. The sense is that Scripture is there in order to enable us to maintain our Christian hope with Christ-like patience, encouraged by its words.

encouragement: the encouragement comes from the Scriptures, but it is only because they speak of Christ. The Scripture which is prophecy of Christ is also precept for us. Cf. 1 C. 10:11 and Wrede, *Paul*, p. 80; also J. Hugh Michael, in *JTS*, XXXIX (1938), p. 154. Michael suggests that we read 'through the Scriptures', omitting 'the patience and comfort of'; it erroneously repeats (by vertical dittography) the same phrase at verse 5. Cf. 1:17 above, p. 35, 76.

5. to live in such harmony . . .: *NEB*: 'that you agree with one another'. The Greek phrase is similar to that at Phil. 2:5: 'Let that *mind* be in you that was also in Christ'; for the expression, cf. Rom. 12:16, 2 C. 13:11, Phil. 2:2, 4:2. The petitionary prayer is that God should create in them the same outlook as Christ had—the same spirit. At 2 C. 13:11, the expression is followed by: 'be at peace (with one another)' (*eirēneuete*).

with one another: i.e. with both groups—liberals and conservatives, 'Jews' and 'Gentiles', 'formalists', 'ritualists' and the advocates of 'freedom'. (**6.**) Only such unity of spirit can lead to common thanksgiving.

7. welcomed you: *NEB*: 'accepted us' (reading *hēmas* for *hymas* with B D★ P etc.) Cf. 14:1, 3, but here of both sides 'accepting' one another, including, no doubt, welcoming one another to common meals. If these had been interrupted or ceased, then the reference could be to the 'acceptance' of each other once more, in a new beginning at the Lord's Table. Christ had 'accepted' them, the unacceptable; he had even died for sinners (5:6; 14:15); also he had 'received' them into his Body, the Church (Eph. 2:13).

8. servant to the circumcised: cf. Gal. 4:4; Wrede, *Paul*, p. 160.

The Servant of the Lord as regards his own people, but also to show the 'reliability', 'trustworthiness', of God.

confirm: i.e. to 'realise' the promises made to the Fathers, yet also to enable the Gentiles to glorify God for his mercy, as is written, etc.

9–13. There follows a *catena* of *OT* verses (cf. *supra*, p. 56, and SH, p. 77). They are Ps. 18:49 (2 Sam. 22:50), Dt. 32:43, Ps. 117:1, Isa. 11:10. It is Paul's usual way of clinching his argument by invoking the authority of Scripture, here using a conventional form of Scripture quotation.

The verses not only sum up the conclusion of the argument between Jewish and Gentile Christian, but also the main theme and purpose of Romans—the furthering of the *Gentile* mission of the Apostle to the Gentiles.

13. Schumacher (*op. cit.*, p. 199, n. 1) remarks that the main subject matter of the Epistle in its teaching and exhortation is concluded in this closing petition invoking the divine blessing. We have here to think of Paul pausing momentarily in his dictation to utter this heartfelt petition.

Paul ends his Christian 'instruction' to the Romans by stressing Christian hope, though not in isolation from faith and the other 'fruits of the spirit'; 'peace and joy'; 'joy and peace' are closely associated (cf. above, 14:17, and Gal. 5:22)—they are specially emphasised in a situation where the Christian fellowship had evidently been disrupted by the tensions between the 'strong' and the 'weak' parties.

in believing: so far from these words being a gloss (cf. Michel, *ad loc.*) they recall the central theme of the Epistle. Faith is the way into the kingdom of joy and peace.

so that by the power of the Holy Spirit you may abound in hope: an alternative is to translate: 'so that you may abound in hope—all in the power of the Holy Spirit', the latter referring, not only to hope, but to joy and peace in which we also abound 'by the power of the Holy Spirit'.

THE CONCLUSION OF THE EPISTLE 15:14–16:27

PERSONAL: THE APOSTLE'S PLANS

15:14–33

The Roman letter is concluded by a personal section which corresponds to the personal introduction at 1:8–17, to a degree, suggesting to some, point by point correspondence (Michel, *ad loc.*). (These two 'personal' portions bracket the main Epistle.) Paul returns to his plans to visit Rome: that he had a firm intention to do so *deo volente* (cf. 15:32f.) is clear from 1:10 and 15:22-4. He repeats in this closing personal part his duty and obligations as Apostle to the Gentiles (1:5, 14ff., cf. 15:15-16), stressing again his apostolic office and authority. Verses 22-23 outline his travel plans after his forthcoming visit to Jerusalem: 30-3 remind the reader of the extreme dangers of this visit (cf. Introduction, p. 5). Cf. J. Knox, 'Rom. 15:14-33 and Paul's Conception of his Apostolic Mission', *JBL*, LXXXIII (1964), pp. 1-11.

14. I myself: or, 'I too (as well as others)'. The emphasis, 'even I, myself', suggests that Paul did not expect to be believed that he could have such a high regard for the virtues of the Roman Church. 'I am convinced; yes, indeed, I am.' No doubt his hearers believed he had been influenced against them.

goodness . . . knowledge: no doubt terms inclusive of all the Christian virtues and qualities of the Roman Church. The choice of words suggests that Paul sets out to compliment the Roman Church on its Christian virtues, but also on its Christian 'knowledge', i.e., its mature Christian wisdom requiring no help from any outside source. 'Goodness' can only be understood of moral qualities (but cf. Michel); for the noun, cf. Gal. 5:22, Eph. 5:9, 2 Th. 1:11. The choice of 'goodness' suggests that Paul deliberately selects a vague, general term. The object of these complimentary references is now, as at chapter 1, to prevent the hearers from taking offence.

15. on some points: *NEB*: 'at times', i.e. in some of his arguments or modes of expression he had been more than bold.
very boldly: lit. 'rather boldly', i.e., much too boldly. Though not the founder of the Roman Church, Paul can write to them 'much too boldly', only by virtue of his apostleship 'of grace' to the Gentiles.
by way of reminder: Paul again strikes an apologetic note; he had nothing to teach the Roman Church they did not already know.
grace given me by God: cf. Gal. 1:15ff.

16. in the priestly service: *hierourgein* means 'to exercise priestly functions'; cf. 1:9 and 12:1f. Cf. C. Wiéner, '*Hierourgein* (Rom. 15:16)', in *Stud. Paulin. Congressus*, 1961, II (Rome, 1963), pp. 399-404.
offering of the Gentiles: the Gentile Christians are the 'offering', and Paul is the priest who offers them to God; cf. Phil. 2:17, where Paul adds the thought of pouring out his blood (life) as the libation accompanying the offering. Cf. Isa. 66:20, where the Diaspora Jews are the 'offering' (*minḥā*) which the Gentiles will bring to Jerusalem (SB, III, p. 153).

The 'offering' of the Gentiles is necessarily unclean; but it is cleansed and sanctified by the Holy Spirit, and so 'well-pleasing' to God. Is Paul thinking of the Christian's baptism?

17. In Christ Jesus, then, I have reason to be proud: Paul boasts of the success of his apostolic mission from vv. 17–21, but his 'boasting' is 'in Christ Jesus'. He boasts of what Christ and the Holy Spirit have accomplished in word and deed, through his ministry.

18. to win obedience from the Gentiles: the main purpose of the Epistle to the Romans. Cf. 1:5.

19. by the power of signs and wonders . . .: a further explication of 'word and deed' (verse 18). These 'signs and wonders' and 'power of the Spirit' were the marks of an apostle (cf. 2 C. 12:12, Heb. 2:4). Note the chiastic arrangement: word, deed; signs, etc.; spiritual power. The 'signs' are wrought by the apostles through the power of the Holy Spirit; it is also the Spirit who inspires the Word.

Paul was only interested in reaching the unevangelised portions of the Levant, and repeats his earlier principle of not entering the 'territory' of another (cf. 1 C. 3:10).

Illyricum: the 'inclusive' geography (from Jerusalem to the edge of the Roman world) is not mentioned simply to supply grounds for St Paul's 'boasting'. It may have been less ambition than eschatology which determined this representative area, just as it was the Apostle's desire to preach the Gospel 'to the ends of the earth' which motivated his planned visit to Spain (cf., especially, J. Munck, *Paul and the Salvation of Mankind*, trans. F. Clarke (London, 1959), esp. pp. 51ff., pp. 298ff.).

Illyricum was an extensive Roman Province stretching along the Adriatic from Italy and Pannonia in the north to Macedonia in the south.

fully preached the gospel of Christ: cf. Col. 1:25 (*AV*: 'to fulfil the word of God'). We are possibly dealing with a familiar expression (so Michel), but one not necessarily meaning the same in every context. Could it mean here that Paul's boast was that he had 'filled the whole of the Mediterranean East with the Gospel of the Messiah' (obj. gen.)? *NEB* is probably correct: 'I have completed the preaching of the Gospel of Christ from Jerusalem as far as Illyricum.' Cf., further, A. S. Geyser, 'Un Essai d'Explication de Rom. 15:19', *NTS*, VI (1959–60), pp. 156–9.

20–21: In customary fashion, Paul concludes this argument by a scriptural quotation (Isa. 52:15), singling out for special emphasis the thought of the previous verse—Paul's policy of not entering the 'territory' of others.

21. who have never been told of him: The quotation originally referred to the Servant of the Lord; now it is applied to Christ as the

Lord's Servant-Messiah; cf. 10:16 (Isa. 53:1). Paul is a missionary of the Servant-Messiah to the world, which, till his kerygma, had neither sight nor hearing of such a one.

Paul's Travel Plans and his Projected Visit to Rome 15:22–30

These verses read very much like an ordinary, personal letter of the period.

22. hindered: a familiar word in Paul (e.g. 1 Th. 2:18, Gal. 5:7) for any let or hindrance from human or other agency. Is there any suggestion that obstacles had been placed in the Apostle's way to any visit to Rome, on the grounds that it was the province of other 'apostles'? (Perhaps Paul considered Rome big enough for all?) The whole passage assumes a sensitive awareness to the possibility that he might be considered an intruder. He is careful to emphasise that it is only a visit in passing on the way to Spain, and is not 'trespassing' on the preserves of others. **23** cf. 1:11.

24. Spain: the Pillars of Hercules marked the limits of the *oikoumenē*. Paul's plan is eschatologically conceived: the Gospel must first be preached 'to the ends of the earth' before the End comes (see note above, p. 203).

At the same time, that there is nothing in this verse to suggest that Paul's plans were not real ones: Spain was frequently visited from Rome (Pausanias, *Hell. Peri.*, x.iv. 6, *CIL* II, No. 1982 (p. 268): cf. Cicero, *Tusc.*, i.45; the tourist centre was Gades, site of the famous Temple of Melkart, the Phoenician Hercules). Ac. 19:21ff. confirms the plans of the Apostle outlined here; Rome was a populous centre of the Roman Empire, and there were probably several active synagogues there (Schürer, II. ii, p. 242, ed. Vermes, Millar, Black, p. 445) (above, p. xvii).

to be sped on my journey: i.e., not only to be given an encouraging farewell, but no doubt also direction, and means, and letters of introduction; cf. Ac. 20:38, 21:5. The phrase was probably a polite formality in current speech (1 C. 16:6; 2 C. 1:16). Dodd, *ad loc.*; SH, p. 411.

enjoyed your company for a little: i.e., 'had some satisfaction out of my visit to you', implying that more of their company would have been even better—again, probably a familiar polite locution in current use.

25. with aid for the saints: or, 'in order to be of service to'. Cf. J. J. O'Rourke, 'The Participle in Rom. 15:25', in *CBQ*, xxix, (1967), pp. 116–18.

26. have been pleased to make: i.e., have freely decided for themselves that it was, after all, no more than their duty. Note the emphatic repetition of this at verse 27: Paul clearly wishes to emphasise that this is no Jewish-Christian 'tax', like those payable by Diaspora synagogues to the Temple, but a freely offered contribution.

the poor among the saints: *NEB*: 'the poor among God's people'. The genitive is partitive, so that the 'poor' here are the physically poor; i.e. the term can hardly be understood here as a *terminus technicus* for the Jerusalem congregation (cf. Michel, *ad loc.*). Cf., however, Gal. 2:10 and, for 'poor' in this specialised sense (applied also to the Qumran sectarians), see *TWNT*, s.v. *ptōchos*, Bd. VI, pp. 885ff. (Bammel). Is Paul here recalling this familiar appellation while reminding his readers that it was also literally true? For 'saints' as a *terminus technicus*, see note on 1:7.

30. to strive together . . . prayers: lit. 'to agonise together with me'. For prayer as an 'agonising', 'wrestling' with God, cf. Col. 4:12; the image no doubt could go back to Gen. 32:24ff. (Jacob). Others think of the struggle being against evil or opposing powers (SH); cf. Mt. 26:42 par.

31. delivered from: especially of physical danger. Used by Paul again at 2 Th. 3:2; cf. Mt. 6:13 of spiritual deliverance.

unbelievers: the chief danger, the hostile Jews who rejected the faith of Christ. The participle 'those who are unbelieving' suggest an active disbelief.

my service: *diakonia*. A variant, *dōrophoria* ('gift-bringing') occurs in the Western text; it has the overtones of 'oblation', but is clearly secondary.

If Paul could be certain of the attitude of the 'unbelieving Jews', one would have expected that he would not be uncertain about the friendly reception of the Jerusalem Christians. But they were probably suspicious of a Gentile mission as were the Jews, so that Paul cannot even be certain that his 'collection' from the Gentile churches would be acceptable. Cf. Ac. 21:21.

32. be refreshed in your company: i.e. enjoy a kind of spiritual holiday after Jerusalem. Cf. Rom. 1:12.

33. the God of peace: occurs again at 16:20; 2 C. 13:11; Phil. 4:9; 1 Th. 5:23; Heb. 13:20. 2 Th. 3:16 has 'the Lord of peace'. The phrase is typically Jewish: it occurs, e.g., in Test. Dan V:2, and in rabbinical sources. See SB, Bd. III, p. 318, Michel, p. 374, n. 3, and especially G. Delling in *Jesus und Paulus*: *Festschrift für W. G. Kümmel*, Göttingen, 1975, pp. 76–84.

A PERSONAL NOTE

A PERSONAL NOTE

16:1–27

For the problem of the connection of chapter 16 with the rest of
the Epistle, see Introduction, pp. 11ff. and Cranfield, pp. 5ff. The
most detailed studies of the names of persons listed are still those
of J. B. Lightfoot, in his *Philippians*, pp. 173ff. and SH, pp. 418ff.

Personal Greeting **16:1–16**

1. Phoebe is usually considered to have been the bearer of the letter.
If this is a separate letter, it could almost be classed as a letter of
recommendation (as common then as now, cf. 2 C. 3:1); even as it
is, as part of Romans, it serves this purpose. The Christian lady in
question appears to have been a Greek Gentile Christian (a Jew
would scarcely have such a name), probably of some social standing
or influence, for she is described as a *prostatis*, or *patrona*. This
would seem originally to have designated an officially recognised
person who had to deal with the rights of 'aliens' and freed slaves.
Here the sense may be a general one; the Roman Christians are
asked to 'stand by' her ('help her'), as she has 'stood by and for'
many, including the Apostle himself—possibly in some legal matter;
see note on verse 2. As a 'deaconess' (cf. 1 Tim. 3:11), she had also
an official function in the congregation at Cenchreae, the port of
Corinth. This seems the only *NT* reference to a deaconess. It has
been conjectured that Phoebe's duties were concerned especially
with women, the sick or 'aliens', or with assisting women at baptism,
but there is very little foundation for these speculations. Cf. further,
C. H. Turner, in *The Ministry of Women* (London, 1919), pp. 93ff.,
M. D. Gibson, 'Phoebe', *ET*, XXIII (1911–12), p. 281, C. C. Ryrie,
The Place of Women in the Church (New York, 1958), pp. 86ff.

2. receive her in the Lord as befits the saints: i.e. 'give her a
Christian welcome', 'welcome her *christiano more*) (Bengel); 'in the
Lord', the phrase occurs again at 11b, 12, 13. All that Christians
are or do is *en kyriō* ('in the Lord'), especially their heavy labours
for others (e.g., 12: 'those that labour in the Lord'—the verb is a
strong one).

help . . . in whatever she may require from you: lit., 'in any affair
where she may need you'. The word for 'help' seems to imply the
kind of help a *prostatis*, or patron, could give, possibly legal aid
('affair' may have this meaning), i.e., assistance, especially that
rendered to aliens entering a country, and particularly Jewish aliens.
This may well have been the kind of 'assistance' Paul himself had
received from Phoebe at Cenchreae when he arrived.

greet: the verb (*aspazesthai*) is repeated fifteen times in this 'greetings' section.

3. Prisca and Aquila: the Jewish Christian couple Paul met in Corinth (cf. Ac. 18:2, 26). The order of the names—wife first—is striking: it occurs again at 2 Tim. 4:19; cf., however, 1 C. 16:19 and Ac. 18:2 (Aquila-Priscilla), 18:26 (Priscilla-Aquila). (The diminutive form 'Priscilla' occurs only in Acts.) They had been refugees in Corinth after the publication of the Edict of Claudius in A.D. 49. They accompanied Paul from Corinth to Ephesus, where evidently they had a residence, like the residence which they had left in Rome, where the local Christian community met (1 C. 16:19; cf. Rom. 16:5). At 2 Tim. 4:19 they appear again in Ephesus. (But cf. Introd., p. 4.) The position of Priscilla *vis-à-vis* Aquila may be explained on the grounds that she was a wealthy Jewish-Christian matron in her own right, able to act as hostess to the Church in these two centres.

If Hort is right in suggestion that Prisca (Priscilla) was a member of a high-born Roman family, this might account for the order; SH thinks they were both 'freed-men'. Aquila came from Pontus in Asia Minor (Ac. 18:1, 2). Their connection with the Roman Church seems probable (SH). The site of their 'house church' in Rome is pointed out at the Church of SS Aquila and Prisca on the Aventine, but the identification does not bear closer examination. There is also a legendary tenth-century *Acts of Prisca* (perhaps significantly named as the leading partner); see, further, SH, pp. 418–20.

4. risked their necks: a current Greek idiom (probably colloquial). See A. Deissmann, *Light from the Ancient East*, pp. 119ff. Is this a reference to a definite incident such as might have happened during the 'riots at Ephesus' (Ac. 18)?
all the churches: the service of this devoted couple to the expanding Church must, indeed, have been great.

5. church in their house: 5a goes with verse 3: the greeting to Priscilla and Aquila includes their house-church. In the first two centuries the Church had no buildings of its own, but met in private houses, usually of a well-to-do family (or widow)—cf. Ac. 12:12; 1 C. 16:19; Col. 4:15; Phm. 2. Cf. also Clement, *Recogn.* x.71.

It has been suggested that the persons greeted in verses 3–16 were members of the 'house-congregation' of Priscilla and Aquila. This would certainly account for Paul's knowing so many Roman Christians since this 'house-church' may have moved from Rome to Ephesus in A.D. 49.

my beloved Epaenetus, who was the first convert in Asia for Christ: a literal and correct translation, but concealing the cultic metaphor of 'first-fruits', the first offering of the harvest, perhaps conferring on Epaenetus a position of special honour in the community. Cf. 1 C. 16:15 and Clement, *Ad Cor. Ep.* 1 xlii. 4, where these 'first-fruits' become the earliest church leaders, bishops, deacons.

Clearly a Greek (the name is common), he may have belonged to the household of Priscilla, and have been their first convert in Ephesus. While the term 'beloved' (*agapētos*) is virtually interchangeable with 'brother' (*adelphos*) (cf. verses 8, 9, 12 and 1 Th. 2:8, 9, Phm. 16 'beloved brother'), the designation here and at verse 8 of Epaenetus and Ampliatus as 'my beloved', 'my beloved in the Lord' does seem to imply a closer personal tie with the Apostle, and a desire to give special honour to these two, probably pioneering *apostoloi* in Rome.

6. Mary, who has worked hard among you: from the name, possibly, but not certainly, a Jewish-Christian, unless we read (with P⁴⁶, ℵ etc.) Miriam. Four women in this chapter are said to have 'laboured' for the Roman congregation; it was a 'Christian work' ('in the Lord'); cf. v. 12. Were they official deaconesses?

7. Andronicus and Junias my kinsmen: or possibly 'fellow-countrymen' (see below on v. 21), perhaps from their names, freedmen, but clearly Jews by birth. The name Junias is not attested as a man's name (Bauer, *Lex.*, s.v.): it is probably best explained as a contraction of Junianus (like Patrobas, Hermas, Olympas). See especially Lightfoot, p. 176. The Greek accusative *Iounian*, however, can be construed to give the common feminine name Junia, which would make Andronicus and Junia a husband and wife pairing, like Prisca and Aquila. Most commentators take the noun as masculine; and in favour of this is the Jewish arrangement for 'pairing' missionary 'apostles' (see Käsemann, p. 395), but the second possibility cannot be so summarily dismissed as it is by Michel (p. 379 'unthinkable'), in view of the prominent role of notable women in the Pauline age. The list here begins with two, Phoebe and Prisca, in the place of honour. SH (p. 423), while favouring the usual view, cite Chrysostom for the second: 'Chrysostom does not appear to consider the idea of a female apostle impossible: ". . . to be apostles at all is a great thing. But to be even amongst these of note, just consider what a great encomium this is! . . . how great is the devotion of this woman that she should be even counted worthy of the appellation of apostle!" ' Cranfield adopts the minority view (pp. 788ff.) Did some or all of the persons greeted on this list belong to 'Caesar's household'? Cf. SH, *ad loc.* Cf. also Phil. 4:22.

my fellow prisoners: in either a literal or a metaphorical sense. Cf. Col. 4:10, Phm. 23. It seems more likely that Paul meant this literally, though when and where Andronicus and Junia(s) were in prison with him it is impossible to say (cf. 2 C. 11:23). Schlatter (*Gottes Gerechtigkeit*, p. 399) thinks the time referred to was when, along with Paul, they belonged to the Antioch congregation; their conversion (older than Paul's) and description as 'distinguished among missionaries' require us to make such an assumption. What evidence, however, is there of imprisonment in this period?

they are men of note among the apostles: i.e. 'themselves distinguished missionaries'.

they were in Christ before me: the perfect tense (*gegonan*) implies that they still are.

8–9. Ampliatus and **Urbanus** are common names in themselves, but are also found in lists of the imperial household (Lightfoot, *loc. cit.*). **Stachys** is a comparatively rare name but attested, and at least one person with this name held important office in the imperial court in St Paul's time (Lightfoot, *loc. cit.*).

10. Apelles: also a name associated with the Roman court (SH). It was also the name of a well-known tragic actor, a native of Ascalon, favoured by the Emperor Gaius.

those who belong to the family of Aristobulus: probably slaves and/or freedmen. Aristobulus was possibly the person of this name who was a grandson of Herod the Great and brother of Agrippa I, who ended his life, as a private individual, in Rome (see Lightfoot, *op. cit.* and Josephus, *BJ*, II. xi. 6 (221–2); *Ant.* xx. i.2 (13). On his death, which probably preceded the writing of Romans, it is likely that, in accordance with established practice, Aristobulus's household was taken over by the Emperor Claudius, of whom Aristobulus appears to have been a friend and adherent. Paul's phrase corresponds to *Aristobuliani*; no doubt such a household would be mainly composed of Jews. (The conjecture that it was this high-born Aristobulos who is here referred to is described by S. Sandmel (*Interpreter's Dictionary of the Bible* (1962), s.v. Herod, p. 593) as far-fetched.

It was obviously through such 'households', where Jews, and later Jewish-Christians, were numerous and influential, that the Gospel penetrated into the higher echelons of Roman imperial society.

11. my kinsman Herodion: obviously a member, probably a freedman, of the Herod family, probably not unconnected with the preceding *Aristobuliani* and the following *Narcissiani*. See Lightfoot, pp. 174ff.

the family of Narcissus: i.e., again, the Narcissians. Lightfoot thinks the reference is to the slaves of the powerful freedman whose wealth was proverbial (Juvenal, *Sat.*, xiv. 329), and who wielded great influence with Claudius. He was put to death by Agrippina just after the accession of Nero. His 'household' would also have been incorporated in the imperial economy.

12. Tryphaena and Tryphosa: two sisters (possibly twins)—or, at any rate, near relatives—for it appears to have been customary to designate such with names from the same root. The second name is commoner than the first.

Persis, singled out by Paul for special praise, is a typical freed-woman's name.

13. Rufus . . . also his mother and mine. Was this the Rufus of Mk 15:21, the son of Simon of Cyrene? Cf. SH, p. 427. He was probably a freed slave. His mother, whom Paul may have known in Palestine or Asia Minor, is specially honoured by the Apostle's skilful compliment; in fact, at some time, she may have protected Paul, rendering him some service.

eminent in the Lord: lit. 'elect in the Lord', but meaning probably more here than an 'elect one', i.e. a Christian; Rufus was evidently a notable Christian. Could there possibly be an allusion to the service his father had rendered?

14. and the brethren who are with them: The names here are mostly attested as names used for slaves or freedmen. **Asyncritus**, e.g., is found in an inscription for a freedman of Augustus. **Hermes** is one of the commonest of slave names occurring frequently among members of the imperial household. **Hermas** is probably an abridged form of a compound name with Hermes, such as Hermog-enes or Hermagoras (so SH). **Patrobas** is probably a variation of Patrobius. It was the name of a wealthy and powerful freedman of Nero, put to death by Galba (Lightfoot, p. 176, Tac. *Hist*. i. 49, ii. 95). If there is any connection with the Patrobas here, it may have been with a member of this Patrobas family. The name **Phlegon** is not attested till the second Christian century, where it is given to a historian referred to by Origen. This last greeting suggests that those here mentioned formed a small group or community by themselves.

15. The name **Philologus** for slaves or freedmen is also attested by inscriptions from the imperial household (See Bauer, *Lex*., s.v.). It can mean 'fond of words/learning' or simply just 'talkative'. Philo-logus is coupled with **Julia**, a common name for slaves or freed-women of the Julian *gens*, also found in the imperial household. (Like Junia(s) at verse 7, Julian may be read as the accusative of Julias, masc. So Barrett, p. 284). They also may have been husband and wife, like Andronicus and Junia at verse 7, or else, if we read Philologus and Julias, two more 'paired' *apostoloi*. **Nereus** is not infrequent as a slave's or freedman's name in the imperial household (were he and his sister children of Philologus and Julia?). **Olympas** is probably a short form for Olympiodôros.

In this list of names as a whole we have to do, for the most part, with the names of slaves or freedmen. Here too, as St Paul wrote to the Corinthians (1 C. 1:26), 'few are powerful or highly born.' Indeed, of this latter class there appears to be no trace. The majority are Greek or Latin names, without the praenomen and cognomen before and after the family name of the Roman citizen. Paul singles out three 'kinsmen' (*syngeneis*), Andronicus, Junia(s) (verse 7) and Herodion (verse 11). The word is usually rendered as 'fellow countrymen', i.e., these three were *native born ethnic Jews, from the 'Holy Land'* (among whom Paul, by implication, includes himself.)[1] There must have been others on the list like Aquila and Prisca, i.e., Jewish Christians from the Diaspora (cf. Ac. 18:2 which describes Aquila as 'a certain Jew . . . a man of Pontus by race.') In fact most of those on the list were probably converted Jews of the Diaspora, including Roman Jews, and the rest either Roman or Greek converts and probably, again, for the most part, converted Jewish proselytes. Persis at v. 12 suggests a family connection with Parthia.

The fact that so many of the names are attested in *Roman* inscriptions, as names for slaves and freedmen, supports the view that Chapter 16 was an integral part of the Roman Epistle. Less important, but perhaps not less significant, is the theory of Lightfoot which associates many with the imperial household, a hypothesis which does not seem to have enjoyed much favour among German exegetes (cf. Käsemann, p. 395). The name Aristobulus, however, links his 'family' with Rome; and the link is further strengthened by Herodion, a slave or freedman of the same family (verses 10 and 11).

As Cranfield notes, the names Tryphaena and Tryphosa are connected, with the word *tryphē*, 'softness, delicacy', but it is doubtful if St Paul had this etymology in mind when he went on to command them as ones 'who toil in the Lord's service'. (*NEB*). It is perhaps worth drawing attention, however, to the kind of names enjoyed by slaves and freedmen. Where these are not derived from the gens or family of their owners, e.g. Julia(s), Herodion, they often (like the cognomen (or agnomen) of a Roman name) refer to some personal characteristic or are virtually nicknames. Thus Epaenetus is the 'estimable' one, Urbanus, the 'city slave' or perhaps even 'the cultivated, urbane one', Rufus the 'red', Asyncritus 'the incomparable'. The names were no doubt given at birth and reflect in some cases more often than not the fond hopes of parents rather

---

[1]See W. C. van Unnik's brilliant study *Tarsus or Jerusalem*, London, 1962.

than any virtues the slaves so named may have ever possessed, although it is always possible that an owner, purchasing a foreign slave with an outlandish name, may have supplied a nickname, such as Rufus or Asynkritus.

16. Greet one another with a holy kiss: the 'holy kiss' was part of the liturgy; cf. 1 Th. 5:26; 1 C. 16:20; 2 C. 13:12; 1 Pet. 5:14; Justin, *Apol.* 1, 65: 'having ended the prayers (of intercession?), we salute one another with a kiss. There is then brought to that one of the brethren who was presiding, bread and a cup of wine mixed with water . . .' (trans. Marcus Dods etc. in *Ante-Nicene Christian Library*, Edinburgh, 1867). There then follows in Justin the prayer of thanksgiving and the celebration of the Eucharist. In 1 Pet. 5:14, the 'kiss of *agapē*' may recall that the 'holy kiss' was already in the *NT* Epistles part of the Eucharist. Cf. Selwyn, 1 *Peter*, p. 244, R. Seeberg, in *Dictionary of the Apostolic Church*, ed. J. Hastings (1915–18), II, p. 443. Tertullian describes it as 'the kiss of peace' (*De oratione*, 18). Embracing and kissing in greeting was as common and just as customary in the ancient Graeco-Roman world as it still is in eastern Europe and the Middle East. The description 'holy kiss' is Pauline, and perhaps served to distinguish the Eucharistic 'greeting' from the more conventional *aspasmos*. Cf. *TWNT*, Bd. 1, pp. 494ff.

It has been thought that Paul's letter was probably read to the congregation assembled to celebrate the Eucharist, and that the brotherly kiss would terminate the reading (Michel, p. 382). By conveying the greetings of 'all the churches of Christ', Paul makes this a specially authoritative greeting. It is the Apostle to the Gentiles speaking.

A Stern Warning Against Factiousness and False Doctrine **16:17–20**

Cf. Gal. 6:11–16 (also Phil. 3:19ff.). The Apostle may have had in mind the divisive influence of judaising or gnosticising tendencies, e.g., behind the 'weak' brethren of 14:1ff., may have been a judaising movement. Cf. W. Schmithals, 'Die Irrlehrer von Röm. 16:17–20', *Studia Theol.*, XIII (1959), pp. 51–69.

Paul's language is strong, bordering on anathema (Michel thinks this particular paraenesis (cf. verse 17) belongs in a cultic setting); cf. especially verse 18: 'their own appetites'; *RSV mg.*: 'their own belly' (Phil. 3:19). If this is understood as the sin of gluttony, it is difficult to see how it fits into the context. Older commentators take the reference to be to the Jewish obsession with 'meats'; but it seems more likely that Paul has in mind the libertarian 'meat-eaters', the people who boasted of 'liberty', including independence of kosher tabus about food. The reference at Phil. 3:18ff. seems to be to a similar group of deviant Christians, and 1 C. 6:12ff. where *koilia*, 'belly', occurs again, perhaps referring to the same kind of Christians. Were they the 'liberated' Christian *pneumatikoi*, charismatic enthusiasts, who went to antinomian extremes, not merely by defying the Jewish kosher rules, but also by sexual indulgence? It is certainly to the latter that 1 C. 6:13ff. refers, and they emerge later, in extreme forms of sexual and sensual licence, among the 'enemies of religion' at Jude (cf. verse 4) and 2 Peter.

A number of commentators have held that these verses (17–20), falling between the lists of greetings, could only have been written to a Church which Paul himself had founded.

18. appetites: Greek *koilia*. Michel takes *koilia* (lit., 'belly') as synonymous with *sarx* ('flesh'). Aramaic *karsa* is idiomatically 'the body' as well as literally 'the belly'; cf. 1 C. 6:13ff., where *koilia* easily passes into *sōma*, 'body'.

by fair and flattering words: lit., 'fine speech and praise (blessing)'. The Romans defined the man who made fine speeches as one to speak well, yet act ill; cf. SH, *ad loc.* The use of the second word in the sense of 'flattery' is rare: its associations in biblical Greek are cultic ('blessing'). Is Paul punning and playing on words? The first word, *chrēstologia*, would sound like *Christologia*. The pun *Christos*, *chrēstos* ('good, kind') was well established in the early Church; cf. 1 Pet. 2:3, Justin, *Apol.* 1, 4, F. W. Beare, *1 Peter* (Oxford, 1958), p. 90; *chrēstologia* follows immediately on *koilia*, 'body', in Aramaic *karsa*, which, itself follows Christos. Is this simply coincidence or is Paul here and at Phil. 3:19 deliberately recalling the Aramaic noun; thus Phil. 3:19 'whose God is *karsa*, i.e. the body, not Christos'? See W. C. van Unnik, in de Zwaan *Festschrift*, above, p. 185. Were they people who had 'Christ' often on their lips, and went in for a specious kind of *eulogia* ('blessing'), but whose doctrine was false and conduct libertarian?

19. obedience is Christian obedience, i.e. the obedience of faith (defined at 1:5, 6:16).

wise as to what is good: experts at goodness, simpletons at evil. The thought is clearly dominically inspired; cf. Mt. 10:16, Phil. 2:15.

20. the God of peace will soon crush Satan under your feet: cf. 15:33. It is the 'God of peace' also who will thus remove the discord in the Church. Cf. 2 C. 11:13ff. where a similar group of 'disturbers of the peace', there described as 'pseudo-apostles', were sowing discord among believers. They are also called 'servants of Satan', and their end is also predicted. The verb 'crush' (*syntripsei*) is used at 1 Mac. 3:22 of the utter destruction of Israel's enemies.

Here it is applied to the archenemy of mankind. See further, *TWNT* Bd. VII, p. 161. 28–34, pp. 923.31–924.11. The verse is both prediction and prayer for the Roman Church.

soon has implicit eschatological overtones, referring to the Parousia.

The grace of our Lord Jesus Christ be with you: The shorter form in *NEB* is to be preferred, i.e., simply 'the grace of our Lord Jesus be with you'. Had the text here read the fuller form 'Our Lord Jesus Christ', as at 1 Th. 5:28, 2 Th. 3:18, it is unlikely that a copyist would have omitted the title 'Christ'. The shorter form is also better supported textually. It occurs again at 1 C. 16:23, but reading 'The grace of *the* Lord Jesus' instead of '*our* Lord Jesus'. As Michel notes (cf. also Cranfield), the Pauline benediction corresponds to the good wishes for health and prosperity which concluded the secular letter of the period, *errōso* (*errōsthe*)', *eutychei* 'Farewell!', *hygiaine*, 'keep well!'

A full trinitarian formula occurs at 2 C. 13:14: 'The grace of the Lord Jesus Christ, and the love of God, and the fellowship of the Holy Spirit be with you all.' In the closing verses of Galatians, Philippians and Philemon, 'with your spirit' is used instead of 'with you', 'the grace of the Lord Jesus Christ be with your spirit', while in Colossians and the Pastorals we find the still further shortened form 'Grace be with you (all)'. Eph. 6:23–24 (trans. *NEB*) has a more elaborate blessing: 'Peace to the brotherhood and love, with faith, from God the Father and the Lord Jesus Christ. God's grace be with all who love our Lord Jesus Christ, grace and immortality' (or who love . . . Christ with 'love imperishable', *NEB mg.*) See, for further details, O. Roller, *Das Formular der paulinischen Briefe* (above, p. 3), pp. 72ff.[1]

As with the epistolary greeting Paul gives his own distinctive Christian salutation (see above on 1:7).

As Cranfield notes, 'In every concluding greeting in the Pauline corpus the word *charis* (grace) occurs.' (p. 804). 'The "grace", which the Lord Jesus is to bestow on the (Roman) congregation . . . embraces the complete fullness of the blessing which the Lord can impart' (Michel, p. 386). It is all this, however, only because it is 'the grace of our Lord Jesus', i.e. the totally unmerited, 'amazing grace', which God freely bestows on the Christian believer.

---

[1]Several mss. (D G Vg ᵐˢ etc.) omit the blessing here, but have one (virtually identical with that at 1 Th. 5:28) with the Received Text, at verse 24, a verse which modern versions, following the best mss., now omit. For textual problems with verses 24–27, see Introduction, p. 13.

Personal Greetings **16:21–23**

These verses list the greetings of Paul's companions, headed by
Timothy, singled out as Paul's colleague ('fellow worker'); the insep-
arable aide-de-camp of the Apostle is usually mentioned at the
beginning of letters (1 C. 4:17, 16:10ff., 2 C. 1:1, Phil. 1:1, Col.
1:1, 1 Th. 1:1, 2 Th. 1:1, Phm. 1:1, etc.). See further, Ac. 16:1–3;
17:14ff.; 18:5; 19:22; 20:4ff., not to mention 1 and 2 Timothy.
The three following names, **Lucius, Jason, Sosipater**, were clearly
Jewish Christians ('my kinsmen'), very probably natives of Palestine
(see above, p. 208). Lucius, a Roman name, recalls Lucius of
Cyrene (Ac. 13:1), but it could also be 'Luke, the beloved phys-
ician', though Luke is generally believed to have been a Gentile.
Cf., however, E. E. Ellis, *The Gospel of Luke* (London, 1966),
pp. 52ff. The other two are also Greek names; there is no evidence
really to connect them with the Jason of Ac. 17:5–7, or the Sopater
of Ac. 20:4. **Tertius** and **Quartus** are both familiar Roman forms
of name. On Tertius as Paul's amanuensis, see *Introduction*, p. 2ff.
Was Quartus 'brother Quartus' or 'the brother of Erastus?' The
latter seems unlikely. Cf. Cranfield and Bruce *ad loc.*
Gaius: There are several persons named Gaius in the New Testament, Ac. 19:29, 20:4, 1 C. 1:14, 3 Jn 1. The most likely among
these mentioned here is the Gaius of 1 C. 1:14. He may well have
been a wealthy Christian who hosted travellers, like Paul, making
their way west via Corinth. The whole of the local church seemed
to have met in his house, perhaps regularly, unless Paul is trying
to say that 'all the Church' passing through Corinth was hosted by
him. **Erastus** is 'city-treasurer': whether the city is Corinth or
Ephesus, the high position of this convert is noteworthy. In Corinth
(or Ephesus), as well as at Rome, Christianity was penetrating all
strata of society; cf. H. J. Cadbury, 'Erastus of Corinth', *JBL*, L
(1931), pp. 42–58.

The Doxology **16:25–27**

For the position of the doxology in the Epistle, see *Introduction*,
pp. 12ff.

That the closing doxology is of later literary vintage than the
original letter to the Romans is widely recognised. It conforms to a
liturgical-literary scheme familiar at Eph. 3:20, Jude 24, and
Martyrium Polycarpi, xx. 2 (all beginning with the words: 'To him
who is able'; for the hymnic style, see E. Norden, *Agnostos Theos*
(Leipzig/Berlin, 1913), p. 255, n. 5; and G. Harder, *Paulus und das
Gebet* (Gütersloh, 1936), pp. 45, 79. Cf. also E. Kamlah, in *Theol.*.

Litzg., LXXXI (1956), p. 492.) Its central thought, the final revelation
of the 'mystery' kept secret for long ages, may derive from the later
Paulines (or deutero-Paulines), Col. 1:26, Eph. 3:9; certainly all
three passages have the same theme. The final editor of the Romans
doxology, however, has worked in a number of expressions from
Romans itself (e.g. 1:2, 5, 2:16). Harnack held that the phrases 'and
the proclamation of Jesus Christ', 'through the prophetic writings',
'made known', were editorial additions by which an original
doxology strongly 'Marcionite' had been "catholicised" ' (*Marcion*,
in *TU* Bd. XIV, p. 146 (²1924), p. 165). Cf. E. C. Blackman, *Marcion
and his Influence*, London (1948), p. 49.

The central theme, shared with the deutero-Pauline Colossians
and Ephesians, and touched on at Rom. 11:25, is of the divine
mystērion, or 'secret', hidden through countless ages, now revealed
through prophetic writings in the eschatological present.

25. strengthen you according to my gospel: the idea of an inner
'confirmation' or 'corroboration' (cf. 1:11, 1 Th. 3:2, 13, 2 Th. 3:3,
etc.), no doubt in sound doctrine and sure convictions, is to be
'according to my gospel and the preaching of Jesus Christ'. Alternatively, one may interpret the two expressions 'my gospel' and 'the
preaching of Jesus Christ' as a kind of hendiadys, and take the
preposition with the verb as instrumental: '. . . who is able to
strengthen you through my proclamation of the gospel of Jesus
Christ'.

26. according to the command of . . . God: God has authorised
by divine command the revelation of the secret plan of salvation—
and its purpose is to bring to faith and obedience *all* the Gentile
nations. Cf. 1:5 for the phrase 'the obedience of faith', another
accommodation to the Roman Epistle.

prophetic writings: i.e., of the old biblical literature (*OT* and apocalyptic writings of the intertestamental period). The meaning
'inspired' for 'prophetic' (and so embracing inspired Christians
writings) is probably to be rejected.

**27. to the only wise God be glory for evermore through Jesus
Christ! Amen:** a traditional type of formula. Cf. 1 Tim. 1:17; Jude
25; 2 Mac. 1:25. An alternative text to *RSV* reads: 'to the only wise
God through Jesus Christ, to whom be glory for evermore' (cf.
NEB mg.). This is the more difficult and the better supported text,
and is to be preferred (it is supported by P[46] B C, etc.); but the
true antecedent of the relative is 'God', not 'Jesus Christ'; the
ambiguity in the position of the relative no doubt led to its removal
or to the substitution of the personal pronoun (*autō*, 'to him'); cf.
J. Dupont, in *Ephemerides Theologicae Lovanienses*, XXII (1946),
pp. 362–75.

GENERAL INDEX

abba, 113f.
Abraham, 65–73, 127f.
Adam
  fall of, 58, 84, 95, 97f.
  and glory, 58, 125, 174
  and law, 82f., 98
  'old', 88, 90, 93f.
  'second', 59, 77, 83, 87, 105
  typology, 10, 41, 77–85, 87
Adoption, 113f., 117
akedah, 120
Alexander Polyhistor, 67
Ambrosiaster, 7
Ampliatus, 208f.
Anathema, 123f., 212
Andronicus, 6, 208–12
Apelles, 209
Apollos, 173
Apostolic office, 6, 18–20, 24
Aquila, 7, 12, 207f., 211
Aristeas, 42
Aristobulus, 8, 209, 211
Aristotle, 40, 48
Asyncritus, 210f.
Augustine of Hippo, 80f.
Authorship, 2f.

Baptism, 76, 86–90, 102f., 111, 114f.
Benediction, 214
Body
  of Christ, 10, 87, 90, 93, 169f.
  of death, 102
  term, 103–6
  works of, 113

Call of God, 24, 119, 129, 133–5, 162
Cenchreae, 4, 206
charaz (string of quotations), 56, 144,
  152, 161
Chiasmus, 3, 78, 203
Chrysosom, 15, 22, 151, 208
Church membership, 165–71
Cicero, 204
Circumcision, 52, 66, 69
Circumstances of letter, 3–5
Claudius, emperor, 6, 12, 207, 209
Clement of Alexandria, 185
Clement of Rome, 42f., 77, 150, 208
Clementine Recognitions, 124
Conscience, 49, 123, 183
Corinth, 4f., 12, 155, 170, 206f., 215
Corporate personality, 87
Corpus Hermeticum, 166f.
Cosmic powers, 121f.
Creation, 115f.
Cynics, 53

Date of letter, 3–5

Day of Atonement, 61f.
Death
  angel of, 89
  and baptism, 88
  'body of', 102
  of Christ, 73, 76f., 88–90, 120, 194,
    196
  and law, 89, 93f., 97f.
  of 'old man', 85
  security from, 119–21
  source, 78–80
  universal, 79–84
  wages of sin, 93
  and works, 113
Decalogue, 97, 185
Derbe, 6
Doxology, 42, 164, 215f.

Eighteen Benedictions, 72
Election, 119, 121, 126–9, 149, 151,
  161f.
Epaenetus, 12, 207f., 211
Ephesus, 4f., 11f., 207f., 215
Epictetus, 42, 53, 99, 177
Erastus, 215
Esau, 128f.
Essenes, 190, 198
Eucharist, 58, 86
Eusebius, 67
Evil inclination (*yētzer hārâ*), 81, 97,
  99f.
Expiation, 60–5

Faith
  of Abraham, 65–73
  and expiation, 62f.
  measure of, 168–70
  and righteousness, 58, 66
  term, 30f., 34–7
Fall, 58, 84, 95, 97f.
Flesh, 21, 66f., 100, 103–7, 110, 125,
  128, 189
Freedom from sin, 89

Gaius (*convert*), 4, 215
Gaius (*emperor*), 209
Galba (*emperor*), 210
Glory
  future, 45, 47, 115
  of God, 41, 58, 88, 125, 133, 216
  term, 58f.
Grace
  and apostleship, 23, 168
  of Christ, 214
  and election, 119, 150
  gift, 59, 70, 75, 83, 150f.
  greeting, 25
  and law, 90

INDEX OF AUTHORS